THE CLASSICS OF WESTERN SPIRITUALITY

MAXIMUS CONFESSOR
Selected Writings

TRANSLATION AND NOTES BY
GEORGE C. BERTHOLD

INTRODUCTION BY
JAROSLAV PELIKAN

PREFACE BY
IRÉNÉE-HENRI DALMAIS, O.P.

PAULIST PRESS
NEW YORK • MAHWAH • TORONTO

Cover Art:
WILLIAM HART McNICHOLS is a Jesuit priest and professional illustrator and painter residing in New York City. Of his cover he says: "Maximus is called Confessor because of his faithful confession of faith; specifically the two natures of Christ represented in the illustration by the blue Greek letter on the open book signifying: Jesus-Christ-Victory. The grief on his face and the two crimson rings about his head portray the severe tortures he endured for his open speech and mystical writings. Yet his compassionate hand is raised in benediction."

Library of Congress
Catalog Card Number: 85-60302

ISBN: 0-8091-2659-1 (paper)
      0-8091-0353-2 (cloth)

Published by Paulist Press
997 Macarthur Boulevard
Mahwah, New Jersey 07430

Printed and bound in the
United States of America

CONTENTS

ABBREVIATIONS

AB	Analecta Bollandiana
ACW	Ancient Christian Writers
Amb. Io.	Ambigua to John
Amb. Th.	Ambigua to Thomas
BZ	Byzantinische Zeitschrift
CWS	Classics of Western Spirituality
Declerck	*Quaestiones et Dubia*, Louvain, 1982
DOP	Dumbarton Oaks Papers
DS	Dictionnaire de Spiritualité
DTC	Dictionnaire de Théologie Catholique
EA	P. Sherwood, *The Earlier Ambigua of Saint Maximus the Confessor and His Refutation of Origenism*, Rome, 1955
EO	Echos d'Orient
GCS	Die Griechieschen Christlichen Schriftsteller
Jaeger	*Gregorii Nysseni Opera* Berlin-Leiden, 1921–1962
JBC	The Jerome Biblical Commentary
KG	Kephalia Gnostica
KL	Kosmische Liturgie (second ed.)
Laga-Steel	*Quaestiones ad Thalassium*, I, Louvain, 1980
Loeb	Loeb Classical Library
LXX	Greek Septuagint translation of the Old Testament
Mansi	*Sacrorum Conciliorum Nova et Amplissim a Collectio*, ed. Mansi, Florence, 1765
MC	Maximus Confessor, Fribourg, 1982
NPNF	Nicene and Post-Nicene Fathers (Eerdmans)
OCA	Orientalia Christiana Analecta
OCP	Orientalia Christiana Periodica
Or.	Oration
PG	Patrologia Graeca
PL	Patrologia Latina
PO	Patrologia Orientalis
Preuschen	GCS 4, 1903
RAM	Revue d'Ascétique et de Mystique
RSPT	Revue des Sciences Philosophiques et Théologiques
RTAM	Recherches de Théologie Ancienne et Mediévale
SC	Sources Chrétiennes
SP	Studia Patristica
TU	Texte und Untersuchungen
VS	La Vie Spirituelle

Translator of this Volume

GEORGE CHARLES BERTHOLD was awarded the doctorate in Theology *avec mention*, in 1975, after he successfully defended his thesis entitled *Freedom and Liberation in the Theology of Maximus the Confessor*. After serving as lecturer at Emmanuel College, Boston, and Merrimack College, North Andover, Massachusetts, he joined the faculty of Saint Anselm College in Manchester, New Hampshire, where he is now an associate professor of theology.

Fr. Berthold has been active in theological and patristic circles on the regional, national, and international levels. He has twice delivered papers at the Oxford Patristic Conference on the subject of Maximus the Confessor, the first one published in *Studia Patristica* 17 (1982) and the second to be published in the same series. In 1980 he was invited to participate in the international symposium on Maximus held at the university of Fribourg in Switzerland, and his paper is published in the volume of that conference (*Maximus Confessor*, Fribourg, 1982).

Author of the Introduction

JAROSLAV PELIKAN received his Ph.D. in 1946 from the University of Chicago, where he also taught from 1953 to 1962. Since 1962 he has been a member of the faculty of Yale University, where he is now Sterling Professor of History. He was Editor of the American edition of *Luther's Works*, and is a member of the editorial board for the *The Collected Works of Erasmus*. Of his books, the best known is probably *The Christian Tradition: A History of the Development of Doctrine* (1971ff.), projected for five volumes. In addition to the second volume of that set, *The Spirit of Eastern Christendom* (600–1700), his publications in the history of Christian doctrine in the East include a monograph on Athanasius, an edition of Chrysostom's commentary on the Sermon on the Mount, and numerous essays dealing with thinkers from Gregory of Nyssa and Basil of Caesarea through Maximus Confessor to Dostoevsky and Tolstoy.

Author of the Preface

IRÉNÉE-HENRI DALMAIS is professor of history at the Institut Catholique in Paris. He is the author of numerous works on Byzantine theology and spirituality and the editor of *Saint Maxime le Confesseur: Le Mystère du Salut* (Namur, Belgium).

To
LAURA F. BERTHOLD
(May 7, 1898–March 22, 1984)

"I assure you, wherever the good news is proclaimed throughout the world, what she has done will be told in her memory." (Mark 14:9)

PREFACE

Only about fifty years ago the name of St. Maximus the Confessor was barely familiar to anyone but historians of Christian doctrine and theologians confronted with the complex controversies of the "Monothelite crisis" and of the existence in Christ of a human will distinct from a divine will. It is, in fact, incontestable that the role played by this monk-theologian and -philosopher in the face of positions he was one of the first to grasp as placing in jeopardy the full reality of the incarnation of the Word of God in its ultimate consequences remains his first claim to be recognized by the Church as one of its Doctors who have defended to the confession of martyrdom what they perceived as an essential point of the orthodox faith.

It is no less true that Maximus is first of all a monk and a spiritual master, one of those great contemplatives who have fixed their gaze on the depths of God's mystery manifested both in the prophetic Word set in the biblical writings and on the living Word of the incarnate Logos. Now the essential message communicated to us is that man has been created by a God who is Love so that he might share in the divine condition itself. Even O. Bardenhewer did not hesitate, in his *Patrology*, to declare, "Maximus is without a doubt one of the most profound mystics which the Greek Church has produced." And yet twenty years later, in 1930, M. Viller had to state, "No comprehensive study has been done of the spirituality of St. Maximus. Even works on individual subjects are not numerous and have to do with two or three points" (RAM 1930, 156). In drawing attention to the relationship between the *Four Centuries on Love* and the works of Evagrius Ponticus, M. Viller was in fact stimulating astonishingly productive research. A few years later, in 1941, H. U. von Balthasar wrote the first lines of his youthful and fascinating synthesis, *Cosmic Liturgy*:

The vision of the world which Maximus the Confessor has left us in his writings is, from more than one point of view, the completion and full maturity of Greek mystical, theological, and philosophical thought. It appears at that happy and fugitive

moment which unites for a last time, before an already close decomposition, the riches
patiently acquired and developed through the effort of a whole culture. . . . The
richness of the spiritual world of Maximus gives for the last time the feeling of or-
ganic fecundity. Already, however, one perceives the decadence and sterility of
Byzantine scholasticism in the lifeless and mechanical accumulation of the past in
florilegia, *anthologies, encyclopedias which Maximus multiplies in the margin of*
his works.

It should indeed be recognized at the outset that reading the texts
of Maximus is arduous—and how much more is translating them. A
rigorous and exacting thought has a hard time mastering an expression
entangled in different vocabularies derived from many traditions.
Among the most notable examples is Origen, who was himself no styl-
ist and whom history has made to pay dearly for the imprecisions of his
own vocabulary and syntax. The Cappadocians, who were the preferred masters of Maximus, certainly corrected this in large part. And
yet it is the "difficult texts" (Ambigua) of a Gregory the Theologian
that will give no end of trouble to their exegete, providing him thereby
the occasion to make his own interpretation clearer. But after them, the
Christological controversies had led the theologians of Justinian's
time—notably the two Leontiuses and their rivals—to make a wider
appeal to a scholasticism that brought into play the subtlest Aristotelian and Stoic distinctions. All of this will come together in the highest
degree in Maximus's more strictly theological writings. But one perceives their reverberations in the more immediately spiritual texts that
have been brought together in the present collection.

But if the shell is hard to break, how tasty is the almond, and how
nourishing. It is only occasionally and briefly that the Confessor has
presented the master strokes of an ample, vigorous, and profound synthesis, without doubt one of the richest of the entire history of Christian thought. As H. U. von Balthasar observed, Maximus has
assimilated the heritage of the most diverse currents of the patristic centuries to set off its ultimate design: how the divine Logos, who is reflected in the various *logoi* of creatures, has pursued to its final
accomplishing "the design of God's great counsel" to bring all creation
into oneness in the communion of the same will with the God-Trinity.
Man should have at least begun this grandiose work by submitting his
own will to that of his Creator, who bore the élan of his love. But greedily man threw himself into the pleasure he thought he found in creatures, thereby introducing the germ of a fatal dissociation. Likewise it

is in humiliation and in renouncement of any superiority that the Logos assumes the human condition, thus radically suppressing all oppositions that broke the unity of the created universe, and rendering it possible for man to share in the filial condition, which is that of the Logos himself. Herein resides the "divinization" that begins for the Christian in baptismal birth that renews the "mode of existence" (*tropos*) without changing the "essential principle" (*logos*) in accordance with which he was created.

These fundamental themes Maximus more often developed or at least sketched out in the form of reconsiderations, of explanatory interpretations, and if the case required, in rectifying the author's teaching itself, whether of Origen in the *Chapters on Knowledge*, of Evagrius in the *Chapters on Love*, of the Cappadocians or the works of the Pseudo-Areopagite in the *Ambigua*, the responses to the *Questions to Thalassius*, or even in the much more personal work of the *Mystagogy*. It is doubtless in the *Ascetic Dialogue* and the Commentary on the *Our Father* that we can best recognize the plan that orients the entire thought of Maximus. But it is in the acts of his trial (*Relatio Monitionis*) that we can recognize the surest testimony, the one on which he lived out his life even to martyrdom.

It is there that we meet the man in his full maturity, the Confessor, the relentless champion of the subtlest consequences of the orthodox faith. How we should wish to be able to follow the stages of a long formation to which this maturity bears witness. Many unknowns and enigmas remain. It has long been known that the traditional biography is not supported by any serious documentation for the forty or forty-five years before Maximus's entry into the Christological controversy, about 634. The discovery by S. Brock of a Syriac biography almost contemporaneous with the rehabilitation of Maximus in 681 can open the field, however tendentious is this spiteful lampoon, to perspectives of the highest interest. If the future confessor is of Palestinian origin or at least if he spent his youth in Palestinian monasteries at a period when the waves of the Origenist crisis were still dangerously stirring opinion, we could better understand the attention with which this young monk read the works of the Alexandrian master and of those in his wake, especially Evagrius, who was formed in the school of Basil and Gregory the Theologian in Cappadocia before coming to the desert of Nitria to distill in strings of brief sayings grouped in centuries the boldest hypotheses of Origen. It is then that he could already have met the Damascene Sophronius, whose disciple he would later become in that monastery of Eukratas which regrouped the Easterners driven from their countries by the Persian invasion of 614–628. And it is Sophronius, elected patriarch of Jerusalem in 634, who recruited Maximus in the struggles for the defense of the orthodox faith. The chronology of the spiritual writings remains uncertain; we agree with Dom P. Sherwood, however, in considering that their serenity invites us to consider them as anterior to this period of struggle. May their reading aid Christians of our day to find root with a comparable sureness for the faith to which they witness.

FOREWORD

The increasing recognition of the importance of Maximus the Confessor in the history of Christian thought has far outstripped the availability of his writings in English translation. It is astonishing that despite the lofty prestige of this great theologian over thirteen centuries no English version of any complete work of his was available until 1955, when Dom Polycarp Sherwood published his translation of *The Ascetic Life* and *The Four Centuries on Charity*. The present work is an attempt to continue the effort to render the writings of Maximus available to the English-speaking public. In keeping with the title of this series, the spiritual works have been chosen for translation. In them the great Confessor reveals himself not only as an admirable thinker but as a wise and practical spiritual master as well.

Critical editions of the texts of Maximus, whenever available, formed the basis of the present translations. In 1963 the critical text of *The Four Hundred Chapters on Love* was established by Aldo Ceresa-Gastaldo. A text of the *Mystagogy* was published by C. Soteropoulos in Athens, 1978. The editors of the Greek section of the Corpus Christianorum series (Louvain) have announced a large-scale project of editions of Maximus, two volumes of which have already appeared. The texts used to translate the other treatises in this book are those of François Combefis, the seventeenth-century Dominican, which are collected in Migne's *Patrologia Graeca*, volumes 90 and 91.

Biblical texts have been translated as they are quoted by the author, without any attempt to make them conform to current English versions. Monastic writers in the tradition of Maximus had a wide familiarity with the text of Holy Writ and could quote it at length from memory. Their consciousness was suffused with biblical language and events, but what was primary was the actuality of the Christian mystery, of what God was effecting in them and in the cosmos. The biblical word was indeed inspired, but in the mystery of the Church they themselves were inspired in the transformation of their beings through the Spirit of the crucified and risen Christ. Toward Scripture they felt a respectful freedom, not a freedom *from* but a freedom *in* the Word. They frequently joined passages from separate sections of the Bible to bring out a theological or spiritual point, even forming chains of such citations which they forged together in a creative way.

The style of Maximus varies greatly, from the generally straightforward aphorisms of *The Four Hundred Chapters on Love* to the dense and involved periods of the *Mystagogy, Our Father,* and other works. The present translation does not seek to conceal this variation but rather to reflect in an accurate manner the stylistic preferences of the author. No one has yet hailed Maximus as a master of Greek prose. The conservative, often literal, style adopted in the translations is intended to allow one to come more directly in contact with the genius of Maximus whose theological splendor vastly outshines the restrictions of language.

I should like to express my gratitude to M.-D. Chenu, O.P., my doctoral father, and to Irénée Dalmais, O.P., both of the Institut Catholique in Paris, and to Professor Ihor Sevčenko of Harvard and Professor Jaroslav Pelikan of Yale for direction and kindnesses.

INTRODUCTION

Maximus Confessor is a member of that small and select group of saints of the Church who belong almost equally to the Western and to the Eastern traditions of Christian spirituality.[1] Significantly, most of the members of that group are Greek church fathers who have been adopted by the Latins, for example, Athanasius of Alexandria, John Chrysostom, John of Damascus. One of the few Latins to have achieved similar standing among the Greeks was, it should be noted, not Augustine of Hippo, despite his unquestionable position as the greatest of all Latin authorities on spirituality and theology, but Pope Saint Leo the Great, because of his magisterial role, through the *Tome to Flavian*, in determining the outcome of the Council of Chalcedon in 451, which continued for centuries to be infinitely more of an issue in the East than in the West. The Byzantine church was confronted, both politically and religiously, by the rivalry of the "non-Chalcedonian" churches, whether Nestorian or Monophysite, throughout most of its history, and therefore Leo's greatest dogmatic achievement, the statement of faith adopted at Chalcedon, stood as *the* line of demarcation between orthodoxy and heresy, as well as between the Byzantine empire and the "confrontation states" on its borders.

It was, indeed, in the aftermath of the Council of Chalcedon that Maximus Confessor attained his historic importance, both for the history of spirituality and for the history of dogma (a distinction that he would not have accepted, since, as every one of these treatises makes abundantly clear, there was for him no spirituality apart from dogma and no dogma apart from spirituality). By the time his long and tumultuous career was finished, Maximus had managed to affirm, for the West no less than for the East, the piety that had always been the underlying presupposition of the Chalcedonian dogma. Sometimes that piety has seemingly been all but submerged by the metaphysical distinctions and disputations of the schools over the chemistry (or alchemy) of the natures (or of the single nature) of the God-man. Only someone like Maximus, who had gone through the schools and who

1

could match the most speculative of their mandarins, point for point, could rescue the spirituality of salvation from the *rabies theologorum* and ground it where it properly belonged. This he did by the study and contemplation of the mystery of the Incarnation, by the recovery of the power and concreteness of the language of Scripture, and thoughtful participation in the drama of the Divine Liturgy. Thus—to invoke a cliché that does have some merit, so long as it is not elevated, as it so often is, to the status of a rigid principle—Maximus combined the speculative genius of the East with the soteriological genius of the West as few before or since have done.

The importance of Maximus Confessor in the seventh century is universally acknowledged by scholars representing many different national traditions of scholarship and articulating several different theological perspectives—Eastern Orthodox, Roman Catholic, and Protestant. In his magisterial history of the Byzantine fathers, the late Georges Florovsky selected him as the only seventh-century figure sufficiently prominent to deserve an entire chapter unto himself.[2] Irénée Hausherr, one of the pioneers in the scholarly study of the history of spirituality, termed him "the great doctor of *philautie* [i.e., the love of self for the sake of God), doctor in the sense both of professor and of physician."[3] Reinhold Seeberg, second only to Adolf von Harnack among Protestant historians of dogma, characterized him as "a star of the first magnitude in the heaven of the Christian Church."[4] Hans-Georg Beck, author of the standard history of Byzantine theological literature, called him "the most universal spirit of the seventh century and probably the last independent thinker of the Byzantine church."[5] Werner Elert, a champion of Lutheran confessional theology at Erlangen earlier in this century, referred to him as "probably the only productive thinker of the entire century."[6] And Aldo Ceresta-Gastaldo, one of his leading interpreters among Italian scholars, identified him as "the most significant theologian of the seventh century."[7]

I

Our information about the life of Maximus comes chiefly from the successive versions of the official *Vita*.[8] That information supplied by the official Greek *Vita* has been enriched and deepened, though not decisively contradicted, by the publication a decade ago of a long-lost Syriac *Vita*, which seems to have been contemporary to his life and death.[9] On the basis of Maximus's own reference to his age as an old man it seems clear that he was born in 580, to a prominent and well-to-do Christian family in Constantinople. From the depth and breadth of his literary acquaintance not only with the Bible and with the fathers and masters of Christian spirituality such as Origen and the fourth-century Cappadocians (Gregory Nazianzus, Basil of Caesarea, and Gregory of Nyssa), but with the major figures of pre-Christian philosophy, including Aristotle and the Neoplatonists Iamblichus and Proclus, scholars have likewise drawn the implication that he must have received the sort of broad humanistic education for which the Christian "university" at Constantinople was renowned throughout these centuries.[10] And from the ease with which he was able to move in official and imperial society even after he was no longer a part of the court, scholars have concluded that he was "to the manner born" and that the family must have belonged to the inner circle of confidants and civil servants who provided most of the intellectual elite and the bureaucratic cadres in the Byzantine capital. Maximus, as a comparatively young man, attained the position of "protosecretary" in the court of the emperor Heraclius (who ascended the throne in 610), although the precise date and the significance of his secretarial appointment are still a matter of some question among scholars.[11]

The most important fact about the appointment as first secretary, however, is that three years or so after receiving it Maximus resigned it. He left the court and the capital to take up residence in the monastery at Chrysopolis (modern Scutari), where he soon become abbot. A few years later, for reasons that are not altogether clear, he transferred to the monastery of St. George at Cyzicus (modern Erdek). Whatever political factors may have been involved in the decision, there is no reason to doubt that the principal reason for his adoption of the practice of the ascetic life was, as he says in an important autobiographical letter,[12] his own devotion to "philosophy," which was a technical term for monastic spirituality.[13] In "the supreme crisis"[14] of the spring of 626, when the Avars, the Slavs, and the Persians were pressing Constantinople, Maximus departed into exile. After stopping over for lengthy sojourns in Crete and probably in Cyprus, he arrived in North Africa, perhaps as early as 628. It would seem highly unlikely that Maximus could have spent such a long time in North Africa without becoming acquainted with the works of its most celebrated Christian thinker, Augustine, who had died almost exactly two centuries earlier; but we have tantalizingly little concrete evidence that he did in fact read Augustine. We do know, however, that this Western exile, which was to last a quarter-century, was punctuated by two major events. In 645 Maximus took part in a theological disputation with the deposed patriarch of Constantinople, Pyrrhus, held at Carthage, of which we have a stenographic transcript. And soon thereafter Maximus paid a visit to Rome, during which he contributed to the decrees of the synod held at the Lateran in Rome in 649—even though, as Polycarp Sherwood points out, "the evidence . . . for Maximus' contribution to the work of the council would not require his physical presence there, however probable it may seem."[15] Both those events were concerned with the controversies that raged throughout this period over whether Christ had one "will" and "activity [*energeia*]" or two. To a superficial or supercilious observer in the twentieth century, this might seem to be a typically useless set of controversies over abstract issues, and there were many in the seventh century who thought so, too, particularly various politicians, both imperial and ecclesiastical. But Maximus recognized what was at stake for Christian faith and spirituality behind the seemingly abstract theological and philosophical issues, and he decisively formulated the orthodox doctrine that since "will" and "activity" pertained to a nature rather than to a person, Christ must have had both a human will and a divine will, since he was one person but, as the Council of Chalcedon had said, "*in* two natures" (or, as a significant variant had it, "*of* two natures"). For, on the basis of the ancient patristic principle that whatever was not assumed in the Incarnation was not healed in the Redemption, the absence of a truly human will in Jesus Christ would have meant that (of all the functions of human nature and personality to be exempted!) the human will of sinful humanity would not have been saved. An introduction to the writings of Maximus on spirituality is not the place to expound his importance as a theologian for the development of this and other central doctrines of Christian orthodoxy during the centuries after the Council of Chalcedon and before the decisive break between East and West.[16] But, as we have already noted, doctrine and spirituality were ultimately inseparable in his thought and life; or, to put it another way, what was at stake for Maximus in his exile and in this controversy over Christological dogma was not simply the rightness of a speculative construct of his own private philosophical theology (though it was certainly also that), but the validity of the spirituality of the entire orthodox and catholic Church, of which he believed himself to be a faithful exponent.

The exile came to an end in 653, with the arrest of Maximus, as well as of Pope Martin I, by order of the emperor Constans II. In a set of proceedings and an interrogation that are movingly described by *The Trial of Maximus* presented here in this volume, they were brought to Constantinople, tried for treason, and banished in 655. Refusing even from his exile in Thrace to assent by silence to the heretical doctrine of one will in Christ, Maximus was returned to Constantinople. After undergoing the third degree and cross examination in 661/662, he was condemned to mutilation: His tongue, by which he had gone on confessing two wills in Christ, and his right hand, with which he had refused to sign a compromise statement of doctrine, were cut off, and he was exiled to Lazica on the southeastern shore of the Black Sea, where he died soon thereafter, on 13 August 662 (the date is observed in both East and West). The title "confessor," which he acquired soon thereafter and which is forever attached to his name, was a tribute to his steadfastness in confessing the faith of the undivided Church in the undivided hypostasis and the distinct natures of the person of the incarnate Son of God.

II

In the history both of Christian spirituality and of Christian thought, Maximus occupies a position whose importance (as Père Dalmais points out in his Preface to this volume) has begun to receive its just due only in the last fifty years, although he was translated into Latin by no less a figure in the history of medieval philosophy than John the Scot and received a critical edition in 1675 from the great seventeenth-century Dominican patristic scholar François Combéfis.[17] Any attempt to locate his position in the history of spirituality must begin with his own view of the place he held, and indeed that all proper theologians and spiritual writers should hold, in that history.[18] According to Maximus, it was characteristic of these theologians and spiritual writers, if they were authentically catholic and orthodox, that they did not invent their own spirituality, but "received the contents of tradition through succession from those who came before them," as he said in commenting on a passage from Gregory of Nazianzus whose opening word had spoken of "innovation [*kainotomia*]" as a blessing wrought by the Incarnation.[19] Ordinarily, of course, "innovation" when used in connection with such words as "succession [*diadochē*]" was anything but a blessing in the judgment of Maximus and the orthodox tradition. In one of his epistles, for example, Maximus attacked a questionable formulation of the doctrine of the person of Christ as a theological innovation that had been perpetrated by those who were depriving the Gospel of its meaning and content.[20] But it would be a grave and superficial oversimplification of Maximus's view both of dogma and of spirituality to conclude from such condemnations of innovation as this that he equated "the heritage of the Faith" with a pedantic adherence to the *ipsissima verba* of the church fathers. Indeed, one of his letters in which that phrase, "the heritage of the Faith," appears consists of a paraphrase of the Nicene Creed that goes far beyond its *ipsissima verba*.[21] And in the conflict with Pyrrhus he refused to accept some sort of *status quo ante bellum*, even though it represented the sayings of the fathers and councils, as an evasion of the questions that had now arisen.

There are several closely related leitmotivs in the spirituality of Maximus Confessor of which a reader ought to be conscious in undertaking to read the spiritual writings presented in this volume. For the history of spirituality, and probably also for the history of dogma, the most crucial test case of Maximus's attitude toward both tradition and innovation was certainly the relation of his spirituality to that of Pseudo-Dionysius the Areopagite. The significance of that great pseudonymous writer for the history of Christian spirituality in both East and West is a topic best reserved for treatment elsewhere.[22] For our purposes here, however, Pseudo-Dionysius looms large because of the major role that Maximus played in making his works acceptable to orthodox spirituality and theology. Partly because of what seems to be an excessively philosophical preoccupation in the scholarly literature about Pseudo-Dionysius, there has been a failure to recognize that the primary achievement of Maximus as an interpreter of the *Corpus Areopagiticum* did not come through his commentaries on that *Corpus* as such. These have, in any case, been conflated (and confused) in the transmission of the literary tradition with those of John of Scythopolis.[23] But Maximus made his principal contribution to the rescue of Dionysius through his orthodox restatement and reinterpretation of the Dionysian structure both in his theology and even more in his spirituality. What Maximus achieved was nothing less than the restoration of the balance between Neo-Platonism and Christian orthodoxy in a Christocentric piety whose roots lie deep in the Cappadocian tradition of Basil and the two Gregories.[24]

The tension between Neo-Platonism and Christian orthodoxy is the crucial problem in the spirituality systematized by Pseudo-Dionysius and transmitted by him to subsequent generations. Long before the sudden appearance of the *Corpus Areopagiticum* in the sixth century, the mutual influences between "Hellenic and Christian [elements] in early Byzantine spiritual life"[25] had been central to what Brooks Otis, in a provocative but neglected article, has called the "coherent system" of "Cappadocian thought."[26] In many ways Dionysius may be said to represent the effort, more or less successful, to spell out in greater detail the philosophical presuppositions that had been at work all along in the system of Cappadocian spirituality. But in the process, the liturgical spirituality embodied in the two fundamental dogmas of the Trinity and the Incarnation was in danger of being engulfed by these Neo-Platonic presuppositions. As Father Florovsky observes, "Dionysius's treatment of the Trinitarian dogma is short and quick [*korotko i beglo*]."[27] Similarly, as John Meyendorff observes in a parallel judgment, "Undoubtedly Dionysius, who probably belonged to the Severian Monophysite party, . . . mentions the name of Jesus Christ and professes his belief in the incarnation, but the structure of his system is perfectly independent of his profession of faith.[28]

As the principal exponent of an orthodox Christological spirituality in the seventh century, Maximus Confessor explained the language of Dionysius in such a manner that he achieved the Trinitarian and Christocentric reorientation of the Dionysian system and thus rehabilitated it. It is noteworthy, for example, that the longest chapter in his *Chapters on Knowledge* should have been one devoted to the doctrine of the Trinity.[29] What may properly be called his "Trinitarian Christocentrism" is probably the overriding theme pervading the texts from Maximus presented in this volume. It is likewise the point at which his status as "confessor" (in the sense of champion of the orthodox Chalcedonian dogma) and his position as "confessor" (in the sense of master of spirituality) converge. When he opposed the Christology of Pyrrhus and of other proponents of the theories of "one nature" or of "one will" or of "one activity," he consistently did so not only with the standard polemical argument that these theories contradicted the authority of the fathers and the councils and the Scriptures (as, in his judgment, they clearly did), but with the recognition that, despite their attractiveness to a Christian spirituality based on a yearning for union with God, such theories would in fact undercut this spirituality by severing the bond between our humanity and the humanity of Jesus Christ. "I have been brought to think," acknowledged the founding father of American scholarship on Maximus, "that this spirituality was in large measure common property not only among the Byzantines but also among the Monophysites," and that it was therefore susceptible of both an orthodox and a heretical interpretation.[30] For that very reason, Maximus had to prove—and, as this collection of texts demonstrates, did prove—that this spirituality demanded, in the celebrated formula of the Council of Chalcedon, for the person of Jesus Christ to be "acknowledged in two natures without confusion, without change, without division, without separation [*asynchytōs, atreptōs, adiairetōs, achōristōs*]." Anyone who is put off by the seeming impersonality of these four adverbs with their alpha-privatives (as many modern believers in all Christian denominations undoubtedly are) can find in the spirituality of Maximus a documentation of the thesis that in fact these are, in meaning though not in grammar, verbs rather than adverbs, because they describe actions that have taken place once and for all in the life, death, and resurrection of Christ and that therefore can continue to transform human life into the image of those actions without destroying it in the process (as the annihilation of the human nature of Jesus by the divine nature of the Logos would do).

Dogmatically explicit and polemically rigorous as they are, the Trinitarianism and Christocentrism of Maximus's spirituality are, however, rescued from presumption by their standing in polarity with his emphasis on the other half of the orthodox doctrine of the knowledge of God: what has come to be known as "apophaticism" (from *apophasis*, the Greek word for "negation"). Maximus was a leading spokesman for the *via negativa* in the knowledge and experience of God.[31] In this respect, too, he showed himself to be a faithful heir of Cappadocian spirituality. Both Basil and Gregory of Nyssa, in their polemical treatises against Eunomius, a heretic and dialectician who had claimed that he knew the being of God as well as God knows it himself,[32] emphasized the transcendence and the otherness of the Divine Nature, "surpassing every mental concept, altogether inaccessible to reasoning and conjecture."[33] But they did not do so—as have some more recent exponents of the *via negativa* in our time, when it seems to have acquired a certain éclat—in order to induce a kind of "sanctified skepticism" that would leave the believer unsure of anything. On the contrary, the purpose of the *via negativa* in Cappadocian spirituality was to affirm the oneness of God with the Logos, through whose Incarnation "that which is completely inexpressible and incomprehensible to all created intellects" became that which "can to a certain extent be grasped by human understanding."[34] Thus someone who claimed to know the essence of God thereby demonstrated the very opposite, his total ignorance of God, who in Christ had made known his power, but never his incomprehensible essence.[35]

One of the most significant ways to identify the place of Maximus Confessor in the history of Christian spirituality, therefore, is to see him, in his role as an interpreter of Pseudo-Dionysius the Areopagite, as the one who turned apophatic theology and spirituality around, from the speculative nihilism that was the potential outcome of apophaticism back to a concentration on the person of Jesus Christ. "The perfect mind," he taught, "is the one that through genuine faith knows in supreme ignorance the supremely unknowable, and in gazing on the universe of his handiwork has received from God comprehensive knowledge of his Providence and judgment in it, as far as allowable to men"—knows in *supreme ignorance*, to be sure, but has *comprehensive knowledge* nevertheless.[36] *Pace* Eunomius, it was, he said earlier in the same treatise, impossible to know God from His being.[37] Even "the holy angels do not know God and the things created by him as God knows himself and the things created by him, [for] God knows himself of his own sacred essence."[38] But from the Incarnation of His Logos in the person of Jesus Christ it *was* possible to know God, though in a special manner. "Who knows," Maximus asked, "how God is made flesh and yet remains God?" And he answered his own question: "This only faith understands, adoring the Logos in silence."[39] It was, then, a genuine understanding, but one that appropriately expressed itself "in silence" rather than in words. Not even the words of the orthodox dogma, for which Maximus contended and suffered all his life, could adequately encompass the mystery of faith. "Theological mystagogy" transcended the dogmas formulated by the councils of the Church.[40] A spirituality shaped by orthodox apophaticism, therefore, was one that gratefully acknowledged those dogmas and was ready to defend them to the death against those who sought to distort them, but that, at the same time, willingly—in fact, worshipfully—acknowledged the limitations that had been placed on all knowledge and all affirmation, be it human or angelic.

Another distinctive characteristic of the spirituality of Maximus, and one that is closely related to this emphasis on worship as the appropriate modality for knowing the unknowable and expressing the inexpressible, is pithily summarized in what is probably the most profound scholarly book ever written about Maximus, the monograph of Hans Urs von Balthasar, originally published in German as *Kosmische*

Liturgie: Höhe und Krise des griechischen Weltbildes,[41] then translated into French as *Liturgie cosmique*,[42] but, unfortunately for most English and American readers, not (or, at any rate, not yet) translated into English. Maximus cannot speak about the salvation of the human race without relating it to the created cosmos of which humanity is a "microcosm"; conversely, he cannot treat the created cosmos as a "nature" ontologically separated from "grace," but must always connect nature and grace.[43] To appreciate this cosmic dimension of his spirituality, we must put Maximus into context by drawing contrasts with other forms of Christian spirituality: on the one hand, with an individualism that is so intent on having the human soul saved *from* the world that it overlooks the biblical emphasis on the salvation of the human soul *with* the world, "that God may be all in all";[44] and on the other hand, with a cosmism in which the individual is obliterated and "salvation" becomes the annihilation of the self rather than the transformation of the self.[45] Like his mentor Gregory of Nyssa and like his spiritual descendant Nicholas of Cusa, Maximus was able to appropriate the valid intention of the spirituality of Origen but to bring it into line with the orthodox Trinitarian and Christological tradition.[46]

In spite of the importance of these several themes in the spirituality of Maximus Confessor, however, most scholars would be obliged to agree with his principal Russian interpreter, S. L. Epifanovich, that "the chief idea of St. Maximus, as of all of Eastern theology, [was] the idea of deification [*obozhenie*]."[47] There is also no idea in Maximus and in Eastern spirituality that is so subject to misinterpretation as this preoccupation with deification. Despite its appearance in the writings of Luther and Calvin—and, for that matter, in the New Testament itself—Protestant histories of the Church and its doctrine have made it almost canonical to dismiss this as a "physical" understanding of salvation and eternal life, with its corresponding view of the human predicament as "corruption" and transiency rather than as sin and guilt.

"The future deification of those who have now been made children of God" was the way the spirituality of Maximus described the stages of salvation: having been transformed into "children of God" in this life, believers could anticipate yet a further transformation in the life to come, into a participation in the very nature of God.[48] That was, for him, the meaning of the New Testament promise that it did not yet appear what was in store for those who were now the children of God, but that the contours of that future had already become discernible in the incarnate Logos and in his humanity, which had been deified but not destroyed in the Incarnation.[49] The most explicit identification of "deification" as the content of the promise of salvation was in the first chapter of the Second Epistle of Peter: "He has granted to us his precious and very great promises, that through these you may escape from the corruption that is in the world because of passion, and become partakers of the divine nature [*theias koinōnoi physeōs*]."[50] This God had done through the Incarnation and the Resurrection of Jesus Christ, which was both the means by which divine life had triumphed over human corruption and "an image of the future deification by grace."[51] "Only by the grace of God" was deification possible.[52] Yet it was, at one and the same time, a gift of divine grace and an act of human free will; for it is "possible for Maximus to say, on the one hand, that there is no power inherent in human nature which is able to deify man, and yet, on the other, that God becomes man *insofar* as man has deified himself."[53] That paradox has been difficult for systematic theology to encompass, as the fifteen centuries of the history of Augustinianism in the West, whether Roman Catholic or Protestant, more than amply attest. But the special gift of Eastern Christian spirituality was that it managed to hold these two emphases together far more successfully than theology ever did. There are some things we can say better on our knees at the altar than on our feet in the classroom, although neither of these postures by itself is sufficient: When we rise from our knees, we also need to reflect critically and systematically about what we have been praying, just as, conversely, the content of spirituality and prayer must in turn become a source for the data of theology and of dogma: *lex orandi, lex credendi.*

It was the genius of Maximus Confessor that, in a measure that has been granted only to a few, he was fully bilingual, affirming by means of negation and speaking both the language of spirituality and the language of theology with equal fluency. From the looks of things within both Western and Eastern Christendom—and beyond—that gift of being bilingual is one that people of faith will need more than ever in the years to come.

NOTES

1. For a presentation of recent scholarship at a symposium in commemoration of the fourteen hundredth anniversary of his birth, see Felix Heinzer and Christoph Schönborn, eds., *Maximus Confessor* (Fribourg, 1982).

INTRODUCTION

2. G. V. Florovsky, *Vizantijskie otci V-VIII veka* [Byzantine fathers of the fifth to the eighth century] (Paris, 1933), pp. 195–227.

3. Irénée Hausherr, *Philautie: de la tendresse pour soi à la charité selon Saint Maxime le Confesseur* (Rome, 1952), p. 7.

4. Reinhold Seeberg, "Maximus Konfessor," *Realenzyklopädie für protestantische Theologie und Kirche*, 3rd ed. (Leipzig,1898–1908), 12:470.

5. Hans-Georg Beck, *Kirche and theologische Literatur im byzantinischen Reich* (Munich, 1959), p. 436.

6. Werner Elert, *Der Ausgang der altkirchlichen Christologie* (Berlin, 1957), p. 259.

7. Aldo Ceresta-Gastaldo, "Maximos Confessor," *Lexikon für Theologie und Kirche*, 2d ed. (Freiburg, 1957–67), 7:208–9.

8. See R. Devreese, "La vie de Saint Maxime le confesseur et ses récensions," *Analecta Bollandiana* 46 (1928): 5–49.

9. S. P. Brock, "An Early Syriac Life of Maximus the Confessor," *Analecta Bollandiana* 91 (1973): 299–346.

10. Ihor Ševčenko's study, "The Definition of Philosophy in the *Life of Saint Constantine*," *For Roman Jakobson* (The Hague, 1956), pp. 449–57, on humanistic education in Constantinople during the ninth century, also pertains, *mutatis mutandis*, to this period.

11. Cf. Irenee H. Dalmais, "Introduction," *Saint Maxime le Confesseur: Le Mystère du Salut* (Namur, Belgium 1964), pp. 8–10.

12. *Epistle 2, PG* 91:392–408.

13. Cf. G. W. H. Lampe, ed., *A Patristic Greek Lexicon* (Oxford, 1961),p. 1483.

14. D. Obolensky, "The Empire and Its Northern Neighbours, 565–1018," *Cambridge Medieval History*, IV-1 (Cambridge, 1966), p. 482.

15. Polycarp Sherwood, *An Annotated Date-List of the Works of Maximus the Confessor* (Rome, 1952), p. 20., n. 92.

16. Cf. Jaroslav Pelikan, *The Spirit of Eastern Christendom (600–1300)*, vol. 2 of *The Christian Tradition: A History of the Development of Doctrine* (Chicago, 1974), pp. 8–90.

17. In this second part of my Introduction I have adapted some of what I have said in my lecture "The Place of Maximus Confessor in the History of Christian Thought," in Heinzer and Schönborn, *op. cit.*, pp. 387–402.

18. See also my study " 'Council or Father or Scripture': The Concept of Authority in the Theology of Maximus Confessor," *The Heritage of the Early Church: Essays in Honor of The Very Reverend Georges Vasilievich Florovsky*, ed. David Neiman and Margaret Schatkin (Rome, 1973), pp. 277–88.

19. *Amb. Io.* 42 (*PG* 91:1304D).

20. *Epistle* 13 (*PG* 91:517C).

21. *Epistle* 12 (*PG* 91:465D).

22. See the introduction to the volume of Dionysius in this series.

INTRODUCTION

23. Hans Urs von Balthasar, "Das Scholienwerk des Johannes von Skythopolis," *Scholastik* 15 (1940): 16–38.

24. Cf. George Berthold, "The Cappadocian Roots of Maximus the Confessor," in Heinzer and Schönborn, *op. cit.*, pp. 51–59.

25. Endre von Ivánka, *Hellenisches and Christliches im frühbyzantinischen Geistesleben* (Vienna, 1948).

26. Brooks Otis, "Cappadocian Thought as a Coherent System," *Dumbarton Oaks Papers* 12 (1958): 95–124.

27. Florovsky, *Vizantijskie otci*, p. 109.

28. John Meyendorff, *Christ in Eastern Christian Thought* (Washington, 1969), p. 81.

29. "Chapters on Knowledge" 2:1, pp. 147–148 below.

30. Sherwood, *Date-List*, p. 3.

31. It will be evident that here, as elsewhere, I have been profoundly shaped by the theological reflections of Vladimir Lossky, "Apophasis and Trinitarian Theology," *In the Image and Likeness of God*, John H. Erickson and Thomas E. Bird (Tuckahoe, N.Y., 1974), pp. 13–29.

32. Cf. Gregory of Nyssa, *Contra Eunomium* III. viii.1–3 (Jaeger 2:226–28); and, more briefly, Basil, *Adversus Eunomium* I.12 (*PG* 29:540A).

33. Gregory of Nyssa, *Orationes de beatitudinibus* VI (*PG* 44:1264C).

34. Gregory of Nyssa, *Homiliae in Cantica Canticorum* XIII (*PG* 44:1045D).

35. Basil, *Epistle* 234, 2–3 (*PG* 32:869B–872A).

36. *Four Hundred Chapters on Love* 3:99, p. 75 below.

37. Ibid., 1:96, pp. 45–46 below.

38. Ibid., 3:21–22, p. 64 below.

39. *Ambigua* 5 (*PG* 91:1057).

40. *Quaestiones et dubia* 73 (*PG* 90:845).

41. Freiburg, 1941.

42. Paris, 1947.

43. Cf. Lars Thunberg, *Microcosm and Mediator: The Theological Anthropology of Maximus the Confessor* (Lund, 1965).

44. 1 Cor 15:28; Jn 3:16–17.

45. For a brief but helpful account, cf. George A. Maloney, *The Cosmic Christ: From Paul to Teilhard* (New York, 1968).

46. Cf. Balthasar, *Liturgie cosmique*, pp. 80–87.

47. S. L. Epifanovich, *Prepodobnyj Maksim Ispovednik i vizantijskoe bogoslovie* [Saint Maximus Confessor and Byzantine theology] (Kiev,1915), p. 125.

48. *Quaestiones ad Thalassium* 9 (*PG* 90:285).

49. 1 Jn 3:2.

50. 2 Pt 1:4 (RSV).

51. *Ambigua* 64 (*PG* 91:1389).

52. *Quaestiones ad Thalassium*, 22 (*PG* 90:321).

53. Thunberg, *op. cit.*, pp. 457–58.

THE TRIAL OF MAXIMUS[1]

AN ACCOUNT OF THE PROCEEDINGS
WHICH TOOK PLACE BETWEEN THE
LORD ABBOT MAXIMUS AND HIS
COMPANIONS AND THE OFFICIALS IN
THE CHAMBER.

On the day when both Maximus and those with him anchored near this royal city at about sunset, two imperial officials came with ten palace guards and ordered them from the boat unclothed and barefoot. Separating them from one another, they guarded them in separate quarters.

After several days they led them to the palace and brought the old man to the place where the senate was gathered with a large crowd as well. They made him stand in the middle of the seated senators, and the bursar[2] said to him with much anger and passion, "Are you a Christian?" He replied, "By the grace of Christ the God of the universe I am a Christian." The former said, "That is not true!" The servant of God answered, "You say I am not, but God says I am and will remain a Christian." "But how," he said, "if you are a Christian, can you hate the emperor?" The servant of God answered, "And how can this be evident? For hatred is a hidden disposition of the soul, just as love is." And he said to him, "From what you have done it has become clear to everyone that you hate the emperor and his realm. For you alone betrayed Egypt and Alexandria and Pentapolis and Tripoli and Africa to the Saracens."[3] "And what is the proof of these things," he asked? They brought forward John, who was the finance minister of Peter, the former general of Numidia in Africa, who said, "Twenty-two years ago the grandfather of the emperor[4] ordered venerable Peter to take an army and go off into Egypt against the Saracens, and he wrote to you as if he were speaking to a servant of God, having confidence in you as a holy man to inquire whether you would advise him to set out. And you wrote back to him and said not to do such a thing since God was not pleased to lend aid to the Roman state under the emperor Heraclius and his family." The servant of God said, "If you are telling the truth, then you surely have both Peter's letter to me and mine to him. Let them be brought forth and I shall be subject to the punishments prescribed in the law." But he said, "I do not have the letter; nor do I even

17

know if he ever wrote one to you. But everyone in the camp spoke of these things to each other at the time." The servant of God said to him, "If the whole camp talked about this, why are you the only one to libel me? Have you ever seen me, or I you?" And he answered, "Never." Then turning toward the senate the servant of God said, "Judge for yourselves if it is just to have such accusers or witnesses brought forward. 'By the judgment you judge you shall be judged, and by the measure that you measure it shall be measured unto you,' says the God of all (Mt 7:2)."

2. And after this they brought in Sergius Magudas, who said, "Nine years ago the blessed abbot Thomas, when coming from Rome, said to me, 'Pope Theodore sent me to the patrician Gregory to tell him not to be fearful of anyone. For the servant of God Maximus saw a vision in his sleep that in the heavens there were factions of angels in the east and west; and those in the east shouted, "Constantine Augustus, you shall conquer"; but those in the west cried, "Gregory Augustus, you shall conquer." And the voice of those in the west overcame the voice in the east.' "[5] At this the minister cried, "God sent you into this city to be burned!" The servant of God said, "I thank God who cleanses me from my voluntary sins through involuntary suffering; but 'Woe to the world because of scandals. It is necessary that scandals arise, but woe to him through whom scandal comes' (Mt 18:7). Such things should not have been said in the presence of Christians. Nor should those be left unpunished who do such things to please men who are here today and gone tomorrow. These things he should have said while Gregory was alive, to inform the emperor of his devotion toward him. The proper thing to do, if you should also concur, is to force my former calumniator to go out and bring in the patrician Peter and he should bring in the abbot Thomas and he in turn should bring in the blessed Pope Theodore. Then in the presence of all I would have said to the patrician Peter; 'Tell me, lord patrician, did you ever write me about what your bursar said, or did I write to you?' And if he should say yes, I would come under liability. Similarly with the blessed Pope: 'Tell me, lord, did I ever recount to you a dream of mine?' And if he should prove me guilty, his would be the crime, not mine who am supposed to have seen it. For a vision is an involuntary thing. The law punishes only voluntary things which are done in defiance of it." Then Troilus said to him, "You are playing with us, abbot; don't you know where you are?" "Oh, I am not playing," he responded, "but I regret that I should have lived long enough to experience such things." The patri-

cian Epiphanios said, "God knows that he is doing well in ridiculing these things if they are not true." After this the bursar again said to him with anger, "Are all these men indeed lying and only you are telling the truth?" In answer the servant of God said as he wept, "You have power with God's permission to give life and to give death; however, if these men are telling the truth, then it is Satan who is really God. But if he is not, as indeed he is not, neither did these people speak the truth. Nor may I be worthy to see with Christians the epiphany of the supersubstantial[6] God, maker and fashioner and creator and provider and judge and savior of all, if ever I have recounted such a dream or heard another recount except at this very time by the lord Sergius, who is very devoted to the empire."

3. Next they proposed a third accuser, Theodore, the son of John called the Candidate, surnamed Chila, who is now the son-in-law of the lord patrician Plato, who said, "In a conversation which took place between us in Rome concerning the emperor he used mocking and abusive language." The servant of God said to him, "I have never communicated with you except once with the most holy priest lord Theocharistos, the brother of the exarch, on behalf of the protonotary when I was summoned to do this by letter. And if I am found to be lying, I accept the consequences."

4. After this one they led in a fourth person, Gregory the son of Photinus, who said, "I went to the cell of the abbot Maximus in Rome and when I mentioned that the emperor is also a priest the monk Anastasius his disciple said, 'He should not be considered a priest.' " The servant of God said right off to him, "Fear God, lord Gregory, my fellow servant did not say anything at all in this conversation on this matter." And he threw himself upon the ground, saying to the senate, "Bear with your servant and I will tell you all as it took place, and he shall convict me if I lie. My lord Gregory on his arrival in Rome deigned to come to your servant's cell. Upon seeing him I prostrated myself upon the earth as is my custom and greeted him. And having kissed him I said to him after we had seated ourselves, 'What is the reason for the welcome presence of my lord?' And he said, 'Our good and God-established lord, having charge of the peace of the saints of God's churches, has issued an order to the God-honored Pope, sending an offering as well to St. Peter, urging him to establish communion with the patriarch of Constantinople; his venerable majesty deigned that this order be sent through your humble servant.' And I said, 'Glory to God who made you worthy of such a ministry. Now on what formula has

his divinely crowned serenity ordered the union to come about? Tell me if you know.' And you said, 'On the Typos.'[7] And I said, 'This, I think, is an impossible thing; for the Romans will not consent that the illuminating statements of the holy Fathers be annulled together with the voices of impure heretics, or that the truth be extinguished with falsehood, or that the light disappear along with the darkness. For nothing will remain for us to worship if we annul the sayings taught by God.' And you said, 'The Typos does not prescribe a denial of the holy statements but rather a silence in order to arrange a peace.'[8] And I said, "Silence according to the divine Scripture is denial as well. For God said through David, "There is no speech, nor are there words whose sounds are not heard (Ps 19:3)." Therefore unless the words concerning God can be spoken and heard then neither do they exist, according to Scripture.' And you said, 'Do not throw me into the water.[9] I am satisfied with the holy creed.' 'And how,' I said, 'can you be satisfied with the holy symbol if you have received the Typos?' 'But how can the reception of the Typos harm the creed?' you asked, 'And what harm is there in both receiving the Typos and reciting the creed?' I said, 'Because the Typos clearly contradicts the creed.' And you said, 'How, in God's name?' 'Recite the creed to me,' I said. And you began to recite it: I believe in One God the Father almighty, creator of heaven and earth, of all things seen and unseen. 'Stop awhile,' I said, 'and learn how the faith of those in Nicea is repudiated. For God would not be a creator were he deprived of a natural will and activity, if it is true that he made heaven and earth willingly and not driven by any necessity, if David speaks the truth in the Spirit, "The Lord made all the things he wanted in heaven and on earth, in the seas and in all the depths (Ps 135:6)." But if the saving faith should be removed along with heresy for the sake of an arrangement,[10] then the arrangement is a thorough separation from God and not a unity with God. For tomorrow the abominable Jews will say, "Let us arrange a peace with one another and unite, and let us remove circumcision and you baptism and we shall not dispute anymore with each other." Once the Arians put this forward in writing at the time of the great Constantine, saying, "Let us remove the Homoousion and the Heterousion and let the churches unite." Our God-fearing Fathers did not consent to this; but rather they preferred to be pursued and put to death than to pass over in silence a term indicating the one supersubstantial godhead of the Father, Son, and Holy Spirit. And the great Constantine concurred with those who were putting such suggestions forward, as is recounted by many who diligently wrote of these matters at the time. No emperor was able to convince the inspired Fathers to come to an agreement with the heretics of that time through the use of equivocal terms. Rather they employed clear and fixed terms corresponding to the dogma inquired about, saying in as many words, "It is for the priests to inquire into and define what concerns the saving dogmas of the Catholic Church." ' And you said, 'What, then, is not every Christian emperor also a priest?' And I said, 'He is not, for neither does he stand at the altar nor after the consecration of the bread does he elevate it saying, "Holy things for the holy." Nor does he baptize, or anoint, or lay on hands and make bishops and priests and deacons; nor does he anoint churches, or wear the symbols of the priesthood, the pallium and the Gospel book as the crown and purple robe are symbols of kingship.' 'And why does Holy Writ say that Melchizedek is king and priest,' you said? And I said, 'Melchizedek was the one symbol of the one king of all things who is by nature God become by nature high priest for our salvation. And since you say there is another king and priest according to the order of Melchizedek, dare also to say the rest, that is, that he is without father, without mother, without genealogy, not having beginning of days or end of life (cf. Heb 7:3). And see the evil growing out of this; for another will be found who is God incarnate according to the order of Melchizedek but not according to the order of Aaron, to work out our salvation.' "

5. Still, why do we wish to go through many things? During the holy anaphora[11] at the holy altar, after the bishops and deacons and the whole priestly rank, the emperors are remembered with the laity when the deacon says, 'And those laymen who have died in faith, Constantine, Constans, and the others.' Thus he makes memory of living emperors after all the clergy." While he was saying this, Menas cried, "In saying these things you split the Church." And he said to him, "If the one who speaks the things of Holy Writ and those of the holy Fathers splits the Church, then the one who destroys the dogmas of the saints, what will he be shown to do to the Church, for without them the Church could not even be such!" And turning about, the bursar said with a loud cry to the exarch's men, "Tell the exarch, 'Should you have let such a man live where you preside?' " And taking him outside, they introduced his disciple, and they demanded that he denounce his master as if he had afflicted Pyrrhus; he answered in a quiet voice what was true, that no one honored Pyrrhus as he honored him; and he was ordered to speak louder. And seeing that he did not consent to give up the

21

decent speech becoming to monks, he ordered him to be beaten by those standing by; and striking him with their fists, they rendered him half-dead.

When they had been dismissed to their prison, Menas went to the old man and said in the presence of the officials, "God has struck you and brought you here in order for you to receive whatever you did to others, leading everyone into the doctrines of Origen."[12] To him the servant of God said in the presence of all, "Anathema to Origen and all his doctrines and to all of the same mind!" And the patrician Epiphanios said, "The rumor which you spread about him, abbot Menas, has been dissipated, or else if he was an Origenist, he freed himself from such a crime when he pronounced the Anathema. I will no longer admit that such a thing be said of him." Each one of them was led out and kept under guard.

6. That same day around nightfall the patrician Troilus and Sergius Euchratas, who was the one in charge of the royal table, came to the elderly servant of God. They sat down and invited him also to sit down. Then they said to him, "Tell us, lord abbot, about the doctrinal dispute which took place between you and Pyrrhus in Africa and Rome, and by what words you persuaded him to condemn his own dogma and to embrace your own."[13] And he recounted everything to them in order, just as memory allowed. He affirmed, "I have no dogma of my own, just the common dogma of the Catholic Church. For I did not promote any formula so that a dogma could be said to be mine." After this explanation they said to him, "You are not in communion with the see of Constantinople?" And he said, "I am not in communion." "For what reason are you not in communion?" they asked. He answered, "Because they have rejected the four holy councils through the Nine Chapters adopted in Alexandria,[14] and through the Ecthesis[15] adopted in this city by Sergius, and recently through the Typos which was published in the sixth indiction;[16] and because what they decreed by the chapters they condemned by the Ecthesis; and what they decreed by the Ecthesis they overturned by the Typos. And they contradicted themselves as many times. Thus those who were condemned by themselves and later by the Romans as well at the council held in the eighth indiction[17]—what kind of liturgy can they celebrate, or what kind of Spirit can settle on those which are celebrated by such people?" And they said to him, "Will you alone be saved and all others be lost?" To which he replied, "The three young men who did not adore the idol

22

when all others adored it did not condemn anyone. They did not attend to what belonged to others but attended to this, that they not lapse from true worship. Likewise, Daniel, when thrown into the lion's den, did not condemn anyone who did not pray to God in accordance with the decree of Darius, but attended to what was his own role, and he preferred to die and not offend God than to be afflicted by his conscience over the transgression of the laws of nature.[18] Thus it is with me as well; may God grant that I neither condemn anyone nor say that I alone am saved. But I prefer to die rather than to have on my conscience that I in any way at all have been deficient in what concerns faith in God."

7. They said to him, "And what will you do if the Romans unite with the Byzantines? For behold, yesterday there came legates of Rome and tomorrow on Sunday they will take communion with the patriarch; it will become evident to all that it was you who turned the Romans away.[19] Doubtless with you removed, there will then be an easy union." And he said to them, "Those who are coming cannot in any way prejudice the see of Rome, even if they should take communion because they have not brought a letter to the patriarch. And I am not at all convinced that the Romans will unite with them unless they confess that our Lord and God by nature both wills and works our salvation according to each of the natures from which he is, in which he is, as well as which he is."[20] And they said, "And if the Romans should come to terms with them at this time, what will you do?" He replied, "The Holy Spirit, according to the Apostle, condemns even angels who sanction anything against what has been preached."[21]

8. Then they asked, "Is it altogether necessary to speak of wills and energies on the subject of Christ?" He answered, "Altogether necessary if we want to worship in truth, for no being exists without natural activity. Indeed, the holy Fathers say plainly that it is impossible for any nature at all to be or to be known apart from its essential activity. And if there is no such thing as a nature to be or to be known without its essential characteristic activity, how is it possible for Christ to be or be known as truly God and man by nature without the divine and human activities? For according to the Fathers, the lion who loses his roaring ability is no lion at all, and a dog without the power to bark is not a dog. And any other thing which has lost something naturally constitutive of it is not any more what it was." And they said to him, "We know well that this is so; still, do not grieve the emperor who issued the

Typos for the sake of peace and that alone, not because he wanted to destroy any of those things understood of Christ but to arrange for the silence of those terms which were causing the dissension."

9. Then casting himself upon the ground with tears, the servant of God said, "Let not the good and pious lord be offended by my lowliness. I cannot grieve God by keeping silent about what he ordered us to speak and confess. For if according to the divine Apostle he is 'the founder in the church first of apostles, secondly of prophets, thirdly of teachers (Eph 4:11),' then it is clear that he is the one who spoke through them. Thus throughout the whole of Holy Writ, both of the Old as well as the New Testament, and also of the holy doctors and councils, we learn that the God incarnate both wills and works in both his divinity and in his humanity. For he is lacking in nothing of those things by which he is known as God and of those things by which he is known as man by nature except sin. If he is complete according to each nature, as nothing is lacking to either, it is obvious that one is corrupting the whole mystery unless he confesses that he is what he is with the natural properties which belong to him according to each nature in which and which he is."

10. After being silent for a while, they said while nodding to each other, "How can you show that those in charge of the see of Constantinople reject the holy councils?" And he said to them, "It has already been shown in part from the things said at Rome by me at the Lord Gregory's, the private secretary. And now if it please the emperor that it be shown, he will order that permission be given to your humble servant and I shall point out a list of books, because mine were taken from me, and I shall make everything clear without any kind of verbal crookedness." Then while they were speaking about many other things they turned both arguments and thoughts to Scripture, nature, and logic. They were pleased with these and came to be of a more cheerful frame of mind, and they began to say, "God knows, we obtained spiritual profit, and we shall not importune you any more."

11. But the lord Sergius said to him, "Often did I go to your cell in Bebbas and listen to your teaching; and Christ will help you and do not be distressed. But there is only one thing in which you grieve everyone, that you are the cause why many are separated from the communion of the Church here." "Is there anyone," said the servant of God, "who claims that I said, 'Do not be in communion with the Byzantine church'?" The lord Sergius replied, "The very fact that you are not in communion is a great exclamation for all not to be in commu-

nion." And the servant of the Lord said, "There is nothing more compelling than an accusing conscience, and nothing more outspoken than a supporting one." When the lord Troilus heard that the Typos had been condemned throughout the whole West, he said to the servant of God, "Is it good that the decree of our venerable emperor be outraged?" The servant of God answered him, "May God pardon those who made the emperor issue the Typos and those who allowed it." He replied, "Those highy placed in the Church made him do it, and the state officials allowed it; and behold, the filth from those who are responsible was shaken out over the one who is innocent and pure of any heresy.[22] But advise him of what his late venerable grandfather did. For when he became aware that some from the West were heaping the blame on him, he made himself free of any censure from the Church through a decree which he composed: 'The Ecthesis[23] is not mine; for I neither dictated it nor ordered its composition; but the patriarch Sergius, having composed it five years before my return from the East, requested upon my return to the happy city that it be published in my name with a signature. And I acceded to his entreaty. Now, however, knowing some are in dispute over it, I make it manifest to all that it is not mine.' He issued this decree to the blessed Pope John, who had condemned the Ecthesis at the time when he was writing to Pyrrhus.[24] And from that time on the Ecthesis was everywhere called the work of Sergius. Let the one who venerably rules over us also do this, and his image will be completely undefiled of any censure." Then shaking their heads they remained silent, saying only this, "The whole problem is difficult and without solution."

12. After they had spoken of these and of other matters, they exchanged reverences and left with all cheerfulness. Once again on the following Saturday they led them into the palace; and they led in first the old man's disciple,[25] in the presence of the two patriarchs.[26] Next they led in Constantine and Menas, the old man's accusers, who demanded that the disciple assent to the things spoken by them. But with all outspokenness the disciple fearlessly said to the senate, "You are bringing Constantine into the palace chamber? He is neither a priest nor a monk, but a stage soldier. It was well known to the Africans and the Romans what kind of loose young girls he kept on his visits there. All knew the craftiness which he used to hide the fact. Sometimes he would say that they were his sisters, sometimes that he took them so that they would not be in communion with the Church of Constantinople lest they be stained by heretical communion. And further, if he

wanted to continue his wantonness, he would find a country where they do not know him yet, and do these same things for the sake of his disgraceful profit and his dirty pleasure. And it is a great shame for anyone who desires to live a decent life even to have any contact with him." Then after this he was asked whether he condemned the Typos and he replied fearlessly, "Not only did I condemn it but also drew up a small document against it." "Why, then," asked the officials, "do you not confess that you acted wrongly?" And he said, "May God not grant that whatever I did rightly according to the law of the Church be said to be evil." And after he was questioned on many other points and having answered as God inspired him, he was led out of the chamber.

13. Once more they led in the old man and the lord Troilus said to him, "Speak, Abbot; look, speak the truth and the emperor will have mercy on you. For if we should go through a legal declaration and it be found that even one of the things against you is true, the law will take away your life." And he said, "I have already said it and say it again, that if only one thing is said to be true then also Satan is God. But if he is not God but an apostate, then also the accusations against me are false and without substance. Still, do whatever you decide to do. I will not be harmed if I worship God." And he said to him, "Did you not condemn the Typos?" He answered, "I have said many times that I did condemn it." And he asked him, "Did you condemn the Typos? Then you condemned the emperor." The servant of God answered, "I did not condemn the emperor but a document alien to the orthodox faith of the Church." And he said to him, "Where was it condemned?" "At the synod of Rome," he replied, "in the Church of the Savior and in that of the Mother of God."[27] Then the eparch said to him, "Are you in communion with the Church of those of this city or are you not?" He answered, "I am not in communion." He said to him, "For what reason?" He replied, "Because it has rejected the councils." And he said, "If it has thrown out the councils, then how is it that they are referred to in the diptychs?"[28] But he said, "And what is the use of the words when the dogmas are rejected?" "And can you?" he said, "demonstrate this?" He answered, "If I have the liberty and you allow it, I will demonstrate this very easily." And everyone became quiet and the bursar said to him, "Why do you love the Romans and hate the Greeks?"[29] In answer the servant of God said, "We have a precept which says not to hate anyone. I love the Romans as those who share the same faith, and the Greeks as sharing the same language." And again the bursar said to him, "How old do you say you are?" He answered, "Seventy-five years

26

old." And he said to him, "How many years has your disciple been with you?" He answered, "Thirty-seven." Then one of the clerics exclaimed, "The lord has rendered to you as much as you did to the late Pyrrhus!" To him he answered nothing at all.

14. As such things were being spoken in the chamber, neither of the patriarchs said anything. But when mention was made of the synod of Rome, Demosthenes cried out, "The synod has no force since the one who summoned it has been deposed."[30] And the servant of God said, "Not deposed but banished. What synodal and canonical act is there among the things accomplished which firmly attests his deposition? Even so, should he be canonically deposed, this does not do prejudice to the things which were written by the late Pope Theodore." And hearing these things the patrician Troilus said, "You do not know what you are saying, Abbot; what is done has been correctly done."

15. Such were the things done and said as far as memory retains them. And the matters concerning them came to such an end when they dismissed the holy old man from the chamber into prison. And on the next day, which was Sunday, the officials of the Church held a meeting and persuaded the emperor to condemn them to that cruel and inhuman exile and to separate them from each other, the holy old man to Bizya, a city of Thrace, and his disciples to Perberis, at the outer limit of the Roman Empire,[31] unprovided for, naked, without nourishment, lacking every resource of life. They did not have access to the sea so that they could not receive helpful visits from those who were merciful. And thus they were, naked and hungry, having only God's help, exhorting all Christians and crying aloud, "Pray through the Lord that God might perfect his mercy with our lowliness, and that he might teach us that those who sail along with him experience a savage sea, like a ship which is driven about by winds and waves but stands firm and unshakeable." For he allowed them to be tried by a great storm, testing their disposition toward him so that they might cry out with a loud voice, "Lord, save us, we are perishing (Mt 8:25)," and so that they might know enough to attribute all the things concerning their salvation to him alone; nor that they should put their trust in themselves but rather attain great calm while the wind and waves are lulled. And he led them out in the midst of wolves (Mt 10:16) and ordered them to enter through the narrow gate and to journey through the straitened path (Mt 7:14). And he offered them hunger and thirst and nakedness, and bonds and prisons and exiles and scourges and a cross and nails and vinegar and gall and spitting and slaps and blows and mockings. Their

end was a radiant resurrection, bringing peace with it to those who had been persecuted on his account, and joy to those who were afflicted for him, and ascension into heaven and accession at the Father's transcendent throne, and an appointed place above every principality and power and virtue and domination, and every name which is named whether in this age or in the one to come. May we obtain all of these things through the prayers and intercessions of the all-holy supremely glorious Mary, truly by nature Mother of God and Ever-Virgin worthy of all praise, and of the holy apostles, prophets, and martyrs. Amen.[32]

NOTES

1. This is, strictly speaking, the first trial of Maximus, which took place in Constantinople in June, 654. According to R. Devreesse ("La vie de saint Maxime le Confesseur et ses recensions," *AB* 46 [1928]: 8) the author of this account is Anastasius, the faithful disciple of Maximus. Because of the detailed character of the report, however, and Anastasius's confinement in a far-off cell at the time of these proceedings, J. M. Garrigues is inclined to attribute authorship to other friends of Maximus, the brothers Theodore and Theodosius of Gangres. Cf. "Le Martyre de saint Maxime le Confesseur," *Révue Thomiste* 76, no. 1 (January-March, 1976): 414.

2. The *sacellarius* was imperial treasurer or keeper of the privy purse. The office developed into one to which was attached much political power. Cf. L. Bréhier, *Les institutions de l'empire byzantin* (Paris, 1970), p. 210; R. Guilland, *Recherches sur les institutions byzantines* (Berlin-Amsterdam, 1967), I 357–58; Arthur E. R. Boak and James Dunlap, *Two Studies in Later Roman and Byzantine Administration* (New York, 1924).

3. The Muslim armies swept over these lands in a wave of conquests in the 640s. The swiftness of their victories was due in no small part to the religious divisions in the eastern half of the empire.

4. Constans II (641–668), son of Constantine III, was the emperor in 654. His grandfather was the emperor Heraclius, who reigned from 610 to 641. On him see A. Pernice, *L'imperatore Eraclio, Saggio di storia bizantina* (Florence, 1905).

5. In 646 Gregory, the governor of Roman Africa, led an abortive revolt against the imperial government in a move to replace the emperor. It is hypothesized that this Gregory was the son of the governor Nicetas, who was first cousin of the emperor Heraclius; cf. Diehl, *L'Afrique Byzantine* (Paris, 1896), p. 525. Maximus himself disposes of this accusation in *Vita ac Certamen*, PG 90:89BC, 112CD, 113A. Even if the accusation is fanciful, it must yet be acknowledged that the West had been sorely tried for some years by the heretical or quasi-heretical policies of the emperor Constans and his predecessors

(excluding Constantine III). Gregory seized his opportunity in 646 by proclaiming himself emperor but was killed a few months later in a battle with an invading Muslim army.

6. "Supersubstantial," that is, transcending all categories of the human mind, including the category of "being" itself; the Greek word, from the Pseudo-Dionysius, is *hyperousios*. See also "The Four Hundred Chapters on Love" 3:27.

7. The Typos was a document promulgated by the emperor in late 648. It enjoined silence on the matter of the number of wills or activities in Christ and carried severe sanctions for those who disobeyed. As Maximus makes clear, to remain silent while an essential truth was being denied was to collaborate in the denial. At issue here, lurking in the background but about to break into the open as the proceedings of the trial make clear, is the question of the emperor's authority *within* the church.

8. The term translated as "arrange" is the verbal form of "economy."

9. That is, do not make things more difficult than they have to be.

10. I.e., economy.

11. The canon, or eucharistic prayer.

12. On the connection between Maximus and Origenism one may read with profit P. Sherwood, *The Earlier Ambigua of Saint Maximus the Confessor and His Refutation of Origenism*, (Rome, 1955); idem, *"Maximus and Origenism," Berichte zum XI Int. Byz. Kongresse* (Munich, 1958); I. H. Dalmais, "S. Maxime le Confesseur et la crise de l'Origénisme monastique," in *Théologie de la Vie Monastique* (Paris, 1961), pp. 411–21; idem, "L'héritage évagrien dans la synthèse de s. Maxime le Confesseur," *Studia Patristica* 8 (1966); 356–63.

13. The successor of Sergius as patriarch of Constantinople, Pyrrhus was forced to resign the see and flee to Africa when the people rose up against him and the unpopular empress-mother Martina. A Monothelite, he allowed himself to be convinced by the persuasive logic of Maximus in the famous debate held in Carthage in 645 (PG 91:288–353) to which reference is here made. Pyrrhus traveled to Rome to make his submission in person to pope Theodore, only to relapse into heresy when the political situation had changed (because of the sudden death of the pretender Gregory). On this see *Liber Pontificalis* (Theodore), L. Duchesne, *L'Eglise au VIème Siècle* (Paris, 1925), pp. 431–85. Reinstalled on the patriarchal seat in late 653 or early 654 he lived only a few months, dying a few weeks before Maximus's trial. On the sources, cf. Andreas N. Stratos, "The Patriarch Pyrrhus" (in Greek) *Studies in 7th Century Byzantine Political History* (London, 1983).

14. These forged a reconciliation between Egyptian Monophysites and Orthodox on the basis of Monenergist formulas in June 633. Cf. Mansi XI; 561–65; *Vita*, PG 90:77C; Theophanes, *Chronographia*, 330.

15. An exposition of the faith signed by the emperor and issued by him in 638. It is openly both Monenergistic and Monothelite. In a letter to pope

John IV the emperor Heraclius rejected authorship and ascribed it to Sergius (PG 90:125 AB).

16. I.e., in 647.

17. The Lateran Synod of 649.

18. Cf. Dn 3 and 6.

19. Emissaries had indeed arrived from Rome to request imperial sanction for the consecration of the new pope, Eugene I, who was elected to replace the exiled Martin I.

20. An expression that is typical of Maximus's defense of the full and functioning humanity and divinity of Christ. Cf. Amb.Th. 5 (PG 91:1052D). On this expression, cf. Pierre Piret, S.J., "Christologie et Théologie Trinitaire chez Maxime le Confesseur, d'après sa formule des natures 'desquelles, en lesquelles, et lesquelles est le Christ,' " in MC 215–22; also idem, Le Christ et la Trinité selon Maxime le Confesseur (Paris, 1983).

21. Cf. Gal 1:8.

22. Maximus is referring to the reigning emperor, Constans II.

23. According to the chronicler Theophanes, Heraclius was confused by the orthodox reaction to his decree, especially by the Synodicon of Sophronius, but was unwilling to undo his work or to admit the error behind it (Chronographia, 330). The text of the Ecthesis has been preserved in the acta of the Lateran Synod of 649 (Third Session), Mansi X. It was in reality a reissue of a document called the Psephos, written by Sergius and published over the emperor's signature.

24. Mansi X, 607, 682–86. Also Theophanes, 508.

25. Anastasius the disciple. On him cf. S. Brock, "An Early Syriac Life of Maximus the Confessor," AB XCI (1973):317.

26. Who were these patriarchs? E. Montmasson ("La Chronologie de la vie de s. Maxime le Confesseur," EO 13 [1910]:149–54) says Pyrrhus and Paul, basing himself on the calculations of E. Brooks ("On the Lists of the Patriarchs of Constantinople from 638 to 715," BZ 6 [1897]: 40–47). R. Devreesse thinks they are Peter of Constantinople and Macedonius of Antioch, then resident in the capital because of the Arab conquest of Syria. Or perhaps, suggests the same author, the second patriarch is Theodore, the patriarchal vicar of Alexandria who had succeeded the Melkite Peter of Alexandria (loc. cit.).

27. The Lateran Synod of 649. On this see E. Caspar, "Die Lateransynode von 649," Zeitschrift Für Kirchengeschichte 51 (1932): 75–137. The first church mentioned is the basilica of St. John Lateran and the second is St. Mary Major.

28. The "diptychs" were the rosters of those for whom prayers were said at the Eucharist. Exclusion of a name from the diptychs was therefore tantamount to excommunication. The argument here is that by including the orthodox councils in the diptychs, the Byzantines continued to affirm them; but

Maximus dismisses this as a mere formality when the content of what the councils had confessed was being denied.

29. Ordinarily the term "Roman" was used of the Byzantines, the eastern Romans. The use of it to denote the Latins and the corresponding use of the term Greeks to refer to themselves represented a shift in traditional usage by the Byzantines. See J. M. Garrigues, *art. cit.*, 423 n. 22.

30. Pope Martin I had been arrested in Rome and forcibly brought to Constantinople. Convicted of having been involved in the treasonous uprising of Olympius of Ravenna, he was banished to Cherson in the Crimea and died there six months later. We have two letters from him where Martin gives information about his imprisonment: Mansi I, 849–53.

31. Bizya, the modern Vize, is near the Turkish-Bulgarian border. Mesembria (Mesemuriya) is in present-day Bulgaria.

32. In exile the great theologian was a sore embarrassment to the emperor and the patriarch. To Bizya were dispatched in August 646 two emissaries in their name to try to reason with the Confessor. The text of this famous disputation is preserved in PG 90:136–72. Despite its promising outcome it issues in no reconciliation because of the emperor's unwillingness to follow through (164B). Instead, Maximus is moved about, winding up in Perberis with his disciple Anastasius. Six years later, in 662, Maximus is again brought to Constantinople to undergo a second trial. With his two associates, both called Anastasius, he is condemned and mutilated by having his tongue ripped out from the root and his right hand amputated, traditional punishment for those who have spoken and written against the emperor (172AB; Theophanes, 351). In this condition the three confessors were led to their last exile in Lazica where they were separated for the last time. Maximus was shut up in the fortress of Schemarum, Tsikhe-Muris near the modern Tsageri in Georgian USSR, where in the eighteenth century, according to the Benedictine editors of the *Vie des Saints* (Paris, 1949, VIII:235), there still existed in the vicinity a monastery dedicated to St. Maximus. He died soon after, on August 13, 662.

THE FOUR HUNDRED CHAPTERS ON LOVE

PROLOGUE

Here, Father Elpidius,[1] besides the discourse on the *Ascetic Life*,[2] I have sent this discourse on love to your Grace, arranged in four centuries[3] in equal number to the four Gospels. While it is perhaps not at all worthy of your expectation, it is yet the best I could do. Your Grace should know that these are not the fruit of my own meditation. Instead, I went through the writings of the holy Fathers and selected from them whatever had reference to my subject, summarizing many things in few words so that they can be seen at a glance to be easily memorized. These I have sent to your Grace requesting that you read them with indulgence and look for only what is of profit in them, over-looking a style which lacks charm, and to pray for my modest ability which is bereft of any spiritual profit. I further request that you not be annoyed by anything that is said; I have simply fulfilled an obligation. I say this because there are many of us who give annoyance today by words while those who instruct or receive instruction by deeds are very few.

Rather, please pay careful attention to each chapter. For not all, I believe, are easily understandable by everyone, but the majority will require much scrutiny by many people even though they appear to be very simply expressed. Perhaps it might happen that something useful to the soul will be revealed out of them. This will happen completely from God's grace to the one who reads with an uncomplicated mind, with the fear of God, and with love. But if someone reads this or any other book whatever not for the sake of spiritual profit but to hunt for phrases to reproach the author so that he might then set himself up in his own opinion as wiser than he, such a person will never receive any profit of any kind.

First Century

1. Love[4] is a good disposition of the soul by which one prefers no being to the knowledge[5] of God. It is impossible to reach the habit of this love if one has any attachment to earthly things.

2. Love is begotten of detachment,[6] detachment of hope in God, hope of patient endurance and long-suffering, these of general self-mastery, self-mastery of fear of God, and fear of faith in the Lord.

3. The one who believes the Lord fears punishment; the one who fears punishment becomes master of his passions; the one who becomes master of his passions patiently endures tribulations; the one who patiently endures tribulations will have hope in God; hope in God separates from every earthly attachment; and when the mind is separated from this it will have love for God.[7]

4. The one who loves God prefers knowledge of him to all things made by him and is constantly devoted to it by desire.

5. If all things have been made by God and for his sake, then God is better than what has been made by him. The one who forsakes the better and is engrossed in inferior things shows that he prefers the things made by God to God himself.

6. The one who has his mind fixed on the love of God disdains all visible things and even his own body as alien.[8]

7. If the soul is better than the body and God incomparably better than the world which he created, the one who prefers the body to the soul and the world to the God who created it is no different from idolaters.

8. The one who separates his mind from love and devotedness toward God and keeps it tied to any sensible thing is the one who prefers the body to the soul and things that are made to God their Creator.

9. If the life of the mind is the illumination of knowledge and this is born of love for God, then it is well said that there is nothing greater than love.[9]

10. When in the full ardor of its love[10] for God the mind goes out of itself, then it has no perception at all either of itself or of any creatures. For once illumined by the divine and infinite light, it remains insensible to anything that is made by him, just as the physical eye has no sensation of the stars when the sun has risen.

11. All the virtues assist the mind in the pursuit of divine love, but above all does pure prayer. By it the mind is given wings to go ahead to God and becomes alien to all things.

12. When through love the mind is ravished by divine knowledge and in going outside of creatures has a perception of divine transcendence,[11] then, according to the divine Isaiah, it comes in consternation to a realization of its own lowliness and says with conviction the words of the prophet:

Woe is me for I am stricken at heart; because being a man having unclean lips, I dwell in the midst of a people with unclean lips and I have seen with my eyes the King, the Lord of hosts.[12]

13. The one who loves God cannot help but love also every man as himself even though he is displeased by the passions of those who are not yet purified. Thus when he sees their conversion and amendment, he rejoices with an unbounded and unspeakable joy.

14. The passionate soul is impure, filled with thoughts of lust and hatred.

15. The one who sees a trace of hatred in his own heart through any fault at all toward any man whoever he may be makes himself completely foreign to the love for God, because love for God in no way admits of hatred for man.

16. "The one who loves me," says the Lord, "will keep my commandments" and "this is my commandment, that you love one another."[13] Therefore the one who does not love his neighbor is not keeping the commandment, and the one who does not keep the commandment is not able to love the Lord.

17. Blessed is the man who has learnt to love all men equally.[14]

18. Blessed is the man who is not attached to any corruptible or transitory thing.

19. Blessed is the mind which has gone beyond all beings and takes unceasing delight in the divine beauty.

20. The one who makes provision for the desires of the flesh[15] and bears a grudge against his neighbor for transitory things—such a man serves the creature rather than the Creator.[16]

21. The one who keeps his body away from pleasure and sickness keeps it as a fellow worker in the service of better things.

22. The one who flees all the world's desires puts himself beyond every worldly grief.

23. The one who loves God surely loves his neighbor as well. Such a person cannot hold on to money but rather gives it out in God's fashion to each one who has need.[17]

24. The one who imitates God by giving alms knows no difference between evil and good or just and unjust in regard to the needs of the body, but distributes to all without distinction according to their need even if he prefers the virtuous person over the wicked because of his good intention.[18]

25. Just as God who is by nature good and free of passion loves all in an equal way as his creatures but glorifies the virtuous man for having become his friend through his intention and has mercy on the wicked out of his goodness and converts him by chastening him in this life, so also does the one who is good and without passion through his intention love equally all men—the virtuous because of his nature and good will and likewise the wicked because of his nature and compassion by which he pities one who is foolish and makes his way in darkness.

26. The disposition of love is made manifest not only in the sharing of money but much more in sharing the word of God and physical service.

27. The one who has genuinely renounced worldly matters and serves his neighbor without pretense through love soon frees himself of all passion and is rendered a sharer of divine love and knowledge.

28. The one who has acquired divine love in himself does not grow weary of closely following after the Lord his God, as the divine Jeremiah[19] says; rather he endures nobly every reproachful hardship and outrage without thinking any evil of anyone.

29. When you are insulted by someone or offended in any matter, then beware of angry thoughts, lest by distress they sever you from charity and place you in the region of hatred.

30. Whenever you are suffering intensely from insult or disgrace, realize that this can be of great benefit to you, for disgrace is God's way of driving vainglory out of you.

31. As the memory of fire does not warm the body, so faith without love does not bring about the illumination of knowledge in the soul.

32. As the light of the sun attracts the healthy eye, so does the knowledge of God draw the pure mind to itself naturally through love.

33. The mind is pure when it is removed from ignorance and illuminated by divine light.

34. The soul is pure when it has been freed from the passions[20] and rejoices unceasingly in divine love.

35. A blameworthy passion is a movement of the soul contrary to nature.[21]

36. Detachment is a peaceful state of the soul in which it becomes resistant to vice.

37. The one who has zealously acquired the fruits of love does not change from it even though he experiences countless ills. And let Stephen, Christ's disciple, and those like him, persuade you, as well as Christ himself who prays for his murderers and asks forgiveness of his Father as for those acting in ignorance.[22]

38. If it is a mark of love to be patient and kind,[23] the one who acts contentiously or wickedly clearly makes himself a stranger to love, and the one who is a stranger to love is a stranger to God, since "God is love."[24]

39. Do not say, as the divine Jeremiah tells us, that you are the Lord's temple.[25] And do not say that "mere faith in our Lord Jesus Christ can save me." For this is impossible unless you acquire love for him through works. For in what concerns mere believing, "even the devils believe and tremble."[26]

40. The work of love is the deliberate doing of good to one's neighbor as well as long-suffering and patience and the use of all things in the proper way.

41. The one who loves God is not sad nor does he grieve anyone because of any passing thing. Only one salutary sadness makes him sad and grieves others, the one which the blessed Paul had and with which he grieved the Corinthians.[27]

42. The one who loves God leads an angelic life on earth, fasting and being watchful and singing psalms and praying and always thinking good of everyone.[28]

43. If anyone desires anything, he naturally strives to obtain it. Now the divine is incomparably better and more desirable than all good and desirable things. What great zeal, then, should we show to obtain what is good and desirable by nature![29]

44. Do not stain your flesh with indecent actions; do not defile your soul with evil thoughts; and God's peace will come upon you and bring love.

45. Afflict your flesh with fasting and vigils. Devote yourself diligently to psalmody and prayer, and holiness in chastity will come upon you and bring love.

46. The one who is deemed worthy of divine knowledge and who through love has attained its illumination will never be blown about by the spirit of vainglory. But the one who is not yet deemed worthy of di-

vine knowledge is easily carried to and fro by it. If such a one, then, should look to God in everything that he does, as doing everything for his sake, he will easily escape it with God.

47. The one who has not yet obtained divine knowledge activated by love makes a lot of the religious works he performs. But the one who has been deemed worthy to obtain this says with conviction the words which the patriarch Abraham spoke when he was graced with the divine appearance, "I am but earth and ashes."[30]

48. The one who fears the Lord always has humility as his companion and through its promptings is led to divine love and thanksgiving. For he recalls his former worldly life and different transgressions and the temptations bedeviling him from his youth, and how the Lord delivered him from all these things and made him pass from this life of passion to a divine life. And so with fear he receives love as well, ever thankful with deep humility to the benefactor and pilot of our life.

49. Do not soil your mind by holding on to thoughts of concupiscence and anger, lest by falling from pure prayer you fall in with the spirit of discouragement.[31]

50. The mind falls from familiarity[32] with God whenever it consorts with wicked and foul thoughts.

51. When the senseless man who is driven by his passions is moved by anger and becomes troubled, he will be eager to flee foolishly from the brethren. But when again he is aroused by concupiscence, he regrets this and runs back to them. The sensible man does the opposite in both situations. In time of anger he cuts off the causes of disorder and frees himself from grief toward the brethren; in time of concupiscence he controls any irrational impulse and relationship.[33]

52. In a period of temptations do not abandon your monastery but bear courageously the waves of thoughts, especially those of sadness and discouragement. Being thus tested with tribulations by divine dispensation, you will have a firm hope in God. But if you leave you will be accounted reprobate, unmanly, and unstable.

53. If you desire not to fall away from divine love, do not let your brother go to bed with anger against you, nor should you go to bed angry against him. Rather, "go, be reconciled with your brother, and come offer" to Christ with a clear conscience the gift of love in fervent prayer.[34]

54. If one has all the gifts of the Spirit, but not love, it profits him nothing, as the divine Apostle says.[35] How great a zeal should we show to acquire it!

55. If "love works no evil to one's neighbor,"[36] the one who envies his brother and is unhappy over his good name and smears his reputation with scoffing or in any way maliciously contrives against him, how does he not render himself a stranger to love and liable to eternal judgment?

56. If "love is the fullness of the law,"[37] how can the one who keeps a grudge against his brother and sets a trap for him and curses him and rejoices over his misfortune be anything but a transgressor and liable to eternal punishment?

57. If "the one who slanders his brother and judges his brother slanders and judges the law,"[38] and the law of Christ is love, how does the slanderer do anything but fall away from the love of Christ and become the cause of his own eternal punishment?

58. Do not lend your ear to the slanderer's tongue nor your tongue to the fault-finder's ear by readily speaking or listening to anything against your neighbor. Otherwise you will fall away from divine love and be found excluded from eternal life.

59. Do not allow any abuse of your father or encourage anyone who dishonors him, lest the Lord become angry at your deeds and destroy you utterly from the land of the living.

60. Silence the one who is slandering in your hearing lest you commit a double sin with him: by accustoming yourself to this deadly vice and by not restraining him from foolish talk against his neighbor.

61. "But I say to you," the Lord says, "love your enemies, do good to those who hate you, pray for those who persecute you."[39] Why did he command these things? So that he might free you from hate, sadness, anger, and grudges, and might grant you the greatest possession of all, perfect love, which is impossible to possess except by the one who loves all men equally in imitation of God, who loves all men equally and "wills that they be saved and come to a knowledge of the truth."[40]

62. "But I tell you to resist evil, but should anyone strike you on the right cheek turn the other to him as well. And if anyone wants to go to court with you and take your tunic, offer him your coat as well; and if one forces you to go one mile, go two with him."[41] Why is this? To keep you free from anger and sadness and to instruct him through your forbearance and to bring you both in his goodness, under the yoke of his love.

63. We carry along with us the voluptuous images of the things we once experienced. Now the one who overcomes these voluptuous images completely disdains the realities of which they are images. In fact,

the battle against memories[42] is more difficult than the battle against deeds, as sinning in thought is easier than sinning in deed.

64. Some of the passions are of the body, some of the soul. Those of the body take their origin in the body; those of the soul from exterior things. Love and self-control cut away both of them, the former those of the soul, the latter those of the body.[43]

65. Some of the passions belong to the irascible, some to the concupiscible part of the soul. Both are moved by means of the senses; and they are moved whenever the soul is found outside of love and self-control.

66. It happens that the passions of the irascible part of the soul are harder to combat than those of the concupiscible. Thus it is that a better remedy for it was given by the Lord: the commandment of love.[44]

67. All the other passions lay hold of either the irascible or the concupiscible part of the soul only, or even of the rational part, as forgetfulness or ignorance. But sloth, by grasping onto all the soul's powers, excites nearly all of them together. In this way it is the most troublesome of all the passions. Well, then, did the Lord tell us in giving the remedy against it, "In your patience possess your souls."[45]

68. Never strike any of the brothers, especially not without reason, lest sometime he not endure the trial and go away. For then you will never escape the reproof of your conscience, always bringing you sadness in the time of prayer and excluding your mind from familiarity with God.

69. Do not tolerate suspicions or people that would be occasions of scandal for you against anyone. For those who take scandal in any way from things which happen, intentionally or unintentionally, do not know the way of peace, which through love brings those who long for it to the knowledge of God.

70. The one who is still affected by human judgments does not yet have perfect love, as for example when he loves one and hates another for one reason or another; or even when he loves and then hates the same person for the same reasons.

71. Perfect love does not split up the one nature of men on the basis of their various dispositions but ever looking steadfastly at it, it loves all men equally, those who are zealous as friends, those who are negligent as enemies. It is good to them and forbearing and puts up with what they do. It does not think evil at all but rather suffers for them, if occasion requires, in order that it may even make them friends if possible. If not, it does not fall away from its own intentions as it ever manifests

the fruits of love equally for all men. In this way also our Lord and God Jesus Christ, manifesting his love for us, suffered for all mankind and granted to all equally the hope of resurrection, though each one renders himself worthy either of glory or of punishment.

72. The one who does not disdain glory and dishonor, riches and poverty, pleasure and pain, does not yet possess perfect love. For perfect love disdains not only these things but also this very transitory life and death.

73. Listen to what those who have been rendered worthy of divine love have to say: "Who shall separate us from the love of Christ? Tribulation, or distress, or persecution, or famine, or nakedness, or danger, or the sword? As it is written, 'for your sake are we put to death the whole day long.' We are accounted as sheep for the slaughter. But in all these things we more than overcome through the one who has loved us. For I am convinced that neither death, nor life, nor angels, nor principalities, nor powers, nor things present, nor things to come, nor height, nor depth, nor any other creature shall be able to separate us from the love of God in Christ Jesus our Lord."[46] All who say and do this concerning the love of God are saints.

74. And concerning love of neighbor, listen again to what they say: "I speak the truth in Christ; I do not lie, and my conscience bears me witness in the Holy Spirit. I have great sadness and continual sorrow in my heart. For I would wish to be anathema myself from Christ for my brethren who are my kinsmen according to the flesh and Israelites."[47] And similarly Moses[48] and other saints.

75. The one who does not disdain glory and pleasure and greed which increases them and which is in turn produced by them cannot cut away the occasions of anger. And the one who does not cut them away cannot attain perfect love.

76. Humility and distress free man from every sin, the former by cutting out the passions of the soul, the latter those of the body. The blessed David shows that he did this in one of his prayers to God, "Look upon my humility and my trouble and forgive all my sins."[49]

77. By means of the commandments the Lord renders detached those who carry them out; by means of the divine doctrines he bestows on them the enlightenment of knowledge.[50]

78. All doctrines are concerned either with God or with visible and invisible things or with Providence and judgment about them.[51]

79. Almsgiving heals the irascible part of the soul; fasting extinguishes the concupiscible part,[52] and prayer purifies the mind and pre-

pares it for the contemplation of reality.[53] For the powers of the soul the Lord has granted us the commandments as well.

80. "Learn of me," he says, "because I am meek and humble of heart."[54] Meekness[55] keeps the temper steady, and humility frees the mind from conceit and vainglory.

81. The fear of the Lord is twofold. The first type is produced in us from threats of punishment, and from it arise in proper order self-control, patience, hope in God, and detachment, from which comes love. The second is coupled with love itself and constantly produces reverence in the soul, lest through the familiarity of love it become presumptuous of God.[56]

82. Perfect love casts out the first fear from the soul which by possessing it no longer fears punishment. The second fear it has always joined to it, as was said. The following passages apply to the first fear: "By the fear of the Lord everyone turns away from evil";[57] and, "The beginning of wisdom is fear of the Lord."[58] And to the second fear: "The fear of the Lord is pure and remains forever and ever,"[59] and, "There is no want in those who fear him."[60]

83. "Put to death your members which are on earth: fornication, uncleanness, lust, evil concupiscence, and greed."[61] He names the care of the flesh "earth"; he speaks of actual sinning as "fornication"; consent he calls "uncleanness"; passionate thoughts he names "lust"; the mere acceptance of a lustful thought is "evil concupiscence"; the matter which gives life and growth to passion he calls "greed." All of these things as members of the wisdom of the flesh the divine Apostle ordered us to put to death.[62]

84. First the memory brings up a simple thought to the mind, and when it lingers about it arouses passion. When it is not removed it sways the mind to consent, and when this happens the actual sinning finally takes place. Thus the all-wise Apostle, in writing to Gentile converts, bids them to remove first of all the effect of the sin, then to backtrack in order to end up at the cause. As previously mentioned, the cause is greed which gives life and growth to passion. And I think that here it signifies gluttony, which is the mother and nurse of fornication. Now greed is evil not only in regard to possessions but also in regard to food, in the same way that self-control is good not only in regard to food but also in regard to possessions.

85. As a little sparrow whose foot is tied tries to fly but is pulled to earth by the cord to which it is bound, so does the mind which does not

yet possess detachment get pulled down and dragged to earth when it flies to the knowledge of heavenly things.

86. When the mind is completely freed from the passions, it journeys straight ahead to the contemplation of created things and makes its way to the knowledge of the Holy Trinity.

87. When the mind is pure and takes on ideas of things it is moved to a spiritual contemplation. But when it has become impure by carelessness, it imagines mere ideas of other things, so that receiving human ideas it turns back to shameful and evil thoughts.

88. When in time of prayer no ideas of the world ever disturb the mind, then know that you are not outside the limits of detachment.

89. When the soul begins to feel its own good health, then does it regard as simple and undisturbing the imaginings which take place in dreams.

90. Just as the beauty of visible things attracts the eye of sense, so also the knowledge of invisible things attracts the pure mind to itself; by invisible things I mean those without a body.

91. It is a great thing not to be affected by things; but it is much greater to remain detached from the thought of them. Therefore, the demons' battle against us through thoughts is more severe than that through deeds.

92. The one who has had success with the virtues and has become rich in knowledge as at last discerning things by their nature does and considers everything according to right reason and is in no way misled. For it is on the basis of whether we make use of things rationally or irrationally that we become either virtuous or wicked.

93. A sign of lofty detachment is that the ideas of the things which are always arising in the heart are just mere thoughts, whether the body is awake or asleep.[63]

94. Through the working out of the commandments the mind puts off the passions. Through the spiritual contemplation of visible realities it puts off impassioned thoughts of things. Through the knowledge of invisible realities it puts off contemplation of visible things. And finally this it puts off through the knowledge of the Holy Trinity.

95. Just as the sun in rising and lighting up the world manifests both itself and the things which it lights up, so the sun of justice in rising on a pure mind manifests both itself and the principles which have been and will be brought to existence by it.[64]

96. We do not know God from his being but from his magnificent

works and his Providence for beings. Through these as through mirrors we perceive his infinite goodness and wisdom and power.[65]

97. The pure mind is found either in simple ideas of human things or in the natural contemplation of visible realities, or in that of invisible realities, or in the light of the Holy Trinity.

98. The mind which is settled in the contemplation of visible realities searches out either the natural reasons of things or those which are signified by them, or else it seeks the cause itself.

99. Dwelling in the contemplation of the invisible it seeks both the natural reasons of these things, the cause of their production, and whatever is consequent upon them, and also what is the Providence and judgment concerning them.

100. Once it is in God, it is inflamed with desire and seeks first of all the principles of his being but finds no satisfaction in what is proper to himself, for that is impossible and forbidden to every created nature alike. But it does receive encouragement from his attributes, that is, from what concerns his eternity, infinity, and immensity, as well as from his goodness, wisdom, and power by which he creates, governs, and judges beings. "And this alone is thoroughly understandable in him, infinity"; and the very fact of knowing nothing about him is to know beyond the mind's power, as the theologians Gregory and Dionysius have both said somewhere.[66]

Second Century

1. The one who truly loves God also prays completely undistracted, and the one who prays completely undistracted also truly loves God. But the one who has his mind fixed on any earthly thing does not pray undistracted; therefore the one who has his mind tied to any earthly thing does not love God.

2. The mind which dallies on a thing of sense certainly has some passion about it, such as desire or sorrow or anger or resentment; and unless he disdains the thing he cannot be freed from that passion.

3. When the passions hold sway over a mind they bind it together with material things, and separating it from God make it to be all-engrossed in them. But when love of God is in control, it releases it from the bonds and persuades it to think beyond not only things of sense but even this transient life of ours.

4. The purpose of the commandments is to make simple the thoughts of things; the purpose of reading and contemplation is to ren-

der the mind clear of any matter or form; from this ensues undistracted prayer.

5. The active[67] way does not suffice by itself for the perfect liberation of the mind from the passions to allow it to pray undistracted unless various spiritual contemplations also relieve it. The former frees the mind only from incontinence and hatred while the latter rid it also of forgetfulness and ignorance, and in this way it will be able to pray as it ought.

6. There are two supreme states of pure prayer, one corresponding to those of the active life, the other to the contemplatives. The first arises in the soul from the fear of God and an upright hope, the second from divine desire and total purification. The marks of the first type are the drawing of one's mind away from all the world's considerations, and as God is present to one, as indeed he is, he makes his prayers without distraction or disturbance. The marks of the second type are that at the very onset of prayer the mind is taken hold of by the divine and infinite light and is conscious neither of itself nor of any other being whatever except of him who through love brings about such brightness in it. Then, when it is concerned with the properties of God, it receives impressions of him which are clear and distinct.[68]

7. What anyone loves he surely holds on to, and looks down on everything that hinders his way to it so as not to be deprived of it. And the one who loves God cultivates pure prayer and throws off from himself every passion which hinders him.

8. The one who throws off self-love, the mother of the passions, will very easily with God's help put aside the others, such as anger, grief, grudges, and so on. But whoever is under the control of the former is wounded, even though unwillingly, by the latter. Self-love is the passion for the body.[69]

9. On account of these five reasons men love one another whether to their praise or blame: for God's sake, as when the virtuous person loves everyone and the one not yet virtuous loves the virtuous person; or for natural reasons, as parents love their children and vice versa; or out of vainglory, as the one who is honored loves the one who honors him; or for greed, as the one who loves a rich man for what he can get; or for the love of pleasure, as the one who is a servant of his belly or genitals. The first of these is praiseworthy, the second is neutral, and the rest belong to the passions.

10. If you hate some people and some you neither love nor hate, while others you love only moderately and still others you love very

much, know from this inequality that you are far from perfect love, which lays down that you must love everyone equally.

11. "Decline from evil and do good."[70] That is, do battle with your enemy to diminish the passions, then keep sober lest they increase. Or again, do battle to acquire virtues, and then remain watchful in order to guard them. This is also what is meant by "working" and "keeping."[71]

12. Those who tempt us with God's permission either arouse the lusts of our soul or stir up our temper or darken our reason, or encompass the body with pain, or plunder our material goods.

13. Either the demons tempt us themselves or they equip those who do not fear the Lord against us: themselves, when we are alone, away from others, just as they tempted the Lord in the desert; through others, when we associate with them, as they tempted the Lord through the Pharisees. It is for us to look to our model and beat them back on both fronts.

14. When the mind begins to make progress in the love of God, the demon of blasphemy begins to tempt him and suggest to him such thoughts as no man but only the devil their father could invent. He does this out of envy for the friend of God, that coming to despair at having such thoughts he no longer dares to approach God in his usual prayer. Nevertheless, the accursed one derives no profit from his plan but rather makes us more steadfast. For engaging in offensive and defensive battle, we become more proven and more sincere in the love of God. "May his sword pierce his heart and may his bows be shattered."[72]

15. In applying itself to visible things the mind knows them in accordance with nature through the medium of the senses, so that neither is the mind evil, nor is natural knowledge, nor the things, nor the senses, for these are all works of God. What then is evil? Evidently it is the passion of the natural representation, which does not have to exist in our use of representations if the mind is watchful.[73]

16. Passion is a movement of the soul contrary to nature either toward irrational love or senseless hate of something or on account of something material. For example, toward irrational love of food, or a woman, or wealth, or passing glory or any other material thing or on their account. Or else it can be toward a senseless hate of any of the preceding things we spoke of, or on account of any one.[74]

17. Or again, vice is the mistaken use[75] of ideas from which follows the abuse of things. For example, in what concerns woman, the proper use of intercourse is its purpose of procreation. So the one who concen-

trates on the pleasure is in error as to its use by considering as good what is not good. Therefore such a person misuses a woman in having intercourse. The same holds true for other objects and representations.

18. When the demons have banished chastity from your mind and surrounded you with thoughts of fornication, then say to the Master with tears, "They have banished me and now they have surrounded me; my joy, deliver me from those who surround me."[76] And you will be safe.

19. The demon of fornication is oppressive, and he violently attacks those who contend against passion. Especially does he do this in their careless living and in their contact with women. For imperceptibly in the softness of pleasure he steals upon the mind and then assails it through the memory when it is in quiet.[77] He inflames the body and presents various forms to the mind to provoke its consent to the sin. If you do not want these things to remain in you, take up fasting and hard work and vigils and blessed solitude with assiduous prayer.

20. Those who are ever seeking our soul do so through passionate thoughts in order to involve it in some sin of thought or deed. When therefore they find that the mind is not receptive, then they will be put to shame and confusion; and when they find it devoted to spiritual contemplation, then they will be quickly turned back and disgraced.[78]

21. The one who anoints his mind for the sacred contests and drives away passionate thoughts from it possesses the character of a deacon. The one who illumines it with knowledge of beings and obliterates counterfeit knowledge possesses that of a priest. Finally, the one who perfects it with the holy perfume of the knowledge of a worshiper of the Holy Trinity possesses that of a bishop.[79]

22. The demons become weak when through the commandments the passions are diminished in us. And they perish when finally they are obliterated through detachment of soul, since they no longer find anything by which they might gain and do battle against it. And this is surely the meaning of "They shall be weakened and perish before your face."[80]

23. Some men abstain from the passions out of human fear; others out of vainglory; others again out of self-control; still others are freed from the passions by the divine judgments.

24. All the Lord's words are embraced in these four: commandments, instruction, threats, promises. Because of them we endure every hardship such as fastings, vigils, sleeping on the ground, hard work and stress in the service of others, outrages, disgrace, tortures, death, and

the like. As the Scripture says, "For the sake of the words of your lips I have kept hard ways."[81]

25. The reward of self-mastery is detachment and that of faith is knowledge. And detachment gives rise to discernment while knowledge gives rise to love for God.

26. The mind that has succeeded in the active life advances in prudence; the one in the contemplative life, in knowledge. For to the former it pertains to bring the one who struggles to a discernment of virtue and vice, while to the latter, to lead the sharer to the principles of incorporeal and corporeal things. Then at length it is deemed worthy of the grace of theology[82] when on the wings of love it has passed beyond all the preceding realities, and being in God it will consider the essence of himself through the Spirit, insofar as it is possible to the human mind.

27. When you intend to know God do not seek the reasons about his being, for the human mind and that of any other being after God [83] cannot discover this. Rather, consider as you can the things about him, for example his eternity, immensity, infinity, his goodness, wisdom, and power which creates, governs, and judges creatures. For that person among others is a great theologian if he searches out the principles of these things, however much or little.[84]

28. He is a powerful man who couples knowledge with action; for by the latter he extinguishes lust and subdues anger, and by the former he gives wings to the mind and flies off to God.

29. When the Lord says, "The Father and I are one,"[85] he is signifying identity of substance. And when he says again, "I am in the Father and the Father is in me,"[86] he indicates the inseparability of the Persons. Therefore the Tritheists in separating the Son from the Father rush in with cliffs all around. For either they say that the Son is coeternal with the Father but separate one from the other and so are compelled to say that he was not begotten of him, and fall off the cliff saying that there are three Gods and three origins, or else they say that he was begotten of him, but insisting on separating are compelled to say that he is not coeternal with the Father and make subject to time the very master of time. For it is necessary both to preserve the one God and to confess the three persons, each one in his individuality, according to the great Gregory.[87] For as he tells us, God is "divided" yet "without division," and "united" yet "with distinction." In this way both the division and the union are extraordinary. But what is so ex-

traordinary in a man being both united with and separated from a man, as the Son to the Father, and nothing more?

30. The one who is perfect in love and has reached the summit of detachment knows no distinction between one's own and another's,[88] between faithful and unfaithful, between slave and freeman, or indeed between male and female. But having risen above the tyranny of the passions and looking to the one nature of men he regards all equally and is equally disposed toward all. For in him there is neither Greek nor Jew, neither male nor female, neither slave nor freeman, but Christ is everything and in everything.[89]

31. From the passions embedded in the soul the demons take their starting base to stir up passionate thoughts in us. Then, by making war on the mind through them they force it to go along and consent to sin. When it is overcome they lead it on to a sin of thought, and when this is accomplished they finally bring it as a prisoner to the deed. After this, at length, the demons who have devastated the soul through thoughts withdraw with them. In the mind there remains only the idol of sin about which the Lord says, "When you see the abomination of desolation standing in the holy place, let him who reads understand."[90] Man's mind is a holy place and a temple of God in which the demons have laid waste the soul through passionate thoughts and set up the idol of sin. That these things have already happened in history no one who has read Josephus can, I think, doubt, though some say that these things will also happen when the Antichrist comes.[91]

32. There are three things that move us to the good: natural tendencies, the holy angels, and a good will. First the natural tendencies, as when what we wish men do to us and we likewise do to them; or as when we see someone in distress and need and we naturally take pity. Second, the holy angels, when for instance we are moved to some good deed and obtain their helpful assistance and are successful. Finally a good will, because when we discern good from evil, we choose the good.

33. Likewise there are three things that move us to evil: passion, the demons, and a bad will. First passion, as when we desire an object beyond reason, such as food outside the time or need, a woman outside the purpose of procreation or one not lawfully ours; or again when we are angered or grieved, for instance against the one who offends or hurts us. Second, the demons, as when they wait for the moment of our carelessness and suddenly set upon us with much violence to rouse

the passions of which we spoke, and similar things. Finally, a bad will, such as when while knowing the good we prefer evil.

34. The reward for the labors of virtue is detachment and knowledge. For these become our patrons in the kingdom of heaven just as the passions and ignorance are the patrons of eternal punishment. Thus the one who seeks these out of human glory and not for their own good should hear the Scripture, "You ask but do not receive because you ask wrongly."[92]

35. There are many things done by men which are noble in themselves but still because of some reason are not noble. For example, fasts and vigils, prayer and psalmody, almsgiving and hospitality are noble in themselves, but when they are done out of vainglory they are no longer noble.

36. God searches the intention of everything that we do, whether we do it for him or for any other motive.

37. When you hear the Scripture saying, "You will render to each one according to his works,"[93] know that God will reward good works but not those done apart from a right intention even if they appear good, but precisely those done with a right intention. For God's judgment looks not on what is done but to the intention behind it.

38. The demon of pride has a twofold wickedness; either he induces the monk to ascribe his virtuous deeds to himself and not to God the bestower of good things and the helper in good behavior, or, unable to persuade him in this, he suggests that he look down on the brothers who are still less advanced than himself. The one who behaves in this way does not realize that he is being induced into denying God's assistance. For if he looks down on them as those who are unable to perform good deeds he is evidently putting himself forward as someone who acts uprightly on his own power; but this is impossible, as the Lord told us, "Outside of me you can do nothing."[94] This is because our weakness, when moved to do good things, is unable to bring anything to completion without the bestower of good things.

39. The one who has come to understand the weakness of human nature has had experience of the divine power, and such a person who because of it has succeeded in some things and is eager to succeed in others never looks down on anyone. For he knows that in the same way that God has helped him and freed him from many passions and hardships, so can he help everyone when he wishes, especially those who are striving for his sake. Although for his own reasons he does not de-

liver all from their passions right away, still as a good and loving physician he heals in his own good time each one of those who are striving.

40. Pride comes along in the quieting of the passions either in the removal of the causes or in the crafty withdrawal of the demons.

41. Nearly every sin is committed for pleasure, and its removal comes about through distress and sorrow whether voluntary or involuntary, through repentance or any predetermined happening brought on by Providence. For, "if we should judge ourselves, we should not be judged. But while we are judged we are chastened by the Lord, lest we be condemned with this world."[95]

42. When a temptation comes upon you unexpectedly, do not inquire of the one through whom it comes but seek the reason for it and you will find correction. Whether it comes from one source or the other, you still have to drink fully the gall of God's judgments.

43. So long as you have evil habits, do not refuse to undergo hardships, so that you may be humbled by them and vomit out pride.

44. Some temptations bring men pleasure, others distress, and still others bodily pain. For according to the cause of the passions rooted in the soul does the Physician of souls apply the medicine of his judgments.

45. The onslaughts of temptations are brought on sometimes to take away sins already committed, or those being committed in the present, or else to cut off those which could be committed. And this is apart from those which come upon one as a trial, as with Job.

46. The sensible man who thinks over the medicine of the divine judgments thankfully bears the misfortunes that befall him because of them, realizing that they have no other cause than his own sins.

47. There are certain things which check the passions in their movement and do not allow them to advance and increase, and there are others which diminish them and make them decrease. For example, fasting, hard labor, and vigils do not allow concupiscence to grow, while solitude, contemplation, prayer, and desire for God decrease it and make it disappear. And similarly is this the case with anger: for example, long-suffering, the forgetting of offenses, and meekness check it and do not allow it to grow, while love, almsgiving, kindness, and benevolence make it diminish.

48. For the mind of the one who is continually with God even his concupiscence abounds beyond measure into a divine desire and whose entire irascible element is transformed into divine love.[96] For by an en-

during participation in the divine illumination[97] it has become altogether shining bright, and having bound its passible element to itself it, as I said, turned it around to a never-ending divine desire and an unceasing love, completely changing over from earthly things to divine.[98]

49. The one who does not envy or is not angry, or who does not bear grudges against the one who has offended him, does not yet have love for him. For it can be that even one who does not yet love does not return evil for evil because of the commandment but in no way does he render good for evil spontaneously. Indeed, deliberately to do good to those who hate you is a mark of perfect spiritual love alone.

50. The one who does not love someone does not necessarily hate him, nor again does the one who does not hate necessarily love; rather, he can be in a neutral position to him, that is, neither loving nor hating. For only the five ways mentioned in the ninth chapter of this century can produce a loving disposition. These are the praiseworthy way, the neutral way, and the blameworthy ones.

51. When you see your mind dallying with pleasure over material things and taking fond delight in thinking of them, know that you love these things rather than God. "For where your treasure is," says the Lord, "there will your heart be also."[99]

52. The mind which attains God and abides with him through prayer and love becomes wise, good, powerful, benevolent, merciful, and forbearing; in short, it carries around almost all the divine qualities in itself. But when it withdraws from him and goes over to material things it becomes pleasure-loving like cattle or fights with men like a wild beast over these things.[100]

53. Scripture calls material things the world, and worldly people are those who let their mind dwell on them. Against these is the very sharp reproof: "Do not love the world nor the things in the world; the concupiscence of the flesh and the concupiscence of the eyes, and the pride of life are not from God but from the world."[101]

54. A monk is one who separates his mind from material things and who devotes himself to God by self-mastery, love, psalmody, and prayer.

55. The active man is allegorically a cattle herder, for moral actions are signified by cattle, as when Jacob said, "Your servants are herders of cattle." But the gnostic is the shepherd, for the thoughts which are tended by the mind on the mountains of contemplation are signified by

sheep, as again, "All shepherds are an abomination to the Egyptians,"[102]; that is, to the powerful enemies.

56. Once the body is moved by the senses to its own lusts and pleasures, the careless mind follows along and assents to its imaginings and impulses. The virtuous mind, in contrast, is in firm control and holds itself back from the passionate imaginings and impulses and instead concentrates on improving its emotions of this type.

57. There are virtues of the body and virtues of the soul. Bodily virtues are, for example, fasting, vigils, sleeping on the ground, service to others, manual labor done so as not to burden anyone or to have something to share, and so forth. The virtues of the soul are love, forbearance, meekness, self-mastery, prayer, and so forth. Now if from some necessity or bodily condition such as ill health or the like it happens that we are unable to accomplish the preceding bodily virtues, we are excused by the Lord, who understands the reasons. But if we do not accomplish the virtues of the soul we shall have no defense, for they are not subject to any necessity.

58. The love of God induces the one who possesses it to despise every passing pleasure and every trouble and sorrow. All the saints, who have suffered so much with joy[103] for Christ, should convince you of this.

59. Keep yourself away from self-love, the mother of vices, which is the irrational love of the body. For from it surely arise the first three passionate and capital thoughts, gluttony, greed, and vainglory, which have their starting point in the seemingly necessary demands of the body and from which the whole catalogue of vices comes about. Therefore, as was said, one must necessarily keep away from and do battle with this self-love with full determination, for when this is overcome then are all its offspring likewise brought into line.

60. The passion of self-love suggests to the monk that he should be kind to the body and to indulge in food more than is appropriate. Thus under the pretense of proper guidance it means to drag him little by little to fall into the pit of voluptuousness. To the worldly person it proposes that he make provision for himself right away in the matter of lust.[104]

61. It is said that the supreme state of prayer is when the mind passes outside the flesh and the world and while praying is completely without matter and form. The one who preserves this state without compromise really "prays without ceasing."[105]

62. Just as the body which is dying is separated from all the realities of the world, so is the mind which dies on the heights of prayer separated from the thoughts of the world. For if it does not die such a death it cannot be and live where God is.

63. Let no one deceive you, monk, into thinking that you can be saved while in the service of pleasure and vainglory.

64. Just as the body which sins through things and has as discipline the bodily virtues to bring it back to its senses, so in its turn does the mind which sins through passionate thoughts likewise have as discipline[106] the virtues of the soul, in order that looking at things in a pure and detached way it might return to its senses.

65. Just as night follows day and winter follows summer, so do sorrow and pain follow vainglory and pleasure whether in the present or in the future.[107]

66. In no way can the sinner escape the judgment to come unless he takes on here below voluntary hardships or involuntary afflictions.[108]

67. It is said that there are five reasons why we are allowed to be warred upon by the demons. First, so that in offensive and defensive battle we come to distinguish virtue and vice. Second, that in acquiring virtue by struggles and toil we shall hold on to it firmly and steadfastly. Third, that while advancing in virtue we do not become haughty but learn rather to be humble. Fourth, that having experienced vice we will hate it with a consummate hate. Fifth, and most important, that when we become detached we do not forget either our own weakness or the power of the one who has helped us.

68. Just as the mind of the one who is hungry imagines bread and that of the one who is thirsty imagines water, so does the glutton imagine a great variety of food and the voluptuous man imagine feminine visions, and the vain person imagine human applause, and the greedy person imagine profits, the vengeful person imagine revenge against the one who offended him, the envious person imagine evil to the one of whom he is envious, and similarly with the other passions. For the mind which is troubled by the passions receives passionate thoughts both when the body is awake and asleep.

69. When lust grows strong, the mind dreams of the objects which give it pleasure; when anger grows strong, it looks on the things which arouse fear. Now it is the impure demons who strengthen the passions and arouse them, making use of the help of our carelessness. On the other hand the holy angels weaken them by moving us to the exercise of the virtues.

70. When the concupiscible element of the soul is frequently aroused it lays up in the soul a fixed habit of pleasure. And when the temper is repeatedly stirred up it makes the mind craven and cowardly. The first is healed by a continual exercise of fasting, vigils, and prayer; the second by kindness, benevolence, love, and mercy.

71. The demons mount their attacks either with things or with the passionate thoughts connected with them: with things, those who are concerned with them, with thoughts those who have withdrawn from things.

72. As much as it is easier to sin in thought than in deed, so is a war with thoughts more exacting than one with things.

73. Things exist outside the mind while thoughts about them are put together inside. Therefore on it depends either their proper or improper use, for the abuse of things follows on the mistaken use of thoughts.

74. The mind receives passionate thoughts from these three sources: sense experience, temperament,[109] and memory. From the senses when things which are the source of passions impress them and move the mind to passionate thinking; from temperament, when because of intemperate living or the working of demons or some sickness, the bodily development is altered and it moves the mind again to passionate thinking or against Providence; finally from memory, when it recalls the thoughts of things that have aroused our passion and moves the mind once more to passionate thinking.[110]

75. Of the things given to us by God for our use some are in the soul, others in the body, and others are concerned with the body. Those in the soul, for example, are its powers, in the body are the organs of sense and the other members; and those which are concerned with the body are food, wealth, possessions, and so forth. Therefore, the good or evil use of these things or of those corresponding to them indicates whether we are virtuous or wicked.[111]

76. Of the accidents in things, some are in the soul, others in the body, and still others concerned with the body. Of those in the soul there are, for example, knowledge and ignorance, forgetfulness and memory, love and hate, fear and courage, sorrow and joy, and so forth. Of those in the body there are, for example, pleasure and hardship, feeling and disability, health and illness, life and death, and similar things. Of those things concerned with the body there are, for example, parenthood and childlessness, wealth and poverty, fame and ill repute, and so forth. Some of these we consider good and others evil,

although none of them is evil in itself but is found to be properly good
or evil according to its use.

77. Knowledge is good by nature, and so likewise is health, but their
opposites have benefited even more than have they. In the wicked
knowledge does not result in good, even though, as was said, it is good
by nature. The same is true for health or wealth or joy: These are not
used profitably by them. So it is, then, that their opposites are profitable, and therefore it happens that they are not evil in themselves even
though they seem to be evil.

78. Do not misuse thoughts, lest you necessarily misuse things as
well. For unless anyone sins first in thought, he will never sin in deed.

79. The image of the earthly man consists in the capital vices, such as
folly, cowardice, intemperance, injustice. The image of the heavenly
man consists in the cardinal virtues, as prudence, courage, temperance,
justice. So, "as we have borne the image of the earthly man, so let us
bear the image of the heavenly."[112]

80. If you wish to find the way that leads to life, look for it and you
will find it in the Way who tells us, "I am the way, and the truth, and
the life."[113] Only seek it very intensely because "few there are who find
it";[114] otherwise you may be left behind by the few and found among
the many.

81. For these five reasons will the soul abstain from sin: the fear of
men, the fear of judgment, the future reward, the love of God, or finally the prompting of conscience.

82. Some say that there would be no evil in beings unless there were
some other power which pulled us on to it, and this is nothing other
than carelessness of the natural functioning of the mind. Therefore
those who are careful about this always do good deeds, never bad. So,
if you too are willing, banish carelessness and you drive evil away as
well, which is the mistaken use of thoughts on which follows the misuse of things.

83. It is according to nature that the rational element in us be sub-
jected to the divine Word and that it govern our irrational element.
Therefore, this order is to be preserved in all things and there will be
neither any evil in beings nor anything available to draw them on to
it.[115]

84. Some thoughts are simple, others compound. The simple are
without passion, but the compound are with passion, as composed of
passion plus representation. In this case, one can see that many simple
thoughts follow on the compound when they have begun to be moved

to sin by the mind. Take money, for example. A passionate thought arises in someone's memory about gold. In his mind he has the urge to steal and with his heart he accomplishes the sin. Now with the memory of the gold will come also the memory of the purse, the chest, the room, and so forth. Now the memory of the gold is compound, for it displayed passion; but that of the purse, chest, and so forth, is simple, for the mind had no passion toward them. And so it is with every thought, with vainglory, with women, and so on. For not all thoughts which accompany an impassioned thought are themselves passionate, as the example has shown. Thus from this we can know what are impassioned representations and what are simple.

85. Some say that the demons get hold of the private parts of the body in sleep and arouse them to the passion of fornication which in turn recalls the female form to the mind through the memory. Others say that they appear to the mind in female guise and then by touching the private parts of the body arouse desire and give rise to imagination. Still others say that the prevailing passion in the approaching demon arouses the passion and in this way the soul is inflamed for evil thoughts by recalling forms through the memory. And similarly for all the other passionate thoughts; some say it comes about in one way, some in another. But in none of these ways are the demons strong enough to arouse any passion whatsoever whether one is awake or asleep when love and self-mastery are present in the soul.[116]

86. It is necessary to observe some commandments of the Law both in letter and in spirit, others only in spirit. For example, the commandments "thou shalt not commit adultery, thou shalt not kill, thou shalt not steal," and the like have to be observed both literally and spiritually, and the latter in three ways. The commandments to be circumcised, to keep the Sabbath, to immolate the lamb and eat unleavened bread with bitter herbs, and so forth, are to be observed only spiritually.[117]

87. There are three general moral states among monks. The first is not to sin in deed, the second is not to dally over passionate thoughts in the soul, and the third is to look with a detached mind on the forms of women or of those who have offended us.

88. The poor man is the one who has renounced all his possessions and owns nothing at all on earth except his body, and having severed his attachment to it has entrusted himself to the care of God and of religious men.

89. Some owners have possessions without attachment, and thus do

not grieve when they are deprived of them, as those who accepted with joy the seizure of their goods.[118] But others possess with attachment and become filled with grief when about to be deprived, like the one in the Gospel who went away sad;[119] and if they are deprived, they grieve until death. So it is that deprivation attests the condition of whether one is detached or attached.

90. The demons make war on those who are at the summit of prayer to prevent them from receiving simple representations of material things. They war on contemplatives to cause passionate thoughts to linger in their minds, and on those who are struggling in the active life to persuade them to sin by action. In every way these accursed beings struggle against everyone in order to separate men from God.

91. Those whose piety undergoes trial in this life by divine Providence are proved by these three temptations: by the gift of pleasant things, such as health, beauty, fine children, wealth, reputation, and the like. Or by the inflicting of sorrowful things, such as the loss of children, wealth, and reputation; or by painful afflictions of the body, such as sickness, disease, and so forth. To the first the Lord says, "If anyone does not renounce all he possesses, he cannot be my disciple."[120] To the second and third he says, "In your patience you shall possess your souls."[121]

92. These four things are said to modify the bodily temperament and thereby to give thoughts to the mind whether passionate or without passion: angels, demons, the weather, and life-style. The angels are said to modify it by reason, the demons by touch, the weather by its variations, the life-style by the quality and quantity of food and drink, whether too much or too little. In addition to these there are the modifications which come to it from the memory, from hearing and sight since it is the soul which is first affected by things which give it grief or joy.[122] And when the soul approves of these, it modifies the temperament of the body; and when this is thus modified, it supplies thoughts to the mind.

93. Death is, properly speaking, separation from God, and "the sting of death is sin."[123] In taking it on, Adam was banished at once from the tree of life, from Paradise, and from God, whereupon there followed of necessity the death of the body. On the other hand life is, properly speaking, the one who says, "I am the life."[124] By his death he brought back to life again the one who had died.

94. The written word is taken down either for one's own memory or

for the profit of others, or both, or to harm certain people, or for ostentation, or out of necessity.

95. The active life is "a place of pasture"; knowledge of created things
is "water of refreshment."[125]

96. Human life is a "shadow of death." Thus if anyone is with God
and God is with him he clearly can say, "For though I should walk in
the midst of the shadow of death, I will fear no evil because you are
with me."[126]

97. A pure mind sees things rightly, a straightforward speech brings
what it sees into view, and a keen hearing hearkens to it. But, the one
who is deprived of these three things abuses the speaker.

98. The one who knows the Trinity and its creation and Providence
and who keeps the emotional part of his soul unattached is with God.

99. The rod is said to signify God's judgment and his staff his Providence. Thus the one who has obtained knowledge of these things can
say, "Your rod and staff have given me comfort."[127]

100. When the mind has become stripped of passions and enlightened
in the contemplation of beings, then it can be in God and pray as it
ought.

Third Century

1. The reasonable use of thoughts and things is productive of mod-
eration, love, and knowledge; the unreasonable use, of excess, hate,
and ignorance.

2. "You have prepared a table for me, etc."[128] *Table* here signifies
practical virtue, for this has been prepared by Christ "against those
who afflict us." The *oil* which anoints the mind is the contemplation of
creatures, the *cup* of God is the knowledge of God itself; his *mercy* is his
Word and God. For through his incarnation he pursues us *all days* until
he gets hold of those who are to be saved, as he did with Paul.[129] The
house is the kingdom in which all the saints will be restored. The *length
of days* means eternal life.

3. The vices, whether of the concupiscible, the irascible, or the rational element, come upon us with the misuse of the faculties of the
soul. Misuse of the rational faculty is ignorance and folly, of the irascible and concupiscible faculty, hate and intemperance. Their right use
is knowledge and prudence. If this is so, nothing created and given existence by God is evil.[130]

4. It is not food which is evil but gluttony, not the begetting of children but fornication, not possessions but greed, not reputation but vainglory. And if this is so, there is nothing evil in creatures except misuse, which stems from the mind's negligence in its natural cultivation.

5. The blessed Dionysius says that among the demons this is what evil is: irrational anger, senseless lust, reckless imagination. But among rational beings unreasonableness, recklessness, and rashness are privations of reason, sense, and circumspection.[131] Now privations follow upon habits; so then the demons once had reason, sense, and religious circumspection. If this is correct, then neither are the demons evil by nature; rather they have become evil through the misuse of their natural faculties.

6. Some passions are productive of intemperance, others of hate, and still others of both intemperance and hate.

7. Excessive and sumptuous eating are causes of intemperance; greed and vainglory cause hatred of neighbor. But their mother, self-love, is the cause of both.

8. Self-love is the passionate and irrational affection for the body, to which is opposed love and self-mastery. The one who has self-love has all the passions.

9. "No one," says the Apostle, "hates his own flesh," of course, "but mortifies it and makes it his slave,"[132] allowing it no more than "food and clothing" and these only as they are necessary for life.[133] So in this way one loves it without passion and rears it as an associate in divine things and takes care of it only with those things which satisfy its needs.

10. When a person loves someone, he is naturally eager to be of service. So if one loves God, he is naturally eager to do what is pleasing to him. But if he loves his flesh, he is eager to accomplish what delights it.

11. What pleases God is love, temperance, contemplation, and prayer. What pleases the flesh is gluttony, intemperance, and what contributes to them. Therefore, "those who are in the flesh cannot please God. And those who are Christ's have crucified their flesh with its passions and lusts."[134]

12. When the mind inclines toward God, it keeps the body as a servant and allows it nothing more than what is necessary for life. But when it inclines toward the flesh, it becomes a servant of the passions and always makes provision for its lusts.[135]

13. If you want to prevail over your thoughts, take care of your pas-

sions and you will easily drive them from your mind. Thus for fornication, fast, keep vigil, work hard, keep to yourself. For anger and hurt, disdain reputation and dishonor and material things. For grudges, pray for the one who has hurt you and you will be rid of them.

14. Do not compare yourself to weaker men, but rather reach out to the commandment of love. For by comparing yourself to these you fall into the pit of conceit; in reaching out for the latter you advance to the heights of humility.

15. If you are really observing the commandment of love of neighbor, for what reason do you bear him the bitterness of resentment? Is it not clearly because in preferring transient things to love and in holding on to them you are making war on your brother?

16. Not so much out of necessity has gold become enviable by men as that with it most of them can provide for their pleasures.

17. There are three reasons for the love of money: pleasure-seeking, vainglory, and lack of faith. And more serious than the other two is lack of faith.

18. The hedonist loves money because with it he lives in luxury; the vain person because with it he can be praised; the person who lacks faith because he can hide it and keep it while in fear of hunger, or old age, or illness, or exile. He lays his hope on it rather than on God the maker and provider of the whole creation, even of the last and least of living things.

19. There are four kinds of people who acquire money, the three just mentioned and the financial administrator. Obviously only he acquires it for the right reason: so that he might never run short in relieving each one's need.

20. All passionate thoughts either excite the concupiscible, disturb the irascible, or darken the rational element of the soul. From this it comes about that the mind is hampered in its spiritual contemplation and in the flight of prayer. And because of this the monk, and especially the solitary,[136] should give serious heed to his thoughts and both know and eliminate their causes. Thus, for instance, he should know that passionate memories of women arouse the concupiscible element of the soul and are caused by incontinence in eating and drinking, as well as by frequent and unreasonable association with these same women. Hunger, thirst, vigils, and solitude eliminate them. Again, passionate memories of those who have hurt us stir up the temper; their causes are pleasure-seeking, vainglory, and attachment to material things, for the aroused person is saddened because he has either lost

these things or not attained them. Disdain and contempt of these things for the love of God eliminates them.[137]

21. God knows himself and the things created by him. The holy angels also know God and they know, too, the things created by him. But the holy angels do not know God and the things created by him as God knows himself and the things created by him.[138]

22. God knows himself of his own sacred essence, and the things created by him from his wisdom, through which and in which he made all things. The holy angels, however, know God by participation, though he is beyond participation, and they know things created by him by a perception of what is contemplated in them.

23. Created things are indeed outside the mind, but it receives their contemplation inside it. This is not so with the eternal, infinite, and immense God, who freely bestows being, well-being, and eternal being on his creatures.[139]

24. A nature endowed with reason and understanding participates in the holy God by its very being, by its aptitude for well-being (that is, for goodness and wisdom), and by the free gift of eternal being. In this way it knows God; and things created by him, as was said, it knows by a perception of the ordered wisdom to be observed in creation. This wisdom exists in the mind as simple and without substance of its own.

25. In bringing into existence a rational and intelligent nature, God in his supreme goodness has communicated to it four of the divine attributes by which he maintains, guards, and preserves creatures: being, eternal being, goodness, and wisdom. The first two of these he grants to the essence, the second two to its faculty of will; that is, to the essence he gives being and eternal being, and to the volitive faculty he gives goodness and wisdom in order that what he is by essence the creature might become by participation. For this reason he is said to be made "to the image and likeness of God":[140] to the image of his being by our being, to the image of his eternal being by our eternal being (even though not without a beginning, it is yet without end); to the likeness of his goodness by our goodness, to the image of his wisdom by our wisdom. The first is by nature, the second by grace. Every rational nature indeed is made to the image of God; but only those who are good and wise are made to his likeness.[141]

26. All national and intelligent nature is divided into two, namely, angelic and human nature. And all angelic nature is again divided into two general sides or groupings, holy or accursed, that is, into holy

powers and impure demons. All human nature is divided as well into only two general sides, religious and irreligious.[142]

27. God as absolute existence, goodness, and wisdom (or rather, to speak more properly, as transcending all these things) has no contrary quality whatever. But creatures, because they all have existence, and rational and intelligent ones their aptitude for goodness and wisdom by participation and grace, do have contrary qualities. To existence is opposed nonexistence, to the aptitude for goodness and wisdom is opposed vice and ignorance. For them to exist forever or not to exist is in the power of their maker. To share in his goodness and wisdom or not to share depends on the will of rational beings.[143]

28. When the Greek philosophers affirm that the substance of beings coexisted eternally with God and that they received only their individual qualities from him, they say that there is nothing contrary to substance but that opposition is found only in the qualities. We maintain, however, that the divine substance alone has no contrary because it is eternal and infinite and bestows eternity on the other substances; furthermore that nonbeing is the contrary of the substance of beings and that their eternal being or nonbeing lies in the power of the one who properly is being, "and his gifts are not subject to revision."[144] And therefore it both always is and will be sustained by his all-powerful might even though it has nonbeing as its opposite, as was said, since it was brought into being from nonbeing by God and whether it has being or nonbeing depends on his will.[145]

29. Just as evil is the privation of good and ignorance that of knowledge, so is nonbeing the privation of being—but not of being properly so called, for it has no contrary—but of true being by participation. Privations of the former depend on the will of creatures; privation of the latter depends on the will of the Creator, who out of goodness ever wills his creatures to exist and to receive benefits from him.

30. Of all creatures, some are rational and intelligent and admit of opposites such as virtue and vice, knowledge and ignorance. Others are various bodies composed of opposites such as earth, air, fire, and water. And there are some completely without body or matter, though some of these are united to bodies, and others have their makeup only of matter and form.

31. All bodies are by nature without movement. They are moved by a soul, whether rational, irrational, or insensitive.[146]

32. The soul's powers are for nourishment and growth, for imagina-

tion and appetite, for reason and understanding. Plants share only in the first powers, irrational animals share in the second as well, and men in the third in addition to the first two. Moreover, the first two powers prove to be perishable, but the third is imperishable and immortal.

33. The holy angels, in communicating their illumination with one another, also communicate to human nature either their virtue or the knowledge which they have. Thus with their virtue, as an imitation of the divine goodness, they benefit themselves, each other, and those beneath them by making them Godlike. With their knowledge, as either something loftier about God ("You, Lord, are forever most high," says Scripture[147]), or deeper about bodies, or more accurate about incorporeal beings, or clearer about Providence, or more manifest about judgment.

34. Impurity of mind means first to have false knowledge; next to be ignorant of any of the universals—I speak of the human mind, since an angel is not ignorant of particular things; thirdly in having passionate thoughts; and fourthly in consenting to sin.

35. Impurity of soul means not acting according to nature, for from this are begotten passionate thoughts in the mind. Now it acts in accord with nature when its sensitive drives, that is, anger and concupiscence, remain free of passion under the assault of material things and the representations they bring.

36. Impurity of body is a sin in deed.

37. The one who is not affected by the things of the world loves solitude; the one who does not love anything human loves all men; and the one who takes no offense at anyone, either because of faults or suspicious thoughts, possesses the knowledge of God and of divine realities.

38. It is a great thing not to be affected by things; but it is far better to remain detached from their representations.

39. Love and self-mastery keep the mind detached from things and from their representations.

40. The mind of the one who loves God does not engage in battle against things nor against their representations, but against the passions joined to these representations. Thus it does not war against the woman nor against the one who offends him, nor against their images, but against the passions that are joined to these images.

41. The whole war of the monk against the demons is to separate the passions from the representations. Otherwise he will not be able to look on things without passion.

42. Thing, representation, and passion are all different realities. A

thing is, for instance, a man, a woman, gold, and so forth. A representation is, for instance, a simple recollection of any of these things. Passion, however, is an irrational affection or senseless hate for any of these things. Therefore the monk's battle is directed against passion.

43. A passionate representation is a thought made up of passion and representation. Let us separate the passion from the representation, and the simple thought will remain. We can, if we wish, make this separation through spiritual love and self-mastery.

44. The virtues separate the mind from the passions; spiritual contemplations separate it from simple representations; then pure prayer sets it before God himself.

45. The virtues are related to the knowledge of creatures, knowledge to the knower, the knower to the one who is known in ignorance and whose knowing transcends knowledge.

46. God who is beyond fullness did not bring creatures into being out of any need of his, but that he might enjoy their proportionate participation in him and that he might delight in his works seeing them delighted and ever insatiably satisfied with the one who is inexhaustible.[148]

47. The world has many poor in spirit, but not in the right way; and many who mourn, but over money matters and loss of children; and many who are meek, but in the face of impure passions; and many who hunger and thirst, but to rob another's goods and to profit unjustly. And there are many who are merciful, but to the body and to its comforts; and clean of heart, but out of vanity; and peacemakers, but who subject the soul to the flesh; and many who suffer persecution, but because they are disorderly; many who are reproached, but for shameful sins. Instead, only those are blessed who do and suffer these things for Christ and following his example. For what reason? "Because theirs is the kingdom of heaven," and "they shall see God," and so forth.[149] So that it is not because they do and suffer these things that they are blessed (since those just mentioned do the same), but because they do and suffer them for Christ and following his example.

48. In everything that we do God looks at the intention, as has frequently been said, whether we do it for him or for any other motive. Therefore when we wish to do something good, let us not have human applause in view but rather God, so that always looking to him we might do everything on his account; otherwise we shall undergo the labor and still lose the reward.

49. In time of prayer chase from your mind the simple representa-

tions of human matters and the ideas of every creature, lest in creating images of lesser things you be deprived of the one who is incomparably better than them all.

50. If we sincerely love God we cast out the passions by this very love. Love for him means to prefer him to the world and the soul to the body. It means to despise worldly things and to devote oneself continually to him through self-mastery, love, prayer, psalmody, and so forth.

51. If we devote ourselves to God for a considerable period and give heed to the sensitive part of the soul, we no longer run headlong into the assaults of thoughts. Rather, in very carefully considering their causes and in eradicating them we become more perceptive and have the words fulfilled in us, "My eye also has looked down on my enemy, and my ear shall hear the malignant who rise up against me."[150]

52. When you see that your mind is conducting itself devoutly and justly in representations of the world, know then that your body, too, remains pure and sinless. But when you see that your mind is giving itself over to sins in thought and you do not resist, know that your body, too, will not be long in falling in with those sins.

53. Just as the body has material things for its world, so does the mind have representations for its world, and just as the body commits fornication with a woman's body, so does the mind commit fornication with the representation of a woman's body through its own body's fantasies. For in its mind it sees the shape of its own body joined with that of a woman. In the same way the mind wards off the picture of the one who has offended us through the shape of its own body. And similarly for other sins. For what the body does through action in the world of material reality, the mind also does in the world of representations.

54. There is no reason to be disturbed, shocked, or astonished by the idea that God the Father judges no one but has given all judgment to the Son.[151] The Son cries out, "Do not judge lest you be judged. Do not condemn lest you be condemned."[152] And the Apostle likewise, "Judge not before the time until the Lord comes," and, "With the judgment that you judge another you condemn yourself."[153] But in neglecting to lament their own sins, men take judgment away from the Son and they themselves, though sinful, judge and condemn each other. And "at this heaven is astonished,"[154] earth is disturbed, but they in their insensitivity are not ashamed.

55. The one who meddles in the sins of others or even judges his brother on a suspicion has not yet laid the foundation of repentance nor

sought to know his own sins (which are truly heavier than an enormous weight of lead). Neither does he know how it comes about that the man who loves vanities and seeks after lies [155] becomes heavy-hearted. Thus as a foolish person going about in the dark he takes no mind of his own sins and imagines those of others whether they actually exist or he only suspects them.

56. Self-love, as has frequently been said, is the cause of all passionate thoughts. From it are begotten the three capital thoughts of concupiscence: gluttony, greed, and vanity. From gluttony the thought of fornication arises; from greed, that of covetousness; and from vanity, that of arrogance. [156] All the rest follow one or the other of these three: the thoughts of anger, grief, resentment, sloth, envy, back-biting, and the rest. These passions, then, bind the mind to material things and keep it down on the earth, weighing on it like a very heavy stone, though by nature it should be lighter and livelier than fire.

57. The beginning of all passions is love of self, and the end is pride. Self-love is irrational love of the body, and if one eliminates this he eliminates along with it all the passions stemming from it.

58. Just as parents have affection for the offspring of their bodies, so also is the mind naturally attached to its own reasonings. And just as to their parents who are emotionally attached the children appear as the fairest and handsomest of all even though in every way they might be the most hideous of all, so it is with the foolish mind. Its reasonings, even though they might be the most depraved of all, still appear in its view as the most sensible of all. However, this is not the case with the wise man and his reasonings. Rather, when it seems convincing that they are true and correct, then especially does he distrust his own judgment but makes use of other wise men as judges of his own reasonings (so as not to run or have run in vain), [157] and from them he receives assurance.

59. When you overcome any of the dishonorable passions, such as gluttony, fornication, anger, or covetousness, suddenly the thought of vanity lights upon you. But when you overcome this, that of pride follows in short order.

60. All the dishonorable passions that hold sway over the soul drive out the thought of vanity from it, and when all these have given way, they set it loose on the soul. [158]

61. Vanity, whether it is eliminated or whether it remains, begets pride. When eliminated it produces conceit, when remaining it produces pretentiousness.

62. Discreet practice eliminates vainglory; ascribing our right actions to God removes pride.

63. A person who has been honored with the knowledge of God and is abundantly enjoying the pleasure it provides disdains all the pleasures begotten from lust.

64. The one who lusts after earthly things lusts after food, or what serves the lower passions, or human applause, or money, or something else associated with them. And unless the mind finds something better than these to which it can transfer its desire, it will not be completely persuaded to disdain them. And better than these by far is the knowledge of God and of divine things.

65. Those who disdain pleasures do so either out of fear or hope or knowledge and love of God.

66. Knowledge of divine things without passion does not persuade the mind to disdain material things completely, but rather resembles the mere thought of a thing of sense. Thus one finds many men with considerable knowledge who yet wallow in the passions of the flesh like pigs in mud.[159] For in reaching through their diligence a certain degree of purification and in acquiring knowledge but in later growing careless they can be compared to Saul, who after being given the kingship conducted himself unworthily and was dismissed from it with terrible wrath.

67. Just as the simple thought of human realities does not oblige the mind to disdain the divine, so neither does the simple knowledge of divine things persuade it fully to disdain human things, for the reason that the truth exists now in shadows and figures. Hence there is a need for the blessed passion of holy love, which binds the mind to spiritual realities and persuades it to prefer the immaterial to the material and intelligible and divine things to those of sense.

68. The one who has eliminated the passions and produced simple thoughts has still not yet completely turned them into divine things but can be drawn neither to human nor to divine things. This is the case of those in the active life who have not yet been given knowledge and who abstain from the passions out of fear or out of hope of the kingdom.

69. "We walk by faith, not by sight," and have knowledge in mirrors and riddles.[160] Because of this we need to be very occupied with these so that through lengthy exercise and discussion we might forge a tenacious habit of contemplation.

70. If after eliminating only to some extent the causes of the passions we devote ourselves to spiritual contemplations but are not constantly

occupied with them, we can while doing this easily revert once more to the body's passions. In this event we can expect to gather no other fruit except simple knowledge with conceit. The result of this is the gradual obscuring of this knowledge and the complete turning of the mind to material things.

71. The blameworthy passion of love engrosses the mind in material things. The praiseworthy passion of love binds it even to divine things. For generally where the mind devotes its time it also expands, and where it expands it also turns its desire and love, whether this be in divine and intelligible things which are its own or in the things of the flesh and the passions.

72. God created the invisible world and the visible world, and naturally he made the soul and the body as well. Now if this visible world is so beautiful, what sort of world will the invisible be? If it is better than the former, how much better than both is the one who created them? If then the Maker of everything that is beautiful is better than all creatures, for what reason does the mind leave the best of all to be engrossed in the worst of all, by which I mean the passions of the flesh? Or is it not clear that having lived and associated with the flesh from birth, the mind has not yet received a perfect experience of the one who is best of all and who transcends all? Therefore if by a prolonged exercise of self-mastery over pleasure and of attention to divine things we gradually break it away from such a relationship, it expands and gradually advances in divine things and recognizes its own dignity and finally transfers its whole longing[161] onto God.

73. The one who speaks in a detached way of his brother's sins does so for two reasons, either to correct him or to help someone else. If he speaks apart from these either to him or to another, he does so with reproach and disparagement. He will not escape being forsaken by God but will surely fall into the same or another failure, and dishonored and reproached by others he will find disgrace.

74. There is not just one reason why sinners commit the same sin in deed, but several. For instance, it is one thing to sin from habit and another to sin by being carried away. In this case the sinner did not fully reflect either before or after the sin but rather was deeply grieved over the incident. The one who sins from habit is quite the reverse, for first he does not cease sinning in thought and after the act he maintains the same disposition.

75. The one who seeks after the virtues out of vainglory obviously seeks after knowledge as well out of vainglory. Clearly such a person

neither does nor says anything for the sake of improvement but is in all circumstances pursuing the approval of the onlookers or hearers. The passion is detected when some of these people impose censure on his deeds or his words and he is enormously grieved thereby, not because he did not edify, for such was not his purpose, but because of his own disgrace.

76. The passion of greed is revealed when one is happy in receiving but unhappy in giving. Such a person cannot be a good steward.

77. A person endures suffering for these reasons: for the love of God, for the hope of a reward, out of a fear of punishment, out of fear of men, through nature, for pleasure, for profit, out of vainglory, or out of necessity.

78. It is one thing to be delivered from thoughts and another to be freed from passions. In fact someone may be often delivered from thoughts of those objects in their absence toward which he has acquired a passion, but the passions are hidden in the soul and are revealed when the objects appear. Therefore it is necessary to observe the mind when the objects are present and determine for which of them it holds an attachment.

79. That is a genuine friend if in time of temptation he supports his neighbor by bearing as his own, without clamor or display, his incidental tribulations, suffering, and misfortunes.

80. Do not disregard your conscience when it always recommends the best choices. In fact, it proposes to you divine and angelic advice; it frees you from your heart's secret defilements, and grants you familiarity[162] before God at the moment of departure.

81. If you want to become judicious and moderate and no servant of the passion of conceit, always seek in things what is hidden from your knowledge. You will indeed find a great many diverse things which have eluded you, and you will be astonished at your own ignorance and temper your pride. And in knowing yourself you will understand many great and wonderful things, since to think that one knows does not allow one to advance in knowledge.

82. A person definitely wants to be healed if he does not put up any resistance to the healing remedies: These are the pains and hurts brought on by many different circumstances. The one who resists does not know what is being worked out here nor what advantage he would draw from it when he leaves this world.

83. Vainglory and greed are mutually begotten of each other, for

while the vain grow rich, the rich grow vain, but only in a worldly sense. Since the monk is without possessions he becomes all the more vain, and when he does have money he hides it in shame as something unbecoming to his calling.

84. It is characteristic of a monk's vainglory that he become vain about his virtue and whatever is associated with it. It is characteristic of his pride that he be elated over his good deeds, dismiss other people, and ascribe these deeds to himself and not to God. It is characteristic of the worldly person's vainglory and pride that he be vain and elated over appearances, wealth, position, and pride.

85. The achievements of those in the world are misfortunes for monks, and the achievements of monks are misfortunes for those in the world. For instance the achievements of those in the world are wealth, fame, position, luxury, bodily comfort, fine children, and what is associated with these. If a monk comes to this, he is lost. On the other hand the monk's achievements are to be without possessions, fame, or influence, also self-mastery, endurance, and what is associated with these. If these things happen to a man of the world against his will he considers it a great misfortune and often comes close to hanging himself; indeed, some have done so.

86. Food was created for two reasons, for nourishment and for healing. Therefore those who take it for any other reason misuse what has been given for their use and are condemned for their luxury. And as with everything, misuse is sin.

87. Humility is continual prayer with tears and suffering. For this constant calling on God for help does not allow us to trust foolishly in our own strength and wisdom nor to be arrogant toward others. These are the dangerous diseases of the passion of pride.

88. It is one thing to fight against a simple thought so as not to arouse passion. It is another thing to fight a passionate thought to avoid giving consent. But in both of these ways the thoughts are not allowed to linger.

89. Hurt is linked to resentment. Thus when someone's mind associates the face of a brother with hurt, it is clear that he bears him a grudge. But "the ways of the resentful lead to death," because, "every resentful man is a transgressor of the law."[163]

90. If you bear a grudge against anyone, pray for him and you will stop the passion in its tracks. By prayer you separate the hurt from the memory of the evil which he did you and in becoming loving and kind

you completely obliterate passion from the soul. On the other hand, if someone else bears you a grudge, be generous and humble with him, treat him fairly, and you will deliver him from the passion.

91. You will check the hurt of the envious person with great difficulty, for he considers what he envies in you as his misfortune. It can be checked in no other way but in hiding something from him. But if the thing is helpful to many yet gives him grief, which side will you choose? It is certainly necessary to be of service to the many while still taking as much care as possible that you be not carried off by the vice of passion, since you could be retaliating not against the passion but against the one who is experiencing it. Instead, you will through humility regard him as above yourself and in every time, place, and situation prefer him to yourself. You will be able to check your own envy if you join the one you envy in rejoicing at what he rejoices at and grieving over what he grieves over. In this way you fulfill the Apostle's words, "Rejoice with those who rejoice and weep with those who weep."[164]

92. Our mind is in the middle of two things, each one active at its own work, the one at virtue, the other at vice, in other words between angel and devil. The mind has the power and strength to follow or oppose the one it chooses.[165]

93. On the one hand, the holy angels urge us on to the good, and natural tendencies and a good will assist us. On the other hand, passions and an evil will support the assaults of the demons.

94. Sometimes God himself lights on a pure mind and teaches it, sometimes the holy angels propose fine things, sometimes the nature of material reality is contemplated.

95. It is necessary that the mind which has been granted knowledge keep its representations of things without passion, its contemplations secure, and its state of prayer untroubled. But it cannot always keep them from the impulses of the flesh, because it is blackened with smoke from the contrivance of demons.

96. We are not grieved by the same things that anger us, for the things which produce grief are more numerous than those which produce anger. For instance one thing is broken, another is lost, such a person dies. For these things we have only grief, but for the others we experience both grief and anger so long as we are irreligiously disposed.

97. When the mind receives the representations of things, it of course patterns itself after each representation. In contemplating them spiri-

tually it is variously conformed to each object contemplated. But when it comes to be in God, it becomes wholly without form and pattern, for in contemplating the one who is simple it becomes simple and entirely patterned in light.[166]

98. The perfect soul is the one whose affective drive is wholly directed to God.

99. The perfect mind is the one that through genuine faith supremely knows in supreme ignorance the supremely unknowable, and in gazing on the universe of his handiwork has received from God comprehensive knowledge of his Providence and judgment in it, as far as allowable to men.[167]

100. Time is divided in three, and faith extends to all three divisions, hope to one, love to two. Faith and hope remain to a certain point, but love for infinite ages in a supreme and ever abounding union with the one who is supremely infinite. And because of this, "the greatest of these is love."[168]

FOURTH CENTURY

1. The mind is first of all in wonder when it reflects on God's universal infinity and that inaccessible and greatly desired ocean. Next it is amazed at how from nothing he has brought into existence everything that is. But just as, "of his greatness there is no end," so is his wisdom unsearchable.[169]

2. How can one help but marvel when considering that immense ocean of goodness which is beyond astonishment? How can one not be struck when reflecting on how and whence rational and intelligent nature came to be, and also the four elements which make up bodies, when there was no matter at all previous to their existence? And what kind of power is it that moved them to reality and brought them into being? But the pagan Greeks do not admit this and remain in ignorance about the all-powerful goodness and its efficacious wisdom and knowledge which is beyond the mind's powers.[170]

3. Eternally existing as Creator, God creates when he wishes by his consubstantial Word and Spirit out of infinite goodness. But do not object: For what reason did he create at this time, since he was always good? Because, I say in turn, the inscrutable wisdom of the infinite nature is not subject to human knowledge.

4. When he willed it, the Creator gave substance to and produced

his eternally preexisting knowledge of beings. It is of course absurd to doubt that an omnipotent God can give substance to something when he wishes.

5. Seek the reason why God created, for this is knowledge. But do not seek how and why he only recently created, for that question does not fall under your mind since while some divine things are comprehended by men others are not. As one of the saints has said, "Unbridled speculation can push you over the precipice."[171]

6. Some say that created things eternally exist with God, which is impossible. For how can what is limited in every way eternally coexist with the wholly infinite? Or how are they really creatures if they are coeternal with the Creator? But this is the theory of the Greeks, who admit God as the Creator not of the substance at all but only of the properties. But we who know the almighty God affirm that he is the Creator not of the properties but of the substance endowed with properties. And if this is true, creatures do not eternally coexist with God.

7. God, along with divine realities, is in one sense knowable and in another sense unknowable: knowable in ideas about him, unknowable in himself.

8. Do not search for states and aptitudes in the simple and infinite substance of the Holy Trinity, lest you make it composite like creatures. To have such notions about God is absurd and impious.

9. Only the infinite and all-powerful substance which created all things is simple, of one form, unqualified, peaceful, and undisturbed. Every creature, on the other hand, is a composite of substance and accident[172] and in constant need of divine Providence since it is not free from mutability.

10. Every intellectual and sensitive substance receives from God, when he brings them into existence, powers which allow them to apprehend beings, the intellectual substance through thoughts and the sensitive substance through sensations.

11. God is participated only; the creature both participates and communicates. He participates in being and in well-being but communicates only well-being, corporeal substance in one way, incorporeal in another.

12. Incorporeal substance communicates well-being by speaking or acting or by being an object of contemplation. Corporeal substance does so by being an object of contemplation only.

13. Whether the rational and intelligent being has eternal being or

nonbeing lies in the will of the one who created all good things. Whether it be good or bad by choice lies in the will of the creatures.

14. Evil is not to be regarded as in the substance of creatures but in its mistaken and irrational movement.

15. The soul is moved reasonably when its concupiscible element is qualified by self-mastery, its irascible element cleaves to love and turns away from hate, and the rational element lives with God through prayer and spiritual contemplation. [173]

16. When one in time of temptation does not bear up under incidental annoyances but cuts himself off from the love of his spiritual brothers, he does not yet have perfect love nor the knowledge of divine Providence in its depths.

17. The purpose of divine Providence is to unify by an upright faith and spiritual love those who have been separated in diverse ways by vice. Indeed it was because of this that the Savior suffered, "to gather together into one the children of God who were dispersed." [174] Therefore, the one who does not endure disturbances or bear up under distress or undergo hardships walks outside divine love and the purpose of Providence.

18. If "love is patient and kind," [175] how can the person who is fainthearted in the troubles that befall him and who consequently deals wickedly with those who offend him, cutting himself away from love for them, help but fall away from the purpose of divine Providence?

19. Be on guard lest the vice that separates you from your brother be not found in your brother but in you; and hasten to be reconciled to him, lest you fall away from the commandment of love.

20. Do not disdain the commandment of love, because by it you will be a son of God. If you transgress it you will become a son of Gehenna.

21. What separates you from the love of friends is this: envying or being envied, hurting or being hurt, insulting or being insulted, and suspicious thoughts. May you never have done or experienced any of these things by which you might be separated from your friend's love.

22. A temptation came upon you from your brother, and the hurt led you to hate. Do not be overcome with hate but overcome hate with love. You will prevail in this way: Pray for him sincerely to God, accept his apology, or else come up with an apology for him yourself, think of yourself as the cause of the temptation, and be patient until the cloud has passed by.

23. A person is patient if he waits out the end of a temptation and awaits the triumph of perseverance.

24. "A patient man is rich in prudence,"[176] because he refers every happening to its end, and while waiting for it he puts up with difficulties. "And the end is everlasting life,"[177] according to the divine Apostle; "and this is eternal life, that they know you, the only true God, and the one you have sent, Jesus Christ."[178]

25. Do not be calm over the loss of spiritual love, because there is no other way to salvation left for men.

26. Do not, because of the hate which has arisen in you today from the evil one's abuse, judge as bad and vicious the brother who yesterday was spiritual and virtuous. Instead, through the patience that love gives, cast out today's hate by thinking of yesterday's goodness.

27. Do not, because you changed from love to hate, disparage today as bad and vicious the one whom yesterday you praised as good and honored as virtuous, and blame your brother for the evil hate within you. Rather, continue in those same praises even though you are still full of hurt, and you will easily return to the same saving love.

28. Do not adulterate a brother's customary praise in the company of the other brothers because of the hidden hurt that you still have toward him by the imperceptible injection of censure into your words. Instead, use only genuine praise in company; pray sincerely for him as for yourself, and you will very swiftly be delivered of this pernicious hate.

29. Do not say, "I do not hate my brother by putting him out of my mind." But listen to Moses who said, "You shall not hate your brother in your heart. Reprove him openly and you will not incur sin through him."[179]

30. Even if in temptation your brother should insist on speaking ill of you, you should not be swept away from your charitable disposition and allow the same wicked demon to upset your mind. But you will not be swept away from it if you bless when being reviled, keep silent when spoken ill of,[180] and remain friendly when being conspired against. This is the way of Christ's wisdom, and the one who will not take it is not in his company.

31. Do not regard as well-meaning those who bring you tales that cause you pain and hate toward your brother, even though they seem to be true. Instead, turn away from such people as deadly serpents in order to cut them off from abusive speech and to deliver your own soul from wickedness.

32. Do not goad your brother by ambiguous language, lest you re-

ceive the same from him in turn and drive away the disposition of love from you both. Instead, go and correct him in loving familiarity, so that you may dissolve the causes of pain and deliver both of you from trouble and pain.

33. Examine your conscience with all honesty to determine whether it is your fault that your brother is not reconciled. Do not be dishonest with it since it knows your hidden secrets, accuses you at the time of your passing, and becomes an obstacle in time of prayer.

34. Do not recall in time of peace what your brother said in time of hurt, even though the offensive things were said to your face, or were said to another about you and you heard them afterward, lest in retaining grudges you revert to pernicious hate for your brother.

35. A rational soul that nourishes hate for a person cannot be at peace with God, who gives us the commandments. "For if," he says, "you will not forgive men their offenses, neither will your heavenly Father forgive you your offenses."[181] But if he does not want to be at peace, still keep yourself away from hate by praying sincerely for him and by not speaking ill of him to anyone.

36. The unutterable peace of the holy angels is attained by these two dispositions: love for God and love for one another. This holds true as well for all the saints from the beginning. Thus we have been beautifully told by the Savior that "on these two commandments depend the whole law and the prophets."[182]

37. Do not be a pleaser of self and you will not hate your brother. Do not be a lover of self and you will love God.

38. If you have determined to live with spiritual brothers, renounce your will at the outset, for in no other way will you be able to be at peace either with God or with those you are living with.

39. The one who has been able to acquire perfect love and who has let it control his whole life can say, " 'Lord Jesus,' in the Holy Spirit."[183] In the contrary case, the opposite will, of course, be true.

40. Love of God is always fond of flying off to hold converse with him; love of neighbor prepares the mind to think always well of him.

41. It is characteristic of the one who still loves empty glory or who is attached to some material thing to take offense at men for the sake of passing things, or to bear them resentment or to have hate for them or to be a slave to shameful thoughts. To the soul that loves God, however, all these things are altogether foreign.

42. When you neither say nor do anything intentionally shameful, nor bear any grudge against the one who has harmed you or spoken ill

of you, and when in time of prayer you always keep your mind free of matter and form, then know that you have reached the full measure of detachment and of perfect love.

43. It is no small struggle to be delivered from vainglory; however, one is delivered by the discreet practice of virtue and more frequent prayer. An indication of this deliverance is to bear no more grudges against anyone who offends us now or has offended us in the past.

44. If you want to be just, assign to each part within you what it deserves, that is, to body and soul. To the rational part of the soul give spiritual reading and meditation and prayer. To the irascible part give spiritual love, which is opposed to hate. To the affective part give temperance and self-mastery. To the bodily part give food and clothing, and only what is necessary.

45. The mind functions according to nature when it keeps the passions subject, when it contemplates the principles of beings, and when it dwells in God's presence.

46. As health and sickness have to do with the body of an animal and light and darkness with the eye, so do virtue and vice have to do with the soul and knowledge and ignorance with the mind.

47. The Christian is wise in these three things: in the commandments, in instruction, and in faith. The commandments separate the mind from the passions, instruction introduces it to the knowledge of beings, and faith brings it to the contemplation of the Holy Trinity.

48. Some of those who contend only beat back passionate thoughts, while others excise the passions themselves. One beats back passionate thoughts, for example, by psalmody, prayer, or uplifting of the mind, or by some other suitable occupation. But another excises the passions by despising the things for which he acquired the passions.

49. The things for which we have acquired the passions are these: women, money, fame, and so forth. And one is able to despise women when with the help of solitude he weakens the body[184] as he should through self-mastery. He despises money when he persuades the mind to be content in everything with just enough, and fame when he loves the secret practice of the virtues known only to God, and similarly for the rest. The one who despises these will never come to hate anyone.

50. The one who has renounced things such as a woman, wealth, and so forth, has made a monk of the outer man but not yet of the inner. The one who renounces the passionate representations of these things makes a monk of the inner man, that is, of the mind. Anyone can easily

make a monk of the outer man if he really wishes to, but it is no small struggle to make a monk of the inner man.[185]

51. Who, then, in this life is entirely freed from passionate representations and has been deemed worthy of pure and immaterial prayer, which is the sign of the inner monk?

52. Many passions lie hidden in our souls. They are exposed when their objects appear.

53. It can be that someone is not troubled by the passions in the absence of the objects, and so enjoys a partial detachment. But if the objects do appear, then the passions immediately distract the mind.[186]

54. Do not think that you have perfect detachment when the object is not present. When it does appear and you remain unmoved toward both the object itself and its subsequent recollection, know that then you have reached its frontiers. But you are not to become presumptuous, because virtue sustained kills the passions but virtue neglected rouses them anew.

55. The one who loves Christ thoroughly imitates him as much as he can. Thus Christ did not cease to do good to men. Treated ungratefully and blasphemed, he was patient; beaten and put to death by them, he endured, not thinking ill of anyone at all. These three are the works of love of neighbor in the absence of which a person who says he loves Christ or possesses his kingdom deceives himself. For he says, "Not the one who says to me 'Lord, Lord,' will enter the kingdom of heaven, but the one who does the will of my Father."[187] And again, "The one who loves me will keep my commandments," and so forth.[188]

56. The whole purpose of the Savior's commandments is to free the mind *from* incontinence[189] and hate and bring it to the love of him and of one's neighbor, from which there springs the splendor of holy knowledge in all its actuality.

57. Once granted a partial knowledge of God, do not be careless about love and self-mastery, for these purify the passionate aspect of the soul and are ever preparing for you the way to knowledge.

58. The way to knowledge is detachment and humility, without which no one will see the Lord.

59. Since "knowledge makes boastful but love edifies,"[190] link up love with knowledge and you will not be puffed up but rather a spiritual architect building up yourself and all those around you.

60. This is the reason why love edifies, because it neither envies nor grows angry with those who do envy, nor does it make a public display

of what is the object of envy, nor think that it has already appre-hended,[191] but confesses unabashedly its ignorance of what it does not know. In this way it renders the mind modest and constantly prepares it to advance in knowledge.

61. It is normal that presumption and envy follow upon knowledge, especially in the beginning, presumption interiorly and envy both in-teriorly and exteriorly: interiorly for those who have knowledge, exte-riorly for those who do not. Thus love overcomes these three: presumption, because it is not puffed up; interior envy, because it is not jealous; exterior envy, because it is patient and kind.[192] It is thus necessary for the one who has knowledge to take hold of love in order to keep his mind from any kind of wound.

62. The one who has been gifted with the grace of knowledge but still has grief, resentment, and hate for his brother is like the person who stings his eyes badly with thorns and burrs. Knowledge is for that rea-son necessarily in need of love.

63. Do not devote all your time to the flesh, but assign it exercises ac-cording to its capacity and turn your whole mind inward. "For bodily exercise is of little profit, but piety is of universal profit, etc."[193]

64. The one who ceaselessly devotes his energies to the interior life is temperate, patient, kind, and humble. Not only this, but he is also con-templative, united to God, and prayerful. And this is what the Apostle says, "Walk in the Spirit, etc."[194]

65. The one who does not know how to walk the spiritual way has no concern over passionate representations but devotes his whole time to the flesh. Either he is gluttonous or intemperate; or he is full of hurt, bitterness, or resentment, and so darkens his mind; or else he is inju-dicious in his ascetical practices and disquiets the understanding.

66. Scripture takes away none of the things given by God for our use but it restrains immoderation and corrects unreasonableness. For ex-ample, it does not forbid eating or begetting children or having money or managing it, but it does forbid gluttony, fornication, and so forth. Nor does it even forbid us to think of these things, for they were made to be thought of; what it forbids is thinking of them with passion.[195]

67. Some of the things we do for God are done because of the com-mandments, some not because of the commandments but through what one can call a free-will offering. For instance we are commanded to love God and our neighbor, to love our enemies, to refrain from adultery, murder, and so on. When we transgress these, we are subject to condemnation. However, there are other things which are not com-

manded, such as virginity, celibacy, poverty, the monastic life, and so forth. These have the nature of gifts, so that if from weakness we have been unable to observe some of the commandments we may propitiate our good Master with gifts.

68. The one who holds celibacy and virginity must necessarily keep his loins girt and his lamp burning,[196] his loins through self-mastery and his lamp through prayer, contemplation, and spiritual love.

69. Some of the brothers suppose that they are excluded from the Holy Spirit's gifts, for through their careless observance of the commandments they do not know that the sincere believer in Christ has within himself all the divine gifts collectively. But since through laziness we are far from having an active love for him, which reveals the divine treasures lying within us, we reasonably suppose that we are excluded from the divine gifts.

70. If, according to the Apostle, "Christ dwells in our hearts by faith,"[197] and "all the treasures of wisdom and knowledge are hidden in him,"[198] then all the treasures of wisdom and knowledge are hidden in our hearts. They are revealed to the heart in proportion to each one's purification by the commandments.

71. This is the treasure hidden in the field of your heart which you have not yet found because of laziness, for if you had found it you would then have sold everything to acquire that field.[199] But now you abandon the field and give your attention to nearby things, in which you find nothing but thorns and burrs.

72. This is why the Savior says, "Blessed are the clean of heart, for they see God,"[200] because he is hidden in the heart of those who believe in him. They will see him and the treasures in him when they purify themselves by love and self-mastery, and the more intensely they strive the fuller will their vision be.

73. This is why he also says, "Sell what you possess and give to the poor and behold all things are clean for you,"[201] that they no longer devote themselves to bodily things but hasten to purify the mind (which the Lord calls heart) from hate and intemperance. For the things which soil the mind do not permit it to see the Lord dwelling in it through the grace of holy baptism.

74. Scripture calls the virtues ways, and the best of all the virtues is love. Therefore the holy Apostle says, "I show you a more excellent way,"[202] because it leads to the despising of material things and to preferring nothing temporal to the eternal.

75. The love of God is opposed to lust, for it persuades the mind to

abstain from pleasures. Love of neighbor is opposed to anger, for it makes it disdain fame and money. These are the two silver pieces which the Savior gave to the innkeeper so that he could take care of you.[203] Now do not show yourself as senseless by joining up with the robbers, lest you be beaten up once again and be found not half dead but completely dead.

76. Purify your mind of anger, resentment, and shameful thoughts, and then you will be able to know the indwelling of Christ.

77. Who enlightened you with the faith of the holy, adorable, and consubstantial Trinity? Or who made known to you the incarnate dispensation[204] of one of the holy Trinity? Or who taught you about the principles of incorporeal beings and those concerning the origin and end of the visible world, or about the resurrection from the dead and eternal life, or about the glory of the kingdom of heaven and the awful judgment? Was it not the grace of Christ dwelling in you, which is the pledge of the Holy Spirit? What is greater than this grace, or what is better than this wisdom and knowledge? Or what is loftier than these promises? But if we are lazy and careless and do not purify ourselves from the passions which defile us and blind our mind, in order to be able to see the principles of these things more clearly than the sun, let us blame ourselves and not deny the indwelling of grace.

78. God who has promised you everlasting happiness and placed in your heart the pledge of the Spirit has enjoined you to tend to your behavior so that the inner man, freed from the passions, might begin here and now to enjoy this happiness.

79. If you have been granted divine and sublime contemplations, pay close attention to love and self-mastery, so that by maintaining your sensitive element undisturbed you will also keep unfailing the splendor of your soul.

80. Curb the irascible element of the soul with love, weaken its concupiscible element with self-mastery, and give flight to its rational element with prayer, and the light of your mind will never be eclipsed.[205]

81. The things which destroy love are these: dishonor, damage, slander (either against faith or against conduct), beatings, blows, and so forth, whether these happen to oneself or to one's relatives or friends. The one who destroys love on account of any of these has not yet learned what is the purpose of Christ's commandments.

82. Be as eager as you can to love every man, but if you cannot do this yet, at least do not hate anyone. And you cannot do this unless you scorn the things of this world.[206]

83. Such a one has offended you; do not hate him but rather the offense and the demon who contrived the offense. If you hate the offender, you hate a person and transgress the commandment, and what he did in word you do in deed. But if you keep the commandment, give proof of your love, and if you in any way can, help him so that he can be delivered from wickedness.

84. Christ does not want you to have hate for anyone, or grief, or anger, or resentment in any way at all or for any temporal reason whatsoever. And this is thoroughly proclaimed in the four Gospels.

85. Many of us talk but few of us act. But no one should falsify the word of God by his own carelessness. Rather, he should confess his weakness and not hide from God's truth, lest he be charged with transgressing the commandments and misrepresenting God.

86. Love and self-mastery free the soul from passions; reading and contemplation deliver the mind from ignorance; and the state of prayer places it with God himself.

87. When the demons see us disdaining the things of the world in order through them not to hate men and fall away from love, they then incite slanders against us, hoping that, unable to bear the hurt, we will come to hate those who slander us.

88. There is no hardship more oppressive to the soul than slander, whether one is slandered in his faith or in his conduct. And no one can disdain it except the one who like Susanna looks to God who alone can rescue in need, as he rescued her, and to reassure men, as he did in her case, and to encourage the soul with hope.[207]

89. To the extent that you pray from your soul for the one who spread scandal about you, God will reveal the truth to those who were told the scandal.

90. Only God is good by nature, and only the one who imitates God is good by his will. His plan is to join the wicked to himself who is good by nature in order that they may become good. So, then, when he is reviled by them, he blesses them; when persecuted, he endures; when slandered, he entreats; when put to death, he intercedes for them.[208] He does all things in order not to fall away from the purpose of love, which is our God himself.[209]

91. The Lord's commandments teach us to use indifferent things in a correct way. The correct use of indifferent things purifies the state of the soul; the pure state of the soul gives rise to discernment, which gives rise to detachment, from which is begotten perfect love.

92. One does not yet possess detachment if when temptation comes

he is unable to overlook the fault of a friend whether it is real or apparent. For when the underlying passions of the soul are aroused, they blind the understanding and do not allow it to look at the rays of truth or to discern the better from the worse. So then neither does such a person possess perfect love, which casts out the fear of judgment.[210]

93. "Nothing can be compared to a faithful friend."[211] This is because he regards his friend's misfortunes as his own and supports him in hardships until death.

94. Friends are abundant—that is, in times of prosperity. In time of trial you can barely find one.

95. You are to love every man from your soul, but in God alone are you to place your hope and to serve him with your whole strength. For so long as he protects us, all our friends respect us and all our enemies can do nothing against us. But if he should ever abandon us, all our friends shall turn away from us and all our enemies will prevail over us.[212]

96. There are four general types of abandonment: The first is in the Lord's incarnation in order that through seeming abandonment those who had been forsaken might be saved. The second type is for testing, as in the case of Job and Joseph, so that they might appear as pillars: one of courage, the other of chastity. The third type is for paternal instruction, as in the case of the Apostle, so that by being humble he might preserve the abundance of grace. The fourth type is a turning away, as with the Jews, so that by being punished they might be brought down to repentance. All of these types are saving and full of the divine goodness and wisdom.

97. Only the diligent observers of the commandments and the genuine initiates into the divine judgments do not forsake their friends who are undergoing trials with God's consent. Those, however, who disregard the commandments and are not initiated into the divine judgments enjoy their friend when he is cheerful; but when he is feeling badly in adversity, they forsake him, and, it is even possible, side with his enemies.

98. The friends of Christ love everyone sincerely but are not loved by everyone. The friends of the world do not love everyone nor are they loved by everyone. The friends of Christ maintain the continuity of their love till the end. The friends of the world, on the contrary, maintain theirs until they clash with each other over the world's goods.

99. "A faithful friend is a strong defense,"[213] for when his friend is prospering he is a good counselor and sympathetic collaborator, and

when he is in distress he is his sincerest supporter and most sympathetic defender.

100. Many people have said much about love, but only in seeking it among Christ's disciples will you find it, for only they have the true love, the teacher of love, of whom it is written, "If I have prophecy and know all mysteries and all knowledge but do not have love, it profits me nothing."[214] Therefore, the one who possesses love possesses God himself, since "God is love."[215] To him be glory forever. Amen.

NOTES

1. We are not informed about the identity of this Elpidius, although it is clear that he is a monk and probably, as Ceresa-Gastaldo asserts, a superior of Maximus: *Massimo Confessore, Capitoli sulla Carita* 49 n. 1.

2. A dialogue between a brother and an old man found in Migne, PG 90: 912–56. Polycarp Sherwood has translated the treatise in ACW 21: 103–35.

3. I.e., sets of one hundred. Maximus proposes to glean from previous spiritual writers various sayings on the subject of Christian love, which sums up the four Gospels, and to arrange them in "century" form, suitable for memorization. Especially in the tradition of Origen, the number one hundred was considered a sacred number because it was seen as a return to unity: cf. I. Hausherr, art. "Centuries" in DS 2, Evagrius, especially, was renowned for this form with his *Praktikos* (critical ed. by A. Guillaumont and C. Guillaumont, SC 171; E.T. by J.E. Bamberger, Cistercian Publications, 1978) and the six centuries of *Gnostic Chapters* (= KG, ed. A. Guillaumont, PO 28/1, Paris, 1958). In the present chapters, Maximus is greatly dependent on Gregory Nazianzen, Origen, Ps. Dionysius, and especially Evagrius. He provides, however, a more genuinely evangelical spirit in which the insightful definitions of the Egyptian monk can be appreciated. Maximus is modest about his own contribution.

4. There are several words in Greek to denote love. Here the word Maximus uses is *agape*, charity, the Christian love of 1 Cor 13, referred to in 1:9. P. Sherwood has noted that in this definition Maximus has subtly reworked that of Evagrius: ACW 21: 248 n. 1. Evagrius, the "philosopher monk *par excellence* of the 4th century," as Hausherr denotes him, had centered his spiritual system on contemplation and had defined love as a state (stasis). In changing "superior state" to "good disposition," however, Maximus is altering the perspective from a static to a dynamic one. This is missed by Hausherr; cf. *Noms du Christ et Voies d'Oraison*, (OCA 157 (Rome, ;1960), 145–46.

5. Knowledge, for Maximus, means mystical experience of God.

6. I. e., *apathia*, passionlessness. This is a creative state of good order when there is nothing troubling the powers of the soul. It bespeaks calm, tran-

quillity, and serenity. Both Pegon and von Balthasar translate the term as "inner freedom," which conveys this positive sense, but I have chosen to retain its negative form and thus render it generally as "detachment." It should be understood as a detachment from excess and disorder. Evagrius also speaks of love as the offspring of detachment in *Prakticos*, prol. (8) and 81.

7. Cf. also "Chapters on Knowledge" 1:16. The mind (*nous*), in the traditional threefold division, is the highest part of the soul. Above the concupiscible and irascible elements, it is the peak of man's spiritual nature.

8. This is to be understood in the light of the previous and following chapters, i.e., in the dynamic choices to be made in life. God must be preferred to any created thing.

9. Cf. 1 Cor 13:13.

10. Maximus here uses the term *eros* as distinguished from *agape*. The expression seems to refer to Gregory of Nyssa, who had spoken of desire (Eros) as the outreach of love: *Cant.* 13, *Pg* 44:1048c (Jaeger VI: 383).

11. The term *aperia* can mean either "infinity" or "beyond experience." Sherwood (ACW 21:249) prefers the former, Hausherr the latter; cf. "Ignorance Infinie," OCP 2 (1936):353 (=OCA 176:40). The term "transcendence" seems to link them both.

12. Isa 6:5.

13. Jn 14:15;15:12.

14. Maximus speaks frequently of this requirement of equal love. It is based on our imitation of God's unstinting love for man.

15. Cf. Rom 13:14.

16. Cf. Rom 1:25.

17. Love as an imitation of God is here seen in the practical form of almsgiving.

18. Cf. Mt 5:45.

19. Cf. Jer 17:16.

20. The soul is the level of human psychological makeup that is subject to the concupiscible and irascible appetites. The passions are the signs of our spiritual instability. God is by nature free from passion. Cf. Gregory of Nyssa, *Beat*, 6 (44,1272 BC).

21. Maximus destinguishes here between passion as a mark of our sinful condition and a *blameworthy* passion, which is contrary to nature. Only the latter is voluntary: Amb. Io. 36 (91, 1308c).

22. Cf. Acts 7:59–60 and Lk 23:34.

23. Cf. 1 Cor 13:4,7.

24. Cf. 1 Jn 4:8.

25. Cf. Jer 7:4.

26. Jas 2:19.

27. Cf. 2 Cor 7:8ff.

28. The monastic life was frequently called the angelic life, and this no-

tion will recur in the treatises included in the present volume. Cf. Origen, C. Cels. 4, 29; Gregory of Nyssa, *cant.* 1 (44,777A; Jaeger VI:30).

29. Cf. Evagrius, *Praktikos*, 4.

30. Gn 18:27.

31. I.e., *akedia*, sometimes translated "sloth." This is "a spirit of restlessness and incapacity for applying oneself to any task," which Sherwood translates as "listlessness" (ACW 21:250 n. 39). In Evagrius's list of eight capital sins it is number six (*Praktikos*, 6); also Hilda Graef, ACW 18:183 n. 26. A useful modern discussion is that of Francis Paget, "Introductory Essay Concerning Accidie," *The Spirit of Discipline* (London, 1891).

32. *Parresia*, a free and open access and relationship, is a term frequently employed by Maximus. Originally a political term, it takes on a moral and religious sense, and is used by both John and Paul: Jn 7:4; Eph 3:12; 6:19; Heb 4:16. For a discussion of the history of this notion see E. Peterson, "Zur Bedeutungsgeschichte von *Parresia*," in *R. Seeberg-Festschrift* (Leipzig, 1929), 283–97. For the notion as it appears in Gregory of Nyssa see J. Daniélou, *Platonisme et Théologie Mystique* (Paris, 1944), 103–15.

33. Cf. Evagrius, *Praktikos*, 22.

34. Cf. Mt 5:24.

35. 1 Cor 13:1–3.

36. Rom 13:10.

37. Ibid.

38. Jas 4:11.

39. Lk 6:27–28; Mt 5:44.

40. 1 Tm 2:4.

41. Mt. 5:39–41.

42. Evagrius speaks often of the damaging force of memories: cf. *Praktikos* 7, 10, 12, 34.

43. Aristotle had distinguished these two types of passion (*Nich. Ethics* 10, 2, 1173b). Self-control (self-mastery, or abstinence) is a very important virtue in the Evagrian system; cf. *Praktikos* prol., 35, 38, 41, 68, 89, 94; also KG 3:35 (ed. Guillaumont, PO 28/1). The present chapter is adapted from ch. 35 of Evagrius: cf. Guillaumont, SC 171, 580–581.

44. Evagrius had spoken of love as the brake on the irascible element (*Praktikos*, 38), an expression, as A. Guillaumont and C. Guillaumont note, that is found in Gregory Nazianzen, *Or.* 6, 6; PG 35:728C.

45. Lk 21:19.

46. Rom 8:35–39. The final sentence of the chapter is not found in the Combefis text published in Migne.

47. Rom 9:1–3.

48. Cf. Ex 32:31–32.

49. Ps 24:18.

50. Gnosis, a mystical insight.

51. Providence and judgment are categories frequently used by Evagrius: KG 2:59, 75, 77; 3:38, 40, 47; 4:89; 5:4, 24; 6:20, 40, 47, 57, 59, 74–76. Maximus also uses them, but only after having first eliminated the fatalistic elements in the Origenist notion of movement, and having reinterpreted the terms with reference to the centrality of Christ. Cf. *Mystagogy* 23; *Q.Thal.* 26 (349A; Laga-Steel 185); *Our Father*.

52. For love and self-control Maximus has here substituted their correlatives, almsgiving (charity in the modern sense) and fasting.

53. Cf. Evagrius, *On Prayer*, 85.

54. Mt. 11:29.

55. On the relationship between meekness and love in the person of Moses see *Praktikos*, 38, with the note of A. Guillaumont and C. Guillaumont (SC 171, 587–9).

56. This twofold fear is discussed in *Q. Thal.* 10 (90, 288A–292A; Laga-Steel 85–87) and in the *Dispute with Pyrrhus* (91, 297CD) as well as in the *Our Father*.

57. Prv 15:27.

58. Ibid. 1:7.

59. Ps 18:10.

60. Ps 33:10.

61. Col 3:5.

62. Cf. Rom 8:6.

63. This is taken from *Praktikos*, 64. Evagrius speaks of dreams also in chapters 54, 55, and 94 of the same work.

64. The principles are the logoi, the true identity of beings that are known in the light of the sun of justice, who is the eternal Logos, Word of God. For a fuller treatment see *Mystagogy*.

65. Goodness, wisdom, and power represent an important triad that reflects the eternal triad of Father, Son, and Holy Spirit.

66. Cf. Gregory Nazianzen, *Or.* 38, 7 (On the Theophany, or birthday of Christ), PG 36:317C, and repeated verbatim in *Or.* 45 (2nd oration on Easter), 628A. Dionysius speaks often enough of the unknowableness of God's essence, but it is significant that Maximus quotes the other "theologian," Gregory.

67. Or practical. This is in contrast to the contemplative way, and both of these general divisions comprised the spiritual life. Cf. *Praktikos*, prol. 9. The division is found in Gregory Nazianzen, the master of Evagrius, but in a way that is closer to Maximus's own understanding. In Evagrius praxis seems to be but a stage—albeit necessary—to contemplation. Viewed in this Middle Platonic sense of dematerialization it does not in itelf seem to possess any intrinsic worth beyond purgation. In a more incarnational scheme, however, such as that of Gregory Nazianzen, praxis, without losing its cathartic function, translates into concrete human actions the redemptive experience of the

individual Christian believer. As such it parallels on one level of human existence what the mind undergoes on another. For a discussion of these terms in
Gregory see J. Plagnieux, *Saint Grégoire de Nazianze, Théologien*, 141–53; also T.
Spidlik, "La *theoria* et la *praxis* chez Grégoire de Nazianze," SP 14/3, 358–64.
For Maximus observance of the commandments makes concrete the union of
the human will with the divine which is the definition of love. "It is said," he
writes, "that virtue is the concrete realization (hypostasis) of wisdom, and that
wisdom is the essence of virtue. That is why the putting into practice in life
(tropos) of contemplated realities is the unerring manifestation of wisdom,
while the contemplation (logos) of practical realities is the solid base of virtue,
and both have as a truly authentic character the attention which does not turn
aside from genuine being." Second Letter to Thomas, 1 (ed. Canart), *Byzantion*
34 (1964): 129.

68. This chapter, as Pegon shows, represents a correcting of the Evagrian scheme: SC 9, 95.

69. Also 2:59. Other definitions of self-love are in 3:8, 57. This vice represents a turning inward of human energy, which by nature was created to be
ecstatic. It is opposed to the union of wills, which is the love of God and of others: cf. Ep. 2, 91, 396D. It is precisely this individualistic principle that com-
promises the integrity of our love in not loving everyone equally: 1:17, 24, 25,
61, 71; 2:10, 30. For a thorough discussion of self-love see I. Hausherr, *Philautie: De la Tendresse pour soi à la charité selon Maxime le Confesseur*, OCA 137 (Rome,
1952).

70. Ps 36:27.

71. An allusion to Gen. 2:15 through Evagrius, *On Prayer*, 48 (tr. Bamberger, p. 62).

72. Ps 36:15.

73. Evil has no positive existence of its own, as Maximus explains in the
prologue to his *Questions to Thalassius*. He sees it as "an irrational movement of
the natural energies through a mistaken judgment to something other than
their end" (90, 253B; Laga-Steel 29–31). Cf. also in the present treatise, 2:17,
3:29, 4:14; also Amb.Io. 37 (1332A), Ep. 24 (609B). The theme is frequent in
Gregory of Nyssa: *Virg.* 12 (*PG*: 46; 372A Jaeger VIII/1,299; *Or. cat.* 5(45,
25A), 6(28C); *An. et res.* (46, 93B, 101A); *Hom. in Eccl.* 7 (44,725AB; Jaeger V,
407).

74. Cf. also 3:42 and 71; 1:35. Thus passion in this sense is not a mere
emotion but rather has an illogical character (cf. Evagrius, *Praktikos*, prol. 6).
Maximus himself tells us that he learnt his teaching from Gregory of Nyssa,
that passions were not originally included in man's nature but were introduced
after the fall into that part of nature inferior to reason: *Q.Thal.* (268D-269D;
Laga-Steel 47–49). On this see von Balthasar, KL, 182–185, 191–194. Cf. Gregory of Nyssa, *virg.* 12, Jaeger VIII/I, 298).

75. I follow Ceresa-Gastaldo, who reads *xresis* for *kresis*. See his expla-

nation, p. 99 n. 7. Cf. Gregory of Nyssa: ". . . according to the use which our free will puts them to, these passions of the soul become the instruments of virtue or of vice" (*Anim. et res.* PG 44:61A; 89A). Also Evagrius: "Things which are good or bad according to their use give rise to virtues or vices. It belongs to prudence, then, to use them for one of these ends," *Praktikos*, 88. In a footnote to their critical edition, A. Guillaumont and C. Guillaumont refer to the Stoic conception of things as indifferent in themselves but becoming good or evil depending on the use to which they are put (SC 171, 681). See below, 2:75 and n. 111.

76. Ps 16:17 and 31:7.

77. I.e., in solitude. The term used is a form of "hesychast" that has become technical in its meaning. Cf. Hausherr, "L'hésychasme. Etude de spiritualité," OCP 22 (1956): 5–40; 247–285 (= OCA 176, 163–237); *Idem, La Méthode d'Oraison Hésychaste, Orientalia Christiana* 9/2, 36 (1927): 101–209.

78. Cf. Ps 6:11.

79. Ps-Dionysius speaks of the hierarchical degrees as reflective of the spiritual orders in *The Ecclesiastical Hierarchy*, 5, 3–7 (PG 3:504A–509C). Von Balthasar sees this as a typical example of Maximus's fusing together of Dionysius with the levels of Evagrius: cf. KL 432.

80. Ps 9:4.

81. Ps 16:4.

82. Theology in this sense means direct communion with God in pure prayer, and "to theologize [*theologein*]" is to pray in spirit and in truth.

83. Agreeing in this translation with Sherwood and Ceresa-Gastaldo against Pegon and von Balthasar.

84. God's essence is beyond the range of human knowledge, a familiar theme with Maximus. It is even beyond the range of angelic knowledge, as he later says in 3:21.

85. Jn 10:30.

86. Jn 10:38.

87. Gregory Nazianzen, perhaps in *Or.* 39 (PG 36:349CD), as Pegon suggests.

88. Cf. Gregory of Nyssa, *Hom. 5 in Eccl.*, Jaeger V. 386, 6ff.

89. Cf. Gal 3:28 and Eph 1:23. In Philo's tradition the concupiscible and irascible appetites were represented as female and male respectively. See R. A. Baer, *Philo's Use of the Categories Male and Female* (Leiden; 1970).

90. Mt 24:15.

91. Cf. *Jewish Wars* 6, 4 and 5–8.

92. Jas 4:3.

93. Ps 61:13.

94. Jn 15:15.

95. 1 Cor 11:31–32.

96. Human eros under the influence of God's grace becomes trans-

formed into divine love. Cf. Gregory of Nyssa, *Life of Moses* 2, 231; SC 1 *ter*, 264–66; CWS 114.

97. Sherwood here notes the indebtedness of Maximus to Gregory of Nazianzen in the use of this word. "In both the illumination is at the summit of the spiritual life." ACW 21, 256 n. 116.

98. The desire for God is never sated even in the next life, as Maximus insists against Evagrian Origenism. Cf. Origen, *First Principles* 2, 9, 2. In this he is influenced by Gregory of Nyssa: "Made to desire and not to abandon the transcendent height by the things already attained, it makes its way upward without ceasing, ever through its prior accomplishments renewing its intensity for the flight," *Life of Moses*, 2, 226; SC 1 *ter*, 262,; Ferguson-Malherbe, CWS, 113. Cf. also below, 3:46.

99. Mt 6:21.

100. Cf. *Q. Thal.* 1 (269A; Laga-Steel 47). Gregory of Nyssa had spoken of exchanging through sin our divine image to a bestial one: *Life of Moses*, 2, 302, CWS 132; *Beat.* 5, ACW 18, 138. Cf. J. Daniélou, *Platonism et Théologie Mystique* (Paris, 1944), 74–79.

101. 1 Jn 2:15–16, adapted.

102. Gen. 46:34. For "contemplative" Maximus here substitutes "gnostic," a common term in the Alexandrian tradition. He will use this term elsewhere in the present works.

103. These two words are missing from the Combefis test in Migne.

104. Maximus uses the vocabulary of Rom 13:14.

105. Cf. 1 Thes 5:17. Pegon points out the strong Evagrian flavor of this language: SC 9, 112–13. To pray without ceasing was the goal of monastic exercise. Besides the present work, Maximus discusses this theme in *Asc.* 24 (90, 929C).

106. *Pedagogia.* Thus does Maximus, in line with the Alexandrian tradition, underscore the pedagogic role of the virtues.

107. Pleasure and pain in Maximus's system are inextricably linked in the disordered state resulting from sin. For Gregory of Nyssa the pleasure craftily offered to our first parents resulted in the pains of the present condition of life: *De Virginitate* 12 (46,373D–76A) Jaeger VIII/1,302. For a good treatment see C. Schönborn, "Plaisir et douleur dans l'analyse de S. Maxime d'après les Quaestiones ad Thalassium," in *Maximus Confessor* (Paradosis 27), ed. Heinzer et Schönborn (Fribourg, 1982), pp. 273–84.

108. Cf. *Acta* (Dispute at Bizya) 2 (90, 137C–140A).

109. Temperament in ancient society and for a long time thereafter was considered to be determined by the proportion of elements and humors in the body.

110. Cf. *Thalassius*, Century 1:46 (PG 91:1432C).

111. Maximus often returns to this thought: 2:17, 73, 76, 78, 82, 84; 3:3, 4, 86; 4:14, 66. Also *Asc.* 7, *Amb. Io.* 2 (1097C), Ep. 1 (91, 369A), 10 (449B).

112. 1 Cor 15:49.

113. Jn 14:6.

114. Mt 7:14.

115. I.e., the logical element must be submitted to the Logos. See *Q.Thal.* 64 (724C). Maximus often discusses the effect in relationship with the cause.

116. The Combefis text in Migne omits the last three words.

117. These commandments are found in Ex 20:13–15 (Dt 5:17–19) and 12:3ff.

118. Cf. Heb 10:34.

119. Mt 19:22.

120. Lk 14:33.

121. Lk 21:19, as in 1:67.

122. Cf. Maximus, *Opusc.* 10 (91, 136B).

123. 1 Cor 15:56.

124. Jn 14:6; 11:25.

125. Ps 23:2. Cf. *Ep. 8 (441B–D)*.

126. Ps 23:4.

127. Ibid.

128. Ps. 23:5–6.

129. Cf. Phil. 3:12–13. The latter verse is a favorite one of Gregory of Nyssa to bring out his notion of *Epektasis*, continual ascent. See *life of Moses*, 1, 5; 2, 225 and 242; and J. Daniélou, *Platonisme et Théologie Mystique*, pp. 296–99.

130. Cf. also 2:75 with its note as well as the following chapter.

131. Cf. *Divine Names*, 4, 23 (PG 3:724).

132. Eph 5:29 and 1 Cor 9:27.

133. Cf. 1 Tm 6:8.

134. Rom 8:8 and Gal 5:24.

135. Cf. Rom 13:14.

136. Or hesychast.

137. See 1:7.

138. Sherwood sees chapters 21–23 as a theological background to the spiritual and ascetic teaching of this work. See his note 150 in ACW 21, 258–259.

139. This triad is found elsewhere in Maximus, as in the following chapter. Cf. *Amb. Io.* 10 and 37.

140. Gen 1:26.

141. The distinction of image and likeness in Maximus is seen by him as that between the logos of nature and the tropos of virtue; cf. *Chapters on Knowledge* 1:13; *Q. Thal.* 53 (505A; Laga-Steel 435–37); *Amb. Io.* 2 (1084A); 37 (1345D). In this he is following an old tradition found in Irenaeus, Clement of Alexandria, and Origen. The idea is also present in Gregory of Nyssa: "I am according to the image by my reason; I become according to the likeness by

making myself Christian" (*Or.* 1, 2 in Gen 1:26; this, however, is generally considered to be a spurious work). On Maximus see T. Didier, "Les fondements dogmatiques de la spiritualité de S. Maxime le Confesseur," *EO* 29 (1930): 296–313, and J. Meyendorff, *Christ in Eastern Christian Thought* (Washington, 1969), pp. 99–115. John Damascene will follow in this tradition: *F.o.* 2, 12 (PG 94:920B). The distinction allows Maximus to stress the hegemonic role of the human will; see below, 3:27 and note; also 4:13.

142. The distinction between ontological and moral orders is seen by Sherwood as a necessary corrective to Origen: ACW 21, 31, and 259–60 n. 155.

143. Stress on the crucial role of the will in the process of deification is here clearly seen. The appreciation of this centrality in asceticism will position Maximus to defend the theological truth of the integrity of Christ's human will in the Monothelite debate. For Gregory of Nyssa human nature is like a mirror that reflects the change of impressions made on its free will: "Thus it is the function of our free will to have the power to take on the form of whatever it chooses" (Cant. 4; 44, 833 AB; Jaeger VI, 104). Also cant. 12 (1017 CD; Jaeger 345, 346).

144. Rom 11:29.

145. This chapter sees the mystery of being and nonbeing in the biblical categories of uncreated and created, and thus traces the mystery to God's will. Cf. Gregory of Nyssa, *or. cat.* 39 (45, 100A).

146. The three levels of the soul were a commonplace of classical Greek psychology. The following chapter elaborates.

147. Ps 91:9.

148. The satisfaction of the creature who possesses God is one that is not vitiated by surfeit, an Origenist notion that Maximus here consciously excludes. On the notion of surfeit see P. Sherwood, *Earlier Ambigua*, 181–204. See above, 2:48.

149. Mt 5:3ff.

150. Ps 91:12.

151. Cf. Jn 5:22.

152. Mt 7:1/Lk 6:37.

153. 1 Cor 4:5 and Rom 2:1.

154. Jer 2:12.

155. Cf. Ps 4:3.

156. This last phrase is omitted in most mss but retained in Combefis's text in Migne and in Ceresa-Gastaldo. As Combefis notes, Maximus here sees covetousness and greed related as offspring to parent (1033D).

157. Cf. Gal 2:2.

158. Cf. Evagrius, *Praktikos*, 31.

159. Cf. 2 Pet 2:22.

160. 2 Cor 5:7; cf. 1 Cor 13:12.

161. *Pothos.* For Maximus this is the basic human affective drive. It can be directed inward to self and thus spawn a multitude of vices, or outward to God and neighbor and thus lead to the genuine liberation of human energies (see 3:98). Maximus often links it with *Phobos*, a reverential and disciplinary fear: e.g., *Mystagogy* 24, Our Father, prol., Second Letter to Thomas 1 (ed. Canart), *Byzantion* 34 (1964): 429.

162. See 1:50, 68; 4:32.

163. Prv 12:28 and 21:24.

164. Rom 12:15.

165. Gregory of Nyssa had spoken of the faculty of free will as directing the contrary motions within us: *Cant.* 12 (44, 1017CD; Jaeger VI, 345–46).

166. This chapter has a pronounced Evagrian tone. Nevertheless, it must ever be borne in mind that while using Evagrian vocabulary, Maximus has demolished the Origenist superstructure. His statements then are to be interpreted in the light of orthodox Christian doctrine. See Sherwood's judicious criticism of Viller and Hausherr on this point in ACW 21, 261–62 n. 187. Indeed, as the whole tenor of the present work makes clear, Maximus is influenced by the perspective of Gregory of Nyssa in stressing human freedom. The present chapter, for instance, can easily be interpreted as an adaptation of Gregory's mirror image in *Cant* 4. See n. 143 to 3:27 of the present treatise.

167. Maximus is here employing both Evagrian and Dionysian language in the same chapter.

168. 1 Cor 13:13. Cf. *Chapters on Knowledge* 1:5. It is not at all clear how Maximus wants us to understand this passage. Pegon, Sherwood, and Balthasar offer interpretations that cannot be judged satisfactory. In any case we can say with Balthasar that in Maximus's view it is love that joins time and eternity: KL 465.

169. Ps 144:3. The first thirteen or fourteen chapters in this set are concerned with the same theme. Sherwood speaks of a "polemic against pagan ways." Besides this one can perhaps see this arrangement as positing the apophatic principle in theology. God's essence (7–9) as well as the how of creation (3, 5) are beyond our comprehension. We are essentially different from him (6, 10–13), and participate in him who does not himself participate (11). Maximus sees the necessity of clearing up errors not only of pagans but of careless Christian writers as well.

170. This argument from creation recalls Gregory of Nyssa: "The one who gazes on the physical universe and perceives the wisdom which is reflected in the beauty of created realities, can reason from the visible to the invisible beauty, the source of wisdom, whose influence established the nature of all reality. So also can one who looks upon this new universe of creation which is the Church see in it the one who is all in all, and thus be led by our faith from things which are intelligible and understandable to a knowledge of the one who

is beyond knowledge." *Cant.* (44, 1049D–1052A; Jaeger VI, 385–86).

171. The exact reference is unknown, although Combefis refers to two of Gregory of Nazianzen's orations. Perhaps the reference is to the swine who ran down the bluff and perished (Lk 8:33), which Gregory brings in to describe the Eunomians who do not respect God's mystery: *Or.* 27 (*Theol.* 1), 7.

172. In using Aristotelian categories Maximus instances his philosophical eclecticism. On the Aristotelian character of his view of the human composite see V. Grumel, "La Comparaison de l'âme et du corps et l'union hypostatique chez Léonce de Byzance et s. Maxime le Confesseur," EO 25 (1926): 393–406.

173. As Sherwood suggests (ACW 21, 263–4 n. 199), this chapter should be read in conjunction with 2:83.

174. Jn 11:52. Maximus treats more fully of this theme of unifying those whom sin has dispersed in the first chapter of *Mystagogy.*

175. 1 Cor 13:14.

176. Prv 14:29.

177. Rom 6:22.

178. Jn 17:13.

179. Lv 19:17.

180. This phrase is missing from the Combefis text in Migne.

181. Mt 6:14–15, adapted.

182. Mt 22:40.

183. 1 Cor 12:3.

184. I.e., the demands of the body's irrational appetites.

185. The use of the Pauline categories of inner and outer man and the identification of the inner man with the mind is a clear indication that Maximus is exorcising the Origenism of Evagrius even while employing his language. See Sherwood, ACW 21, 264 n. 218.

186. Cf. *Praktikos,* 60. Sherwood here refers to *Q.Thal.* 55 (544C; Laga-Steel 493) for a discussion of the degrees of detachment.

187. Mt 7:21.

188. Jn 14:15. The theme of imitating Christ is very strong in Maximus. On this theme in Eastern writers generally, including Maximus, see Hausherr, "L'imitation de Jésus-Christ dans la spiritualité byzantine," in *Mélanges offerts au P. P. F. Cavallera* (Toulouse, 231–59 = *Etudes de Spiritualité Orientale* [Rome, 1969], pp. 217–245).

189. *Akrasia,* incontinence, is the opposite of *ekratia,* self-mastery. Cf. Liddell-Scott, *Greek-English Lexicon,* s.v.

190. 1 Cor 8:1. The text from Paul justifies Maximus in his reaction against an overly gnostic and intellectualized spirituality. The following chapters drive home the point.

191. Cf. Phil 3:12; also referred to above in 3:2. Interestingly, Maximus here views the apprehension of God from an intellectual point of view. Such a

contemplation can have no end but the apophatic darkness of infinite knowledge, just as our love and enjoyment of God require endless and insatiable delight.

192. 1 Cor 13:4.

193. 1 Tm 4:8.

194. Gal 5:16.

195. The balanced perspective of this chapter reflects a healthy appreciation of the nature of created realities. Balthasar attributes this to Maximus's synthesis of Aristotle and Chalcedon and in this regards him as a genuine forerunner of Aquinas: KL 63.

196. Cf Lk 12:35.

197. Eph 3:7.

198. Col 2:3.

199. Cf. Mt 13:44.

200. Mt 5:8. The following clause is missing in the Combefis text in Migne.

201. Lk 12:33; 11:41.

202. 1 Cor 12:31.

203. Cf. Lk 10:35.

204. I.e., economy.

205. Gregory of Nyssa had regarded anger and lust as warts growing out of the rational element of the soul: *An. et res.* (46, 56C).

206. Scorn, i.e., the pursuit of them.

207. Cf. Dn 13:35.

208. Cf. 1 Cor 4:12–13.

209. The Combefis text in Migne does not include the final words.

210. Cf. 1 Jn 4:18.

211. Sir 6:15.

212. The same thought is expressed in the treatise on the Ascetic Life. Cf. *Asc.* 43 (953CD).

213. Sir 6:14.

214. 1 Cor 13:2.

215. 1 Jn 4:8.

COMMENTARY ON THE OUR FATHER[1]

A BRIEF EXPLANATION OF THE
PRAYER OUR FATHER TO A CERTAIN
FRIEND OF CHRIST BY SAINT
MAXIMUS, MONK AND CONFESSOR.

PROLOGUE

My Lord in divine keeping, it is yourself that I received, you who come to me through your very praiseworthy letters. Indeed, you are always present and totally incapable of being absent in spirit, and likewise you do not refuse to converse in imitation of God[2] with your servants by the abundance of your virtue and the utterance which God has given to your nature.

For this reason, admiring the greatness of your condescension, I blended my fear with affection,[3] and from these two, fear and affection, I created a single thing, love, made up of modesty and benevolence, in such manner that a fear devoid of affection did not become hatred, nor did an affection not joined to a prudent fear become presumption, but on the contrary that love be shown to be an immanent law of devotedness which harmonizes whatever is related by nature. By benevolence it masters hatred, and by reverence it pushes away presumption. Realizing that it (that is, fear) confirms divine love more than anything else, the blessed David has said, "The fear of the Lord is chaste and remains from age to age."[4] He well knew that this fear is different from the fear which consists of being afraid of punishments for faults of which we are accused, since for one thing this (fear of punishment) disappears completely in the presence of love, as the great evangelist John shows somewhere in his words, "Love drives out fear."[5] For another thing, the former (fear of the Lord) naturally characterizes the law of true concern; it is through reverence that the saints keep forever completely uncorrupted the law and mode of life of love toward God and toward each other.

Thus, as I was saying, having myself joined to affection the fear I have toward you, my Lord, I established the present day this law of love: by reverence I refrained from writing lest I open myself to presumption while by kindness I was driven to write lest the complete re-

101

fusal to write be not interpreted as hatred.[6] I write then because I must, not what I think, "since the thoughts of men are vile,"[7] as Scripture says, but what God wants and grants through grace to begin this undertaking. Indeed, "the counsel of God," says David, "remains forever, the thoughts of his heart from generation to generation."[8] Undoubtedly he calls "counsel" of God the Father the mysterious self-abasement of the only-begotten Son with a view to the deification of our nature,[9] a self-abasement in which he holds enclosed the limits of all history; while by "thoughts of his heart" he means the principles of Providence and judgment[10] according to which he directs with wisdom as different generations our present life and the life to come, imparting differently to each the mode of activity which is proper to it.

1. If then the realization of the divine counsel is the deification of our nature, and if the aim of the divine thoughts is the successful accomplishment of what we ask for in our life, then it is profitable to recognize the full import of the Lord's prayer, to put it into practice and to write about it properly. And since you, my Lord, in writing to me your servant, have mentioned this prayer under God's influence, I thus make it of necessity the theme of my words, and I ask the Lord who taught us this prayer to open my mind to understand the mysteries it contains and to give me a power of expression in proportion to the meaning of the mysteries apprehended. Indeed this prayer contains in outline, mysteriously hidden, or to speak more properly, openly proclaimed for those whose understanding is strong enough, the whole scope of what the words deal with. For the words of the prayer make request for whatever the Word of God himself wrought through the flesh in his self-abasement. It teaches us to strive for those goods of which only God the Father through the natural mediation of the Son in the Holy Spirit is in all truth the bestower, since according to the divine Apostle the Lord Jesus is "mediator between God and men":[11] Through his flesh he made manifest to men the Father whom they did not know, and through the Spirit he leads the men whom he reconciled in himself to the Father. For them and on their account, he became man without any change[12] and he himself worked and taught many new mysteries whose number and dimension the mind can in no way grasp or measure. There are seven in number which are more general than the others which he appears to have given to men in his extraordinary generosity. The scope of the prayer, as I have said, mysteriously contains their meaning: theology,[13] adoption in grace, equality of honor with the angels,[14] participation in eternal life, the restoration of

nature inclining toward itself to a tranquil state, the abolition of the law of sin, and the overthrowing of the tyranny of evil which has dominated us by trickery. Let us now examine the truth of what has just been said.

2. In becoming incarnate, the Word of God teaches us the mystical knowledge of God[15] because he shows us in himself the Father and the Holy Spirit. For the full Father and the full Holy Spirit are essentially and completely in the full Son, even the incarnate Son, without being themselves incarnate. Rather, the Father gives approval and the Spirit cooperates in the incarnation with the Son who effected it, since the Word remained in possession of his own mind and life, contained in essence by no other than the Father and the Spirit, while hypostatically realizing out of love for man the union with the flesh.[16]

He gives adoption by giving through the Spirit a supernatural birth from on high in grace, of which divine birth the guardian and preserver is the free will of those who are thus born. By a sincere disposition[17] it cherishes the grace bestowed and by a careful observance of the commandments it adorns the beauty given by grace. By the humbling of the passions it takes on divinity in the same measure that the Word of God willed to empty himself in the incarnation of his own unmixed glory in becoming genuinely human.[18]

He rendered men equal in honor to the angels[19] not only in that "reconciling through the blood of his cross what is in heaven and what is on earth"[20] and destroying the hostile forces which fill up the middle space between heaven and earth, he showed there was only one gathering of earthly and heavenly powers for the distribution of divine gifts which sings with joy the glory of God with one and the same will with the powers on high.[21] But even more than this, after the fulfillment of the dispensation[22] toward us, and after having ascended with the body he had assumed, he united through himself heaven and earth, joined sensible to intelligible things, and showed the unity of created nature, internally coherent in its furthest parts, by virtue and exact knowledge of the first cause. He showed, I think, by what he accomplished in a mysterious way, how the Word is the uniting of what is distant and how unreason is the division of what is united.[23] And we learn how to strive for the Word by practice so as to be united not only to angels by virtue but spiritually to God by the separation from creatures.

He gives a sharing in the divine life by making himself food for those whom he knows and who have received from him the same sensibility and intelligence. Thus in tasting this food they know with a true knowledge that the Lord is good,[24] he who mixes in a divine quality to deify those who eat, since he is and is clearly called bread of life[25] and of strength.

He restores nature to itself not only in that having become man he kept a free will tranquil and undisturbed in the face of nature and did not allow it to become unsettled in its own movement in a way contrary to nature[26] even in the face of those who were crucifying him; he even chose death at their hands rather than life, as the voluntary character of the passion shows, which was accomplished by the disposition of love for men by the one who underwent this passion. But even more than this, he abolished enmity in nailing to the cross the bond[27] by which nature waged implacable war against itself, and having called those who are far and those who are near (that is, of course, those who are under the Law and those who are outside the Law), "and having broken down the dividing wall of hostility, by abolishing in his flesh the law of commandments and ordinances, [he created] in himself one new man in place of the two, so making peace, and reconciling"[28] us through himself to the Father and with each other in such a way that we no longer have a will opposed to the principle of nature and that thus we be as changeless in our free decisions as we are in our nature.

He purified nature from the law of sin in not having permitted pleasure to precede his incarnation on our behalf. Indeed his conception wondrously came about without seed, and his birth took place supernaturally without corruption: with God being begotten of a mother and tightening much more than nature can the bonds of virginity by his birth. He frees the whole of nature from the tyranny of the law which dominated it in those who desire it and who by mortification of the sensuality of the earthly members[29] imitate his freely chosen death. For the mystery of salvation belongs to those who desire it, not to those who are forced to submit to it.[30]

He effects the destruction of the tyranny of evil which has lorded over us by trickery. He conquers the flesh which had been overcome in Adam by brandishing it as an instrument against evil. Thus does he show how the flesh, which had been bruised first by death, captures its captor and destroys its life by natural death.[31] The flesh has become both a poison strong enough to make him vomit out all those whom he had swallowed by confining them in death's dominion,[32] and also a life for the human race, which causes the whole nature to rise like a loaf for a resurrection of life. It is wholly on account of this life that the Word who is God has become man (certainly an incredible fact and story) and willingly accepts the death of the flesh.[33] All of this, as I have said, the words of the Prayer are found to request.

3. It speaks, in fact, of the Father, of the Father's name, and of his kingdom.[34] Moreover, it sets before the one who prays in grace the Son of this Father. It asks that those in heaven and on earth come to be of a single will. It enjoins the request for daily bread. It establishes reconciliation as a law for men, and by the fact of forgiving and being forgiven it binds the nature to itself to be no longer mutilated by the difference of will.[35] It teaches us to beg not to be led into temptation, which is the law of sin, and it exhorts us to be protected from evil. It was necessary, indeed, that he who effects and gives the benefits to those who believe in him and imitate his conduct in the flesh give and teach them as well as his disciples the words of the prayer as precepts of this life. By these words he pointed out the hidden treasures of wisdom and knowledge[36] which exist as such in himself, in furthering the desire of those who pray it toward the enjoyment of these treasures.

This is why, I think, Scripture calls this teaching a prayer because it makes a request for the gifts which God gives to men by grace. Indeed, just as our fathers inspired by God explained and defined prayer by saying that it is a request of what God gives to men in a way which is fitting to himself, so they defined that the vow[37] is a profession or promise of what men offer to God in genuine and worshipful service. They have often explained that Scripture witnesses to this by its own language; thus, "Make vows to the Lord our God and fulfill them,"[38] and, "What I have vowed I will offer you, Lord our God."[39] This is what is said for vow; and for prayer, "Hannah prayed to the Lord and said, 'Lord Adonai, Eloi Sabaoth, if you deign to hear your servant and give fruit to my womb!' "[40] and, "Hezechiah, king of Judah, as well as Isaiah, son of Amos, prayed to the Lord,"[41] and also what the Lord says to his disciples, "When you pray, say, 'Our Father who art in heaven.' "[42] Thus the vow can be a keeping of the commandments ratified by the will of the one who makes the vow; and prayer is the petition that the one who observes them be brought to the enjoyment of what they contain. Or else, vow is the combat of virtue, an offering that God accepts with the greatest pleasure, and prayer is the reward of virtue, that God gives back with the greatest joy.

Thus, since it has been shown that prayer is a petition for blessings which come from the Word incarnate, let us by setting at the head the very one who taught us the words of the prayer, advance with confidence, carefully unraveling by contemplation the meaning of each word, as far as possible, as the Word himself is accustomed to furnish profitably and to give the power to understand the meaning of what is said.

OUR FATHER WHO ART IN HEAVEN, HALLOWED BE THY NAME: THY KINGDOM COME.

4. First of all the Lord, by these words, teaches those who say this prayer to begin as is fitting by "theology," and he initiates them into the mystery of the mode of existence of the creative Cause of things, since he himself is by essence the Cause of things.[43] Indeed, the words of the prayer point out the Father, the Father's name, and the Father's kingdom to help us learn from the source himself to honor, to invoke, and to adore the one Trinity. For the name of God the Father who subsists essentially is the only-begotten Son, and the kingdom of God the Father who subsists essentially is the Holy Spirit. Indeed, what Matthew here calls kingdom another evangelist elsewhere calls Holy Spirit: "May your Holy Spirit come and purify us."[44] The Father indeed has no acquired name and we should not think of the kingdom as a dignity considered after him. For he did not begin to be, as if he had a beginning as Father and King, but he always is, and is always both Father and King, not having in any way begun to exist or to be Father or King. And if he who always is, is always Father and King as well, then also the Son and Spirit always coexisted in essence with the Father. They are by nature from him and in him beyond cause and understanding, but they are not after him as if they had come about subsequently as being caused by him. For relation has the capacity of joint indications without at the same time allowing the terms of the relationship to be thought of as coming one after the other.[45]

Our Father. Thus at the beginning of this prayer we are directed to honor the consubstantial and superessential Trinity as the creative Cause of our coming into existence. Further, we are also taught to speak to ourselves of the grace of adoption, since we are worthy to call Father by grace the one who is our Creator by nature. Thus by respecting the designation of our Begetter in grace, we are eager to set on our life the features of the one who gave us life: We sanctify his name on earth in taking after him as a Father, in showing ourselves by our actions to be his children, and in extolling by our thoughts and our acts the Father's Son by nature, who is the one who brings about this adoption.

Hallowed Be Thy Name. We sanctify the name of the Father in grace who is in heaven by mortifying earthly lust, of course, and by purifying ourselves from corrupting passions, since sanctification is the total immobility and mortification of sensual lust. Arrived at that point, we quiet the indecent howling of anger which no longer has, to excite it and persuade it to be carried over to familiar pleasures, the lust which is already mortified by a holiness conformed to reason. Indeed, anger, as a natural ally of lust, ceases to rage once it sees that lust is mortified.[46]

Thy Kingdom Come. It is right, then, that after the elimination of anger and lust there comes, according to the prayer, the victory of the kingdom of God the Father for those who, having rejected them, are worthy to say, "thy kingdom come," that is to say, the Holy Spirit, for by the principle and path of meekness they have already become temples of God by the Spirit.[47] For it is said, "On whom shall I rest if not on the one who is meek, on the one who is humble and who fears my words?"[48] From this it is obvious that the kingdom of God the Father[48] belongs to the humble and the meek. For it is said, "Blessed are the meek, for they shall inherit the earth."[49] It is not this earth which by nature occupies the middle place of the universe which God promised as an inheritance to those who love him since he speaks the truth in saying, "When they rise from the dead they neither marry nor are given in marriage but are like the angels in heaven,"[50] and, "Come, blessed of my Father, inherit the kingdom prepared for you since the foundation of the world."[51] And again elsewhere to another who served with devotion, "Enter into the joy of your Lord."[52] And after him the divine Apostle says, "For the trumpet will sound, and those who have died in Christ will rise first, incorruptible; then we the living who remain here will be taken up together with them into the clouds to meet the Lord in the air, and thus we shall always be with the Lord."[53]

Since such promises have been made to those who love the Lord, who would then say, if he has his mind fixed squarely on the word of Scripture, if he is moved by the Word and wishes to be his servant, that heaven, the kingdom prepared from the world's foundation, the joy of the Lord mysteriously hidden, the continuous and completely uninterrupted dwelling place and home with the Lord for those who are worthy, is in any way identical to the earth? On the contrary, I think I can now say that the earth is the solid and thoroughly unalterable habit and force of inflexibility in the good which the meek possess.[54] Because they are always with the Lord and possess an endless joy, they have acquired a kingdom prepared from the beginning and have been judged worthy of a place and position in heaven as a kind of land occupying the mid-point of the universe, that is, the principle of virtue. According to this principle the meek man, situated midway between the good and evil said of him, dwells in tranquillity, without being puffed up because he is well spoken of nor saddened because he is ill spoken of. For since reason is free by nature it has rejected appetite and is not sensitive to its regard and has settled the complete force of its soul on the immovable divine freedom. Wishing to give this to his disciples the Lord says, "Take my yoke upon you and learn of me for I am meek and humble of heart, and you will find rest for your souls."[55] He calls rest the victory of the divine kingdom, insofar as it produces in those who are worthy a sovereignty released from any bondage.

If the indestructible might of the unfading kingdom is given to the humble and the meek, who would at this point be so deprived of love and desire for the divine gifts as not to tend as much as possible toward humility and meekness to become, to the extent that this is possible for man, the image of God's kingdom by bearing in himself by grace the exact configuration in the Spirit to Christ, who is truly by nature and essence the great King? In this configuration, says the divine Apostle, "there is neither male nor female,"[56] that is to say, neither anger nor lust. Indeed, anger tyrannically destroys the exercise of reason and makes thought take leave of the law of nature. And lust takes beings which are inferior to the one and only desirable and impassible cause and nature and makes them more desirable than it. Thereby it sets up flesh as more valuable than spirit, and renders the enjoyment of what is visible more delightful than the glory and brightness of spiritual realities. By the sensual softness of pleasure it leads the mind from the divine perception of spiritual things which is connatural to it. Rather, there is reason alone which has by an abundance of virtue stripped itself of that tenderness and affection which are not only supremely without passion but are natural for the body as well.[57] The spirit is then perfect master of nature and persuades the mind to take leave of moral philosophy whenever it should unite itself to the super-essential Word by simple and undivided contemplation, even if practical reason contributes to it for an easy separation and transition from the course of temporal events. Once this transition is accomplished it is not reasonable to impose as a heavy coat[58] the burden of a moral condition on the one who has shown himself unrestrained by sensible things.

And this is the mystery which the great Elijah clearly shows in the actions which he accomplished by way of figure.[59] For during his rapture he gives Elisha his coat (that is, mortification of the flesh in which the magnificence of the good moral order is firmly grounded) as an ally of the spirit in the struggle against any enemy force and as a blow against the unstable and flowing nature figured by the Jordan so that the disciple be not held back from crossing over to the Holy Land by being swamped in the mud and slipperiness of the craving for matter. As for himself, he advances toward God free and uncontrolled by any attachment to beings at all, simple in his desire and uncomplicated in his intention, and makes his dwelling with the one who is simple by nature through general virtues spiritually harnessed to each other as fiery horses. For he knows that it is necessary for Christ's disciple to keep away from unequal dispositions whose differences prove an estrangement since the passion of lust produces an outpouring of blood around the heart and a movement of anger evidently produces a boiling of blood.[60] When he reaches the point of having life, movement, and being[61] in Christ, he has put far from him the monstrous origin of inequalities and he no longer carries within himself the contrary dispositions of these passions, as I was saying, after the manner of the male-female opposition. In this way reason is not enslaved by them, having remained aloof from their unstable fluctuations. In it the holiness of the divine image has been naturally included to persuade the soul to transform itself by its free will to the likeness of God and to belong to the great kingdom which subsists substantially with God, the Father of all. It becomes a radiant abode of the Holy Spirit and receives, if one can say it, the full power of knowing the divine nature insofar as this is possible. By this power there is discarded the origin of what is inferior, to be replaced by that of what is superior, while the soul like God keeps inviolable in itself by the grace of its calling the realization of the gifts which it has received. By this power, Christ is always born mysteriously and willingly, becoming incarnate through those who are saved. He causes the soul which begets him to be a virgin-mother[62] who, to speak briefly, does not bear the marks of nature subject to corruption and generation in the relationship of male and female.[63]

No one should be astonished to hear corruption placed before generation. For the one who examines without passion and with a correct reason the nature of things which come to be and which pass away will clearly discover that generation takes its beginning from corruption and ends up in corruption. The passions associated with this generation and corruption, as I was saying, do not belong to Christ, that is, to the life and logic of Christ and according to Christ, if we can believe the one who says, "For in Christ there is neither male nor female," thus clearly indicating the characteristics and the passions of a nature subject to corruption and generation. Instead, there is only a deiform principle created by divine knowledge and one single movement of free will which chooses only virtue.

"Neither Greek nor Jew." This refers to a difference, or more properly a contradiction, in opinions about God. The Greek notion foolishly introduces a multiplicity of principles and divides the single principle into contrary energies and forces. It fashions a polytheist cult which becomes factious by reason of the multitude of its objects and ludicrous because of the various ways of veneration. The Jewish notion introduces a single principle but one which is petty and imperfect, almost impersonal as deprived of reason and life. Through opposite ways it results in the same evil as the first notion, a disbelief in the true God. It limits to a single person the one principle which would subsist without the Word and the Spirit, or which would be qualified by the Word and the Spirit. It does not see what God would be if he had no part with the Word and Spirit, nor how he would be God in having part with them as if they were accidents, by a participation close to that of rational beings subject to generation. In Christ, as I have said, there is none of these things, but only the reality of genuine piety, a steadfast law of mystical theology which rejects any expansion of the divinity as the first notion does, while not allowing any contraction as does the second.[64] Thus there is no dissension by a plurality of natures, the Greek error, nor an affirmation of the oneness of hypostasis, the Jewish error, because being deprived of the Word and the Spirit or qualified by the Word and the Spirit, God is not honored as Mind, Word, and Spirit. This teaches us, who have been introduced to the perfect knowledge of truth by a calling of grace in faith, to recognize that the nature and the power of the divinity is one, and therefore that there is one God contemplated in the Father, Son, and Holy Spirit. This means a single Mind essentially subsisting without being caused, who begot the one Word subsisting by essence without a principle, and who is the source of the one eternal life essentially subsisting as Holy Spirit. Trinity in Unity and Unity in Trinity: not one in the other, for the Trinity is not related to the Unity as an accident in an essence, nor conversely the Unity in the Trinity, for it is unqualified. Nor as one and the other, for the Unity does not differ from the Trinity by a difference of nature since it is a simple and single nature. Nor as one after the other, for the Trinity is not distinguished from the Unity by a lessening of power, nor the Unity from the Trinity. And the Unity is not distinguished from the Trinity as something common and general considered only by the mind as distinct from the parts which make it up, since it is an essence which exists properly by itself, and a force which is absolutely mighty. Nor as one through the other, for there is no mediation of relation as from effect to cause between what is completely identical and absolute. Nor as one from the other, for the Trinity is not a derivation of the Unity, since it is without origin and self-manifesting.

On the contrary, we say and know that the same God is truly Unity and Trinity: Unity according to the principle of essence and Trinity according to the mode of existence.[65] The same reality is wholly Unity without being divided by the Persons, and wholly Trinity without being confused in unity. In this way polytheism is not introduced by division, nor atheism by confusion. By avoiding both, the understanding of God in the light of Christ shines forth. I call Christ's understanding the new proclamation of truth, "In him there is neither male nor female," that is, no signs or passions of a nature subject to corruption and generation; "neither Jew nor Greek," that is, no conceptions opposed to God; "neither circumcision nor uncircumcision," that is, no different religions issued from these opposed conceptions. The religion of circumcision, through the symbols of the Law, considers the visible creation evil and accuses the Creator of being the author of these evils. The religion of uncircumcision deifies the visible creation through the passions and sets the creature against the Creator. Both of these together end up at the same evil, insolence against God. "Neither barbarian nor Scythian," that is, no tension of will pushing the single nature to revolt against itself, by which there has been introduced among men the unnatural law of mutual slaughter. "Neither slave nor freedman," that is, no division of the same nature by opposition of will, which makes dishonored what is by nature of equal honor and has as an auxiliary the attitude of those who exercise a tyrannical sway over the dignity of the image. "But Christ is in all," creating by what surpasses nature and the Law, the spiritual configuration of the kingdom which has no beginning, a configuration characterized, as has been shown, by humility and meekness of heart. Their concurrence shows forth the perfect man created according to Christ.[66] For every humble man is also thoroughly meek, and every meek man is also thoroughly humble: humble because he knows that his being has come to him as a loan, meek because he knows how to use the natural powers which have been given to him, since he gives them over to the service of reason to give rise to virtue and because he restrains in a perfect way their sense activity. That is why this man is always in movement toward God by his mind.[67] Even if he experiences at one time everything that can afflict the body, he is not at all moved according to the senses, nor does he mark his soul with any trace of affliction as a substitute for a joyful attitude, for he does not think that physical suffering means a loss of happiness. Indeed there exists but one happiness, a communion of life with the Word, the loss of which is an endless punishment which goes on for all eternity.[68] And that is why by abandoning his body and whatever is the body's he strives intensely toward that communion of life with God, thinking that the only loss—even if he were master of everything on earth—would be in the failure of the deification by grace which he pursues.

Let us therefore purify ourselves from all defilements of the flesh and of the spirit[69] so that we may sanctify God's name by extinguishing lust which indecently flirts with the passions, and let us by reason rein in anger which pleasures incite to a reckless fury. Thus will we welcome the kingdom of God the Father which comes through meekness. And to these opening words let us join the following words of the prayer in saying,

THY WILL BE DONE ON EARTH
AS IT IS IN HEAVEN.

The one who mystically offers God worship through the spiritual power alone separated from concupiscence and anger has accomplished the will of God on earth as the angelic orders do in heaven. He has become in every way the companion of the angels in their worship and in their life, as the great Apostle somewhere says, "Our citizenship is in heaven,"[70] where there is no concupiscence to relax the mind's reach by pleasures, nor raging anger to bark indecently against one's kinsmen, but where there will be reason all by itself to lead naturally rational beings to the first Principle. It is this alone which gladdens God and which God requests of us his servants. It is what he shows in saying through the great David, "What exists for me in heaven, and besides you what did I wish for on earth?"[71] There is nothing which is offered to God in heaven by the holy angels except the spiritual worship[72] he expects of us when he teaches us to pray in saying, "Thy will be done on earth as it is in heaven."

Our reason also should therefore be moved to seek God, the force of desire[73] should struggle to possess him and that of anger[74] to hold on to him, or rather, to speak more properly, the whole mind should tend to God, stretched out as a sinew by the temper of anger, and burning with longing for the highest reaches of desire. Thus indeed we will be found to be giving God worship in every way in imitation of the angels in heaven, and we shall exhibit on earth the same manner of life as the angels in having as they do the mind totally moved in the direction of nothing less than God. For by such a manner of life according to our vows, we shall receive as a supersubstantial and life-giving bread to nourish our souls and to keep in good condition the goods with which we have been favored, the Word who said, "I am the bread which has come down from heaven and which gives life to the world."[75] He becomes everything for us in proportion to the virtue and wisdom with which we have been nourished, taking a body in a variety of ways, as only he knows, in each of the saved, while we are yet in this age according to the force of the text of the prayer which says,

GIVE US THIS DAY OUR DAILY BREAD.

I think, in fact, that "this day" means in present history.[76] Thus to understand this passage of the prayer in its clearest meaning we should say, "Our bread," which you prepared in the beginning for the immortality of nature, "give us this day," to us who belong to the mortal condition of the present life, so that nourishment by the bread of life and knowledge triumph over the death of sin. The transgression of the divine commandment did not allow the first man to become a sharer in this bread. For if he had satisfied himself with this heavenly food, he would not have fallen prey to the death brought in by sin.

But, in fact, the one who prays to receive this supersubstantial bread does not receive it altogether as this bread is in itself, but as he is able to receive it. For the Bread of Life, out of his love for men, gives himself to all who ask him but not in the same manner to everyone: to those who have done great works, he gives himself more fully, to those who have done smaller ones, less; to each, then, according to the spiritual dignity enabling him to receive it.[77]

The Savior has led me to this understanding of the present word when he expressly enjoins his disciples not to be overly concerned with sensible food. "Do not worry," he says, "about your life, what you will eat or what you will drink; nor for your bodies, what you will wear.

For all these things the people of the world worry about. But seek first the kingdom of God and his justice, and all of this will be given to you in abundance."[78] How then does he teach us to pray for what he had previously ordered us not to seek after? It is obvious that he did not enjoin us to ask in the prayer what he had exhorted us not to seek in his commandment. For we should ask in the prayer only what should be sought after according to the commandment. Therefore it happens that what he did not by commandment allow us to seek, he did not set up as lawful to ask for in the prayer. And if the Savior has commanded us to seek only the kingdom of God and his justice, then it is evidently this that he suggested that those who desire the divine gifts should ask for in prayer. Thus, by confirming through prayer the grace of what is natural to seek after, he will join to the will of the one who supplies the grace the free will of those who request it, by rendering it identical to it in a union of relation.[79] If we are also charged in the prayer to ask for this day's bread which sustains the present life, let us not go beyond the borders of the prayer in greedily speculating on periods of many years, and let us not forget that we are mortal and possess a life as fleeting as a shadow. On the contrary, let us without anxiety ask in prayer for one day's bread and let us show that in the Christian way of life we make life a preparation for death,[80] by letting our free will overtake nature, and before death comes, by cutting the soul off from the concerns for bodily things. In this way it will not be nailed down to corruptible things, nor pass on to matter the use of the natural desire, nor learn the greediness which deprives one of the abundance of divine gifts.

Let us then flee, as much as we can, a fondness for matter and wash our involvement from it as dust from our spiritual eyes. Let us be satisfied only with what makes us subsist and not with what serves for our pleasure in the present life, and moreover, let us ask God, as we have been taught, to be strong enough to keep the soul from servitude and entirely without any surrender of the body to visible things. Let us prove that we eat to live and let us not be convicted of living to eat. For one is clearly proper to a rational nature and the other to a nature without reason. Let us be scrupulous observers of the prayer in showing by our very acts that we hold on tightly to the one and only life in the Spirit and that we make use of the present life with a view to acquiring it. On account of life in the Spirit we are content to use the present life in such a way as not to refrain from sustaining it by bread alone or from keeping up its good physical health; as far as this is permitted us, not in order to live but rather to live for God.[81] We thus make of the body rendered spiritual by its virtues a messenger of the soul, and by its stead-fastness in the good we make the soul a herald of God. We naturally limit this bread to but one day without daring to extend the request to a second one after this because of the giver of the prayer. Indeed, by setting our actions in good order according to the power of the prayer, we can in all purity go on to the following words and say,

FORGIVE US OUR TRESPASSES
AS WE FORGIVE THOSE WHO TRESPASS AGAINST US.

The one who, according to the first contemplative reading of the preceding words, seeks in the prayer according to present history of which we said that "this day" is the symbol, the incorruptible bread of wisdom of which the transgression in the beginning deprived us (as he knows that the only pleasure is the attainment of divine things whose giver by nature is God and whose guardian by will is the free choice of the one who receives them and that the only sorrow is their loss, suggested by the devil but accomplished by whoever grows weary of divine things by relaxing his free will and who does not keep up the love of what is honorable by a firm disposition of will), that person does not at all incline his free choice toward anything visible, and because of this he is not subject to painful things befalling his body.[82] In truth he forgives, in spiritual detachment, those who sin against him because no one at all can lay his hand on the good he zealously seeks with all his desire and which we believe is by nature unattainable. And for God he makes himself an example of virtue, if one can say this, and invites the inimitable to imitate him[83] by saying, "Forgive us our trespasses as we forgive those who trespass against us." He summons God to be to him as he is to his neighbors. For if he wishes that as he forgave the debts of those who have sinned against him, he also be forgiven by God, and it is obviously in detachment from passion that God forgives those who forgive, then also the one who remains in detachment in what befalls him forgives those who have offended him, without allowing the memory of whatever painful that has happened to him to be imprinted in his mind, so as not to be accused of dividing nature by his free will by separating himself as man from any other man.[84] For since free will has been thus united to the principle of nature, the reconciliation of God with nature comes about naturally, for otherwise it is not possible for nature in rebellion against itself by free will to receive the inexpressible divine condescension. And it is perhaps for this reason that God wants us first to be reconciled with each other, not to learn from us how to be reconciled with sinners and to agree to wipe away the penalty of their numerous and ugly crimes, but to purify us from the passions and to show that the disposition of those who are forgiven accords with the state of grace. He has made it very clear that when the intention has been united to the principle of nature, the free choice of those who have kept it so will not be in conflict with God since nothing is considered unreasonable in the principle of nature, which is as well a natural and a divine law, when the movement of free will is made in conformity with it. And if there is nothing unreasonable in the principle of nature it is likely that the intention moved according to the principle of nature will have an activity habitually corresponding in all things to God. This will be a fruitful disposition, produced by the grace of the one who is good by nature, for the purpose of giving rise to virtue.[85]

Such, then, is the disposition of the one who asks in prayer for spiritual bread, and the one who out of natural need seeks only the bread of today is disposed in the same fashion. Forgiving the debtors their debts inasmuch as knowing himself mortal by nature, and waiting each day with uncertainty for what makes him live by nature, he outstrips nature by his intention and voluntarily he dies to the world according to the passage which says, "For your sake we are put to death the whole day, we are considered as sheep of the slaughterhouse."[86] That is why he pours himself out in libation for everyone[87] so as not to bring away with him the mark of the wretchedness of the present life, in passing into the life which does not grow old and to receive from the Judge and Savior of all the reward equal to what he had undergone here below. For a pure disposition in regard to those who have caused pain is necessary for the mutual advantage of both, because of all that precedes and not least because of the force of the words which remain to be said and which present themselves in this manner:

And Lead Us Not Into Temptation, But Deliver Us From Evil.

In these words Scripture makes us see how the one who does not perfectly forgive those who offend him and who does not present to God a heart purified of rancor and shining with the light of reconciliation with one's neighbor will lose the grace of the blessings for which he prays. Moreover, by a just judgment, he will be delivered over to temptation and to evil in order to learn how to cleanse himself of his faults by canceling his complaints against another. He here calls "temptation" the law of sin which the first man did not bear when he came into existence, and "evil" the devil, who mingled this law of sin with human nature and who by trickery persuaded man to transfer his soul's desire from what was permitted to what was forbidden, and to be turned around to transgress the divine commandment. And the result of this transgression was the loss of incorruptibility given by grace.

Or again we can also call "temptation" the soul's voluntary inclination to the passions of the flesh, and "evil" the manner of the passionate disposition which fulfills itself in act. The just Judge will exempt from neither of these things anyone who does not forgive his debtors their debts, even if he uses the words to ask for this in the prayer. On the contrary, he allows such a man to disgrace himself by the law of sin and leaves the stubborn and immature will to the domination of the evil one, since it has preferred dishonorable passions, whose sower is the devil, to nature, whose creator is God. He does not prevent him from voluntarily directing himself to the passions of the flesh nor ransom him from the habit which carries out this passionate disposition in act, because in paying less attention to nature than to formless passions out of his ardor for them, he has ignored the principle of nature. In the movement of this principle he should know what is the law of nature and what is that of the passions, whose tyranny comes about by a choice of free will and not by nature.[88] He should also preserve the law of nature by an activity conformed to nature and keep the law of passions far away from his intention. He should safeguard by reason the nature which of itself is pure and spotless, without hatred or dissension. He should on the contrary make free will a partner of nature which does not involve itself in anything beyond what the principle of nature gives out, and thereby to reject all hatred of and estrangement from the one who is akin to him by nature. Thus in saying the prayer he will be heard and will receive from God a double instead of a single grace, the forgiveness of past offenses as well as the protection and ransom from future sins. God will not let him enter into temptation, nor allow the Evil One to enslave him on the sole basis of his having readily forgiven his neighbor's debts.

5. This is why, to step back and review briefly the import of what has been said, if we wish to be rescued from evil and not enter into temptation, we also should have faith in God and forgive the trespasses of those who trespass against us, "for," it is said, "if you do not forgive men their sins, neither will your heavenly Father forgive you yours."[89]

In this way not only shall we acquire forgiveness for our sins but we shall also be victors over the law of sin without being left behind to undergo the experience of it. We shall trample underfoot the evil serpent which gave rise to this law[90] from whom we beg to be delivered. When Christ who has overcome the world[91] has become our leader, he will fully arm us with the law of the commandments by which he makes us reject the passions and thus binds the nature back to itself by love.[92] He sets in movement in us an insatiable desire[93] for himself who is the Bread of Life, wisdom, knowledge, and justice. When we fulfill the Father's will he renders us similar to the angels in their adoration, as we imitate them by reflecting the heavenly blessedness in the conduct of our life. From there he leads us finally in the supreme ascent in divine realities to the Father of lights[94] wherein he makes us sharers in the divine nature[95] by participating in the grace of the Spirit, through which we receive the title of God's children and become clothed entirely with the complete person who is the author of this grace, without limiting or defiling him who is Son of God by nature, from whom, by whom, and in whom we have and shall have being, movement, and life.[96]

6. The aim of the prayer should direct us to the mystery of deification so that we might know from what things the condescension through the flesh of the Only Son kept us away and whence and where he brought up by the strength of his gracious hand, those of us who had reached the lowest point of the universe where the weight of sin had confined us. Let us love more intensely the one who so wisely prepared for us such a salvation. By what we do let us show that the prayer is fulfilled, and manifest and proclaim that God is truly a Father through grace. Let us show clearly that we do not at all have as a father of our life the Evil One who, by the dishonorable passions, always tries to impose tyrannically his domination over nature. Let us not unwittingly exchange death for life, since each of the adversaries (God and the devil) agrees to make an exchange with his associates, one bestowing eternal life on those who love him and the other causing death in those who come near him through the stratagem of voluntary temptations.

For according to Scripture there are two kinds of temptation, one pleasurable and the other painful, the first being intentional and the other unintentional. The former begets sin, and the Lord's teaching instructs us to pray not to enter into this when he tells us, "And lead us not into temptation,"[97] and "Watch and pray that you do not enter into temptation."[98] The latter, a penalty for sin, chastises the disposition of loving sin by involuntary recurrences of troubles. If we endure them and especially if we are not attached to them by the nails of wickedness,[99] we shall hear the great Apostle James who clearly proclaims, "Count it all joy, my brethren, when you meet various trials, for the testing endured by your faith produces constancy, constancy produces fidelity, and fidelity accompanies a perfect work."[100] The Evil One mischievously uses both types of temptations, voluntary and involuntary, the first by sowing and greatly provoking the soul with bodily pleasures and scheming first to take away the desire of divine love. Then he cunningly works on the other type, hoping to corrupt the nature by pain so as to constrain the soul, struck down by the weakness of sufferings, to set in motion the attitudes of hatred of the Creator.

But we who know well the designs of the Evil One pray to avoid voluntary temptation so that we will not turn aside our desire from divine love. As far as involuntary temptation is concerned, let us endure it nobly as coming with God's consent, so that we might show that we prefer the Creator of nature to nature itself. And may it happen that all of us who call on the name of our Lord Jesus Christ be ransomed from the devil's present delights and be freed from future sufferings by the participation in the formal realization of the blessings to come, which we shall attain in Christ our Lord himself, who alone with the Father and the Holy Spirit is glorified by the whole creation. Amen.

NOTES

1. By reason of the dignity of its origin and its liturgical use, the Our Father is the subject of many patristic commentaries. Prior to the time of Maximus, widely read treatises or sermons were composed by Tertullian, Cyprian, Ambrose, Augustine, John Cassian, and Peter Chrysologus in the West and by Origen, Cyril of Jerusalem, Gregory of Nyssa, John Chrysostom, and Theodore of Mopsuestia in the East. A handy collection of texts has been gathered in A. Hamman, *Le Pater Expliqué par les Pères* (Paris, 1962).

2. For the theme of imitation of God, see *Chapters on Love* 4:55 and note. We do not know to whom this treatise is addressed.

3. *Phobos/Pothos*, two qualities that Maximus likes to see in dynamic interplay. Their union without confusion becomes love (*agape*), as Maximus affirms, which functions as the harmonizing principle of the redeemed cosmos. Nicholas Madden has examined the structure of their relationship in "The Commentary on the Pater: An Example of the Structural Methodology of Maximus the Confessor," MC 147–55. The numbering of sections has been made according to the suggestions of this work.

4. Ps 19:10.

5. 1 Jn 4:18.

6. Cf *Chapters on Love* 1:81 and *Q.Thal.* 10 (289AB; Laga-Steel 85).

7. Wis 9:14.

8. Ps 33:11.

9. The term self-abasement or self-emptying (*kenosis*) is a common patristic term for the incarnation and is founded in St. Paul's use of the verb form in Phil 2:7. Here in very clear language Maximus directly relates human deification to the divine incarnation, echoing thereby the classic expressions of St. Athanasius, "He became man that we might become God" (inc. 54; SC 199, 458) and Gregory Nazianzen, Or. 30 (4th Theol.) 14 and 21 (SC 250, 256 and 272). Like Maximus, Gregory cites the same verse from 1 Timothy. Ps. Dionysius often uses the term "deification" but without the very explicit correlative of incarnation. For Maximus see also *ascet.* 43 (953B) and *Q.Thal.* 63 (668ff, 681ff.): The incarnation is Providence's plan of man's deification. In question 22 of the latter work Maximus sees history as divided into two sections, represented by the incarnation of God and the deification of man.

10. These categories were seen in the *Chapters on Love* 1:78, 96, 100; 3:33, and again in *Mystagogy* 23 and 18. Maximus here sees providence and judgment as expressions of God's counsel for man's salvation. Cf. also *Q.Thal.* 22 (317BC; Laga-Steel 137), and 63 (681C–685A).

11. 1 Tm 2:5; cf. Heb 8:6.

12. I.e., without compromising his divinity: *apathos*.

13. Theology here means dwelling with and contemplation of God. Cf. Evagrius, *On Prayer* 60: "If you are a theologian you truly pray. If you truly pray you are a theologian" (Bamberger, 65). Maximus speaks of this state in *Chapters of Love* 2:26.

14. This New Testament term (Lk 20:36) becomes a common theme in monastic literature. It is found in Origen himself and in his tradition, cf. c. Cels. 4, 29: "We know that men, when they are tendered perfect, become equal to the angels." Also Comm. on John 2, 22. In Origen's system this state is a return to the primordial condition; this does not hold as such for Maximus. See below and note 18.

15. I.e., theology, understood as a mystical, not an academic, reality.

16. Maximus speaks often of man's salvation in trinitarian terms. Cf., e.g., *Q.Thal.* 2 (272B; Laga-Steel 51), 60 (624BC). In doing so he is viewing the Trinity from an *economic* perspective. A little later in this treatise he will view it from a *theological* one. On this theme see F. Heinzer, "L'Explication trinitaire de l'Economie chez Maxime le Confesseur," MC 159–72.

17. As the context makes clear, the term "disposition" is not used in the psychological sense of temperament but in the deliberative sense of a state of will. The new birth into Christ is a voluntary one and is in need of constant ratification through observance of the commandments. It is in this sense that we

must understand Maximus's definition of love as a "good disposition of the soul" (*Chapters on Love* 1:1). Elsewhere Maximus speaks of the spirit of adoption as a seed that leads to likeness with God: *Q.Thal.* 6 (281AB; Laga-Steel 71).

18. The *tantum-quantum* relationship brings out the necessary and intrinsic connection between incarnation and deification.

19. For the theme of equality with the angels see Evagrius, *On Prayer* 113, as well as *Chapters on Love* 2:17 and *Mystagogy* 23. Angels live a life in accordance with the intelligence while men live in accordance with their bodily passions. Cf. I. Hausherr, *Leçons d'un contemplatif*, p. 147.

20. Col 1:20.

21. The union of wills, of course, means a union in love without discord. It bespeaks a reconciliation in love between angelic and human creations where the natural distinctions of each are respected. It is clear that Maximus is cleansing this term ("equal in honor to the angels") of its Origenist taint of implying a return to a primordial henad. Unfortunately, in substituting "will" for "nature" Maximus will have obviated only the Origenist error, not that of the Monothelite movement, which was soon to become the chief issue.

22. I.e., the span and experience of his life on earth.

23. This cosmic scope of salvation, based on the Pauline epistles, will be discussed further in the *Mystagogy*. In *Amb.Io.* 36 and *Q.Thal.* 48 Maximus presents Christ as systematically reconciling all the disruptions in nature. On this important point one may consult with profit KL 269–73 and L. Thunberg, *Microcosm and Mediator* (Lund, 1965), pp. 396–459.

24. Cf. Ps 34:9.

25. Jn 6:35, 48, 51. The theme of the Logos as food is very common in Origen: hom. in Lev. 16, 5 (SC 287, 285); Comm. on Jn 20, 35 (28), 313; 19, 6, 39; etc.

26. In accordance with the definition that disorderly passion is a movement contrary to nature: *Chapters on Love* 1:35. This contrasts with the Lord's passion mentioned just afterward.

27. Cf. Col 2:14.

28. Eph 2:14–16.

29. Cf. Col 3:5.

30. The emphasis on the human will in this and the preceding paragraph points out its central role in the mystery of salvation and deification as Maximus sees it. His anthropology, strongly Cappadocian in tone, is one centered on human freedom. In this way he was well positioned to judge the Monothelite compromise as poisoning the very root of the Christian mystery. As the arena in which the drama of love or rejection of God takes place, the will of man though wounded must be integral, free, and operative. *Chapters on Love* 3:27 with its note.

31. Death, then, is seen as a providential disposition by which sin and its effects, having run their course, can be eliminated. Here Maximus is influ-

enced by Gregory of Nyssa: "Man, like some earthen potsherd, is resolved again into the dust of the ground, in order to secure that he may part with the soil which he has now contracted, and that he may, through the resurrection, be reformed anew after the original pattern." *Or. cat.* 8 (45,358ff.), NPNF (Series Two) 5, 482.

32. The image of poison and antidote is also found in *Q.Thal.* 1 (269BC; Laga-Steel 48–50), a question where Maximus acknowledges his indebtedness to Gregory of Nyssa. In the latter father the image is found in Or. cat. 37 (45,93AB).

33. Thus Christ's death was redemptive as was his birth because of its voluntary character; cf. *Q.Thal.* 21 (313C; Laga-Steel 129).

34. A trinitarian allusion, as Maximus explains further on.

35. Both this phrase and that of the "single will" above will later be regarded by Maximus as insufficiently precise. By the former he means "opposition of wills" and by the latter, "united in the object of their wills."

36. Cf. Col 2:3.

37. The discussion is based on the etymology of the words prayer (*proseuche*) and vow (*euche*), and is based on Evagrius, *On Prayer* 21, and through him on Mt. 5:24. Here vow, or votive offering, is usually translated simply as gift. Cf. also *Q.Thal.* 50 (469A; Laga-Steel 383). In his commentary on The Lord's Prayer, Gregory of Nyssa offers definitions similar to those by Maximus and is clearly one of the inspired fathers to whom he refers: or. dom. 2 (44, 1137C–1140A).

38. Ps 76:12; also quoted by Gregory of Nyssa.

39. Joh 2:10.

40. 1 Sm 1:11.

41. 2 Chr 32:20.

42. Mt. 6:9; also quoted by Gregory of Nyssa.

43. The proper beginning of Christian prayer and thought is the recognition of God's transcendent existence: *lex credendi*.

44. There is indeed a very rare manuscript that has this variant of Lk 11:2 but Maximus undoubtedly got this reading from Gregory of Nyssa, *The Lord's Prayer* 3 (PG 44, 1157C and 1160). Cf. Hilda Graef in ACW 18, 187 n. 69. According to Hausherr, certain Coptic documents say that Evagrius composed a treatise on the Our Father where the Holy Spirit is spoken of as the kingdom that is prayed for: *Leçons*, 83–84. The variant is also found in Tertullian in the West. A. Hamman speculates that as the Lord's Prayer was solemnly recited in the baptismal liturgy, the variant reading could have been suggested by the rubric of imposition of hands as Tertullian describes it in *On Baptism* 8 (PL1, 1316A). Cf. *Le Pater expliqué par les Pères*, 13.

45. The theological precisions here and further on are meant to be confessions of praise.

46. Lust and anger, or the concupiscible and irascible drives of the soul, were treated of in *Chapters on Love*.

47. Cf. Eph 2:22.

48. Is 66:2 (LXX).

49. Mt 5:4.

50. Mt 22:30.

51. Mt 25:34.

52. Ibid., 25:21.

53. 1 Thes 4:15, 16; 1 Cor 15:52.

54. This inflexible habit is the same as the good disposition which is spoken of elsewhere. It underscores the ethical concern of Maximus in the perfecting of the Christian and the primacy of the will in its attainment. Maximus's classic defense of the full integrity and redemptive role of Christ's human will in his more directly dogmatic and polemical writings gives the proper Christological setting to this ascetical truth.

55. Mt 11:29.

56. Gal 3:28. Cf. *Chapters on Love* 2:30 and note 89 (p. 92).

57. Cf. *Q.Thal.* (269A; Laga-Steel 47); *Chapters on Love* 4:80, etc.

58. A coat of sheep- or goatskin. In Origen's tradition, animal skins are the symbol of mortification because they are no longer living. Evagrius, *Practikos* prol. 6; see note by A. Guillaumont and C. Guillaumont. Gregory of Nyssa takes up the image in or. cat. 8 and *Life of Moses* 2, 187 (SC 1 ter, 232; CWS 102).

59. Cf. 2 Kgs 2:11, 12.

60. According to contemporary medicine. The image is found in Gregory of Nyssa, beat. 2 (44, 1216C); an. et res. (46,56A); cant. 3 (828A; Jaeger VI, 94).

61. A Pauline triad borrowed from the pagan poet (Acts 17:28), which Maximus finds useful.

62. On this point see A. Squire, "The Soul as Virgin and Mother in Maximus the Confessor," SP 8 (Berlin, 1966): 451–61.

63. Sexual generation, like time and death, is for Maximus a sign of the present fallen condition, which is overcome in the cosmic reconciliation of Christ.

64. In this analysis of expansion and contraction in the understanding of the Trinity, the errors of Greek and Jew respectively, Maximus is indebted to Gregory Nazianzen. Cf. *Or.* 38 (On the Theophany), 8, (36, 320B). The theological precision of what follows is clearly regarded by Maximus as doxological. See also *Mystagogy* 23 and *Chapters on Knowledge* 2:1–10.

65. Utilizing here the distinction logos-tropos.

66. Cf. Col 1:28.

67. Creaturely movement has God as its term, but man's capacity for

God, as Maximus showed in his refutation of the Origenist myth, never reaches a term.

68. In spite of this clear language on the eternity of hell, E. Michaud has argued that Maximus held to a universal restoration as did the Origenists; "S. Maxime le Confesseur et l'apocatastase," *Revue internationale de théologie* 10 (1902): 257–72. This has been refuted in an admirable study by Brian Daley, "Apokatastasis and 'honorable silence' in the Eschatology of Maximus the Confessor," MC 309–39.

69. Cf. 2 Cor 7:1.

70. Phil 3:20. For references to the life of virtue as angelic and worshipful see, *Chapters on Love* 1:42; 4:36; *Mystagogy* 23, 24, as well as below.

71. Ps 73:25.

72. Spiritual worship is a theme found in Origen (c. Cels. 8, 17; 3, 34; 6, 14; 7, 65; h. in Lev. 9,1; SC 287, 72–74). See J. Daniélou, *Origène* (Paris, 1948), pp. 42–52.

73. *Pothos*, that yearning and affective drive of the human person.

74. The irascible element in the human makeup. Maximus is saying that the entire thrust of human psychological powers should be directed toward God.

75. Jn 6:33.

76. *Aeon:* understood in the Cappadocian perspective of history as a sign both of sin and of hope. Cf. *Chapters on Love* 3:100; *Q.Thal.* 15 (297A–300A; Laga-Steel 101–03); *Chapters on Knowledge* 1:5, 68–70.

77. This passage on a theme dear to Origen is repeated verbatim in *Chapters on Knowledge* 2:56. For references cf. its note.

78. Mt 6:25, 31,33.

79. The context makes clear, even explicit, that Maximus is speaking of a union of divine and human wills in grace. That he feel no pressure to insist that this union is not one of nature is an indication that this work predates the Monothelite crisis (Sherwood, *Datelist*, 31). Moreover, the term *gnome* is here employed to signify will, that is, intentionality. This was a common enough usage in contemporary Greek. With the outbreak of the Monothelite heresy, however, Maximus had to restrict the use of this term to the human condition of the will which lies subject to sin. Cf. Pyrrh. (312Aff).

80. Or, meditation on or training for death. The phrase is found as early as Socrates (Plato, *Phaedo* 67DE and 80E–81A) and had passed into patristic usage. Clement of Alexandria (Strom. 5, 11, 67, 1) had pointed out the Platonic origin of this idea (Viller, RAM 258, n. 195). Evagrius uses the expression in *Practikos* 52 and Gregory of Nazianzen as well, but as A. Guillaumont and C. Guillaumont note in their critical edition (SC 171, 621), the context in which Maximus speaks of it is closer to Gregory than to Evagrius.

81. In using the traditional Platonic imagery of withdrawal from the body, Maximus is yet standing it on its head by speaking in the dynamic

framework of Christian freedom. Having made clear that all things are good in themselves as logoi, he is intent on restoring the balance to creation by liberating human drives to seek their true end.

82. This sentence gives evidence of the tortuous and convoluted style to which Maximus is often subject and which called down the criticisms of Photius, *Library* 192A (critical ed. R. Henry [Paris, 1962], pp. 80–81).

83. Cf. *Chapters on Love* 4:55 and note. Elsewhere Maximus speaks of God and man as "examples for each other," God becoming man out of love for him and man becoming deified through love for God: *Amb.Io.* 5 (1113BC).

84. Cf. ibid., 4:34, 76, 84, etc.

85. The correspondence of free will with nature is thus posited as a necessary requirement for deification.

86. Ps 44:23 and Rom 8:36.

87. Cf. Phil 2:17.

88. These two "laws" are norms of behavior according to which one directs his life. The law of sin spoken of above introduced deception into human behavior in such a way that man is ruled by the passions. The law of nature must be restored, and the tyranny of the passions overcome, by a voluntary conformity of our wills with God's in virtue. Maximus's interpretation of "temptation" and "evil" (cf. *Q.Thal.* 26) is thus to be seen in the dynamic realm of existential freedom. We are here, of course, in another theological climate from that which developed in the West with its distinction between nature and the supernatural. This anthropology owes much to Gregory of Nyssa.

89. Mt 6:15.

90. Cf. Gn 3:1ff.

91. Cf. Jn 16:33.

92. Love, the moral union of free wills, is thus the reconciling agent and curative element in a fallen world as well as the goal of human activity.

93. Insatiable because the human capacity for the infinite God is itself infinite. *Epektasis*, the notion of continual progress, was a favorite theme of Gregory of Nyssa; see his *Life of Moses* 2, 226–7; 162, etc.; cf. Daniélou, *Platonisme et Théologie Mystique*, pp. 291, 307.

94. Cf. Jas 1:17.

95. Cf. 2 Pt 1:4.

96. Cf. Acts 17:28.

97. Mt 7:13.

98. Mt. 26:41.

99. See *Chapters on Knowledge* 1:99 with its note.

100. Jas 1:2–4.

CHAPTERS ON KNOWLEDGE

TWO HUNDRED CHAPTERS OF OUR
HOLY FATHER MAXIMUS THE
CONFESSOR ON THEOLOGY AND THE
ECONOMY IN THE FLESH OF THE SON
OF GOD.

First Century

1. God is one, without beginning, incomprehensible, possessing in his totality the full power of being, fully excluding the notion of time and quality in that he is inaccessible to all and not discernible by any being on the basis of any natural representation.[1]

2. God is in himself (insofar as it is possible for us to know) neither beginning, nor middle, nor end, nor absolutely anything that is thought of as coming after him by nature; for he is unlimited, unmoved, and infinite in that he is infinitely beyond every essence, power, and act.[2]

3. Every essence, which implies in itself its own limit, is naturally a principle of movement contemplated in potency to it. Every natural movement toward act, discerned after essence and before act, is a middle insofar as it is taken naturally between the two as midpoint. And every act, circumscribed naturally by its own principle, is the end of essential movement logically preceding it.[3]

4. God is not essence, understood as either general or particular, even if he is principle; nor is he potency understood as either general or particular, even if he is means; he is not act, understood as either general or particular, even if he is end of essential movement discerned in potency.[4] But he is a principle of being who is creative of essence and beyond essence, a ground who is creative of power but beyond power, the active and eternal condition of every act, and to speak briefly, the Creator of every essence, power, and act, as well as every beginning, middle, and end.[5]

5. Beginning, middle, and end are characteristics of beings distinguished by time and it can be truly stated that they are also characteristics of beings comprehended in history. Indeed time, which has measured movement, is circumscribed by number, and history, which includes in its existence the category of when, admits of a separation in-

129

sofar as it began to be. And if time and history are not without beginning, so much less are those things which are contained in them.[6]

6. God is always properly one and unique by nature. He encloses in himself in every way the whole of what being is in that he is himself even well beyond being itself. If this is the case, absolutely nothing that we call being has being at all of its own. Consequently, absolutely nothing that is different from him by essence is seen together with him from all eternity: neither age, nor time, nor anything dwelling in them.[7] For what is properly being and what is improperly being never come together with each other.

7. Every beginning, middle, and end does not totally exclude every category of relation. God, on the contrary, being infinitely infinite, well above every relationship, is obviously neither beginning nor middle nor end nor absolutely anything of what the category or relation can be seen to possess.[8]

8. It is said that all beings are objects of knowledge because they bear the demonstrable principles of their knowledge. God, however, is called the unknown, and among all knowable things only his existence can be perceived.[9] This is why no knowable object can compare in any way with him.

9. The knowledge of beings includes naturally, in view of demonstration, their own principles which naturally circumscribe them in a definition. But with God, only his existence can be believed through the principles in beings. He gives to those who are devout a proper faith and confession which are clearer than any demonstration. For faith is a true knowledge from undemonstrated principles, since it is the substance of realities which are beyond intelligence and reason.[10]

10. God is the beginning, middle, and end of beings in that he is active and not passive, as are all others which we so name. For he is beginning as creator, middle as provider, and end as goal, for it is said, "From him and through him and for him are all beings."[11]

11. There is no rational soul which is by essence more valuable than another rational soul. Indeed, God in his goodness, creating every soul to his image, brings it into being to be self-moving. Each one, then, deliberately either chooses honor or accepts dishonor by its own deeds.[12]

12. God is the sun of justice,[13] as it is written, who shines rays of goodness on simply everyone. The soul develops according to its free will into either wax because of its love for God or into mud because of its love of matter. Thus just as by nature the mud is dried out by the sun and the wax is automatically softened, so also every soul which

loves matter and the world and has fixed its mind far from God is hardened as mud according to its free will and by itself advances to its perdition, as did Pharaoh. However, every soul which loves God is softened as wax, and receiving divine impressions and characters it becomes "the dwelling place of God in the Spirit."[14]

13. The one who has illumined his mind with divine thoughts, who has accustomed his reason to honor ceaselessly the Creator with divine hymns, and who has sanctified his sense with uncontaminated images has added to the natural beauty of the image the voluntary good of likeness.[15]

14. One keeps his soul uncontaminated for God if he strives to direct his thought to think on God alone and on his virtues, who sets up his reason as a true interpreter and exegete of his virtues, and who teaches his senses to reflect honestly on the sensible world and whatever it contains so as to announce to the soul the magnificence of the principles of things.[16]

15. In freeing us from the bitter bondage of tyrannical devils, God has given us the loving yoke of holy piety, which is humility. By it all diabolical power is subdued, and for those who choose it everything becomes good and remains inviolate.

16. The believer comes to fear. The one who has fear is humbled. The one who is humbled becomes gentle; he has adopted a behavior which renders inactive the movements of the anger and lust. The one who is gentle keeps the commandments. The one who keeps the commandments is purified. The one who is purified is illumined. And the one who is illumined is judged worthy to sleep with the Word-Spouse in the inner chamber of the mysteries.[17]

17. As a farmer in examining a suitable place to transplant wild trees falls upon an unhoped for treasure, so it is with every genuine and humble ascetic whose soul is smooth of the roughness of matter, as the most blessed Jacob, asked by his father on the manner of his knowledge, "How did you find it so quickly, my son?" replies, "The Lord God granted me success."[18] For when the Lord will have given us who did not expect it the wise contemplations of his own wisdom without labor, it will be granted us suddenly to find a spiritual treasure. For the proven ascetic is a spiritual farmer who transplants as a wild tree the sense contemplation of visible things into the region of the spiritual and who finds a treasure: the manifestation by grace of the wisdom which is in beings.

18. Falling suddenly through humility on the ascetic who did not ex-

131

pect it, the knowledge of divine contemplations overcomes the thinking of the one who seeks it with effort and toil for the sake of show but does not find it. It foolishly engenders in the senseless one any envy toward his brother, a thought of murder, and for himself a sadness in not having the vanity of praises.[19]

19. Those who search for knowledge with toil and do not succeed fail because of a lack of faith or else because being foolishly in rivalry with those who have knowledge they are at the point of rebelling against them, as once the people did against Moses. Against them let the law rightly say that some, using force, climbed the mountain, and the Amorite who dwelt on that mountain came out and slaughtered them.[20] For it is necessary that those who simulate virtue through ostentation be not only defeated for having deceived piety but also be wounded by their conscience.

20. The one who seeks knowledge for the sake of display and does not succeed should not be jealous of his neighbor nor should he be sad, but let him make the Preparation with some neighbor as it is prescribed;[21] he must be diligent in readying himself for knowledge by practice, first on the body, then on the soul.

21. Those who deal rightly and piously with beings and who conceive no sort of love of ostenation will find coming to meet them their most precise apprehension. To these the Law says, "Enter and inherit big and beautiful cities and houses which you did not build, filled with all kinds of goods, and wells dug in stone, which you did not dig, and vines and olive trees which you did not plant."[22] Indeed he who lives not for himself but for God becomes filled with divine graces which had not been manifested till then because of the pressing disturbance of the passions.

22. Just as we speak of the two types of sense, the first a habitual one which is ours even when we are asleep and which does not perceive any object (it has no utility since it does not tend to an act), the second, in act, by which we perceive sensible things, so are there two types of knowledge. The first is intelligent, which picks up the principles of beings by its habit alone; it has no usefulness since it does not tend toward the observance of the commandments. The second is practical, in act, and admits this true understanding of beings through experience.[23]

23. The hypocrite, so long as he thinks himself hidden, is quiet and seeks after glory in having it believed that he is righteous. But when he is detected, he hurls death-bearing words, thinking in abusing others to hide his own deformity. Scripture compares him to a brood of vipers

because of his duplicity and calls upon him to produce fruits worthy of repentance, that is, to transform the hidden disposition of the heart into honest behavior.[24]

24. Some call beast every being living in the air, on land, or in the sea which is not adjudged clean by the Law even if it seems domesticated in its ways. By their names, the Scripture denotes each man according to his passion.[25]

25. The one who counterfeits friendship to harm his neighbor is a wolf who hides his wickedness under his fleece,[26] and when he encounters a simple behavior or a word according to Christ done or said with innocence, he robs them and corrupts them, showering many censures. He attacks these words and this behavior as a spy on the freedom of the brothers in Christ.[27]

26. The one who simulates silence because of wickedness contrives deceit against his neighbor. He gives up without success, having inflicted sorrow on himself by reason of his own passion. On the other hand, the one who keeps silence for the sake of spiritual profit has increased friendship and is made happy for having received an illumination which puts darkness to flight.

27. The one who in a gathering interrupts rashly the flow of conversation does not hide in his illness his love of glory. Caught in the act, he proposes countless escapes and circumlocutions in an attempt to quarrel with the sequence of what is said.

28. The wise man who gives or receives instruction wishes to give or receive it only in useful matters. However, when the man who appears wise seeks information or is questioned, he advances only more contrived things.

29. The goods which one has received by the grace of God should be shared without jealousy with others. For it is said, "You have freely received, freely give."[28] For the one who hides the gift under the earth accuses his master of being harsh, declining virtue by caring for the flesh.[29] And the one who sells the truth to the enemy and is later convicted of glory-seeking cannot bear the shame and hangs himself.[30]

30. Those who are still timid in the war against the passions and who fear the inroads of invisible enemies should be quiet, that is, not engage in warlike behavior above their strength, but by prayer abandon the care of themselves to God's concern. For we read in Exodus, "The Lord will fight for you and you will keep quiet."[31] Those who have already overcome their pursuers and who seek virtuous behavior for right-minded instruction must only keep open the ear of the mind. To

them is said, "Listen, Israel!"[32] To him who by purification energetically aims at the divine knowledge there corresponds a reverent boldness. It will be said to him, "Why do you cry out to me?"[33] Thus to the one to whom silence is prescribed because of fear, only refuge in God is helpful. To the one to whom it is recommended to listen there corresponds a readiness to hearken to the divine commandments. As for the gnostic, it is fitting that he cry out endlessly in supplication to turn away evils and to give thanks for the sharing of good things.

31. The soul would never be able to reach out toward the knowledge of God if God did not allow himself to be touched by it through condescension and by raising it up to him. Indeed, the human mind as such would not have the strength to raise itself to apprehend any divine illumination did not God himself draw it up, as far as it is possible for the human mind to be drawn, and illumine it with divine brightness.[34]

32. The one who imitates the Lord's disciples is not deterred on account of the Pharisees from walking through the grain fields on the Sabbath and picking the ears of grain,[35] but arrived at detachment through spiritual practice he gathers up the principles of creatures and is religiously nourished with the divine knowledge of beings.

33. The one who is a simple believer according to the Gospel moves the mountain of his wickedness through practice, rejecting for himself from the unstable course of sensible things the former disposition based on them. The one who is capable of being a disciple receives in his hands from the Word the fragments of the loaves of knowledge and nourishes thousands of people,[36] showing that by practice the power of the word is multiplied. The one who has received the strength of being an apostle heals every sickness and weakness by expelling demons, that is, by putting to flight the activity of the passions, in caring for the sick, in recalling to a habit of devotion by words of hope those who are deprived of it, and in converting by the word of judgment those who have been weakened by laziness. For exhorted to crush underfoot both serpents and scorpions,[37] he obliterates the beginning and end of sin.

34. The one who is an apostle and a disciple is also completely a believer. But the one who is a disciple is not wholly an apostle, but is wholly a believer. The one who is only a simple believer is neither disciple nor apostle. Still, by his manner of life and contemplation, the third can be moved to the rank of dignity of the second, and the second to the rank of dignity of the first.

35. All things created in time according to time become perfect when they cease their natural growth. But everything that the knowledge of

God effects according to virtue, when it reaches perfection, moves to further growth. For the end of the latter becomes the beginning of the former. Indeed, the one who by practicing the virtues keeps in check the substance of past things begins other, more divine patterns. For God never ceases from good things, as he never began them. For just as it is the property of light to illumine, likewise is it the property of God to do good. Under the Law which regulates the ordering of what is in time subject to becoming and corruption, the Sabbath is honored by rest. But under the Gospel, which brings in the restoration of intelligible things, it is brightened by the noble performance of good works. Only those who did not yet know that "the Sabbath was made for man, and not man for the Sabbath," and again that the "Son of Man is Lord even on the Sabbath" would be indignant.[38]

36. For the Law and the Prophets there is the Sabbath,[39] the Sabbaths,[40] and the Sabbaths of Sabbaths, just as there is the circumcision and the circumcision of circumcision, and also the harvest and the harvest's harvest, as it is written, "When you harvest your harvest."[41] The first is the completion of practical, natural, and theological learning. The second is the release of becoming and of the principles of becoming. The third is the bringing in and enjoyment of the more spiritual principles of sense and mind. And this comes about, of course, in each of the three categories mentioned. In this way the gnostic knows the principles according to which Moses observes the Sabbath in dying outside the Holy Land.[42] Joshua, son of Nun, performs circumcision in crossing the Jordan[43] and those who inherited the good land present to God the gathering in of the doubly abundant harvest.

37. Sabbath is the detachment of the rational soul which has by practice completely thrown off the marks of sin.[44]

38. Sabbaths are the freedom of the rational soul which by natural contemplation in the Spirit has put down this natural activity oriented toward sensibility.

39. Sabbaths of Sabbaths are the spiritual peace of the rational soul which, having withdrawn the mind even from all the more divine principles which are in beings, dwells entirely in God alone in a loving ecstasy,[45] and has rendered itself by mystical theology totally immobile in God.

40. Circumcision is the soul's putting off of its disposition of being affected by becoming.[46]

41. The circumcision of circumcision is the total loss and stripping even of natural movements of the soul with respect to becoming.

42. The harvest is the rational soul's collecting and recognition with understanding of the more spiritual principles of things by virtue and nature.[47]

43. The harvest of harvests is the understanding of God, not accessible to all, beyond the mystical contemplation of the intelligibles, arranged around the mind in an unknowable manner. This understanding God presents to the one who worthily honors the Creator from visible and invisible creatures.

44. There is another more spiritual harvest which is said to be from God himself, and another more mysterious circumcision and another more secret Sabbath in which God rests in doing Sabbath from his own works. Thus it is said, "The harvest is plentiful but the laborers are few,"[48] and "the circumcision of the heart in Spirit,"[49] and "God blessed the seventh day and sanctified it because on it he rested from all the works that he had begun to create."[50]

45. The harvest of God is the future home and dwelling in him for the end of ages of those who are completely worthy.

46. The circumcision of the heart in spirit is the complete stripping away of the natural actions of sense and mind with respect to sensible and intelligible things by the presence of the Spirit, who directly transfigures the entire body and soul altogether into something more divine.

47. The Sabbath of God is the full return to him of all creatures whereby he rests from his own natural activity toward them, his very divine activity which acts in an ineffable way. For God rests from his natural activity in each being by which each of them moves naturally. He rests when each being, having obtained the divine energy in due measure, will determine its own natural energy with respect to God.[51]

48. Zealous people should look among God's works to know which of them he began to create and which, on the contrary, he did not begin. Indeed, if he has rested from all the works that he began to create, it is clear that he did not rest from those which he did not create. God's works which began in time are all beings which share, for example, the different essences of beings, for they have nonbeing before being. For God was when participated beings were not. The works of God which did not happen to begin to be in time are participated beings, in which participated beings share according to grace, for example, goodness and all that the term goodness implies, that is, all life, immortality, simplicity, immutability, and infinity and such things which are essentially contemplated in regard to him; they are also God's works, and yet they did not begin in time. For what does not exist is not older than vir-

tue nor than anything else of what was just listed, even if beings which participate in them in these things began their existence in time. For all virtue is without beginning, not having any time previous to itself. Such things have God alone as the eternal begetter of their being.

49. God infinitely transcends all things which participate or are participated. For everything claiming to have the term attributed to it happens to be a work of God, even if some begin their existence through becoming in time and others are implanted by grace in creatures, for example, an infused power which clearly proclaims that God is in all things.

50. All immortal things and immortality itself, all living things and life itself, all holy things and holiness itself, all virtuous things and virtue itself, all good things and goodness itself, all beings and being itself, are clearly found to be works of God. But some began to be in time, for there was a time when they were not, and others did not begin to be in time. Thus there was never a time when there existed neither virtue nor goodness nor holiness nor immortality. What began in time is and is said to be what it is and is said, by participation with what did not begin in time. God is the creator of all life, immortality, holiness, and virtue, for he transcends the essence of all which can be thought and said.[52]

51. According to Scripture, the sixth day brings in the completion of beings subject to nature. The seventh limits the movement of temporal distinctiveness. The eighth indicates the manner of existence above nature and time.[53]

52. The one who spends the sixth day solely according to the Law in fleeing the tyranny of the passions which strongly oppress the soul fearlessly crosses the sea toward the desert; he observes the Sabbath only by the inactivity of the passions. But the one who crosses the Jordan, having gone even beyond the simple state of inactivity of the passions, comes into the inheritance of the virtues.[54]

53. The one who spends the sixth day according to the Gospel, having already given up the first movements of sin, acquires by his virtues the state of detachment which is removed from all evil; he makes Sabbath in his mind of the simple representation of the passions. The one who has crossed over the Jordan is transported to the region of knowledge where the mind, mystically built by peace as a temple, becomes "the dwelling-place of God in the Spirit."[55]

54. The one who has divinely accomplished in himself the sixth day by appropriate works and thoughts, and who has with God nobly

brought his works to an end, has crossed by comprehension all the ground of what is subject to nature and to time. He is transported to the mystical contemplation of the immortal ages, and in an unknowable manner he makes Sabbath in his mind in leaving behind and totally surpassing beings. The one who has become worthy of the eighth day is risen from the dead, that is, from what is less than God: sensible and intelligible things, words, and thoughts; and he lives the blessed life of God, who alone is said to be and is in very truth the Life, in such a way that he becomes himself God by deification.[56]

55. The sixth day is the full accomplishment of the natural activities of those who practice virtue. The seventh is the fulfillment and rest of the natural activities of those who contemplate the ineffable knowledge. The eighth is the promotion and transition to deification of those who are worthy. The Lord has perhaps never allowed a more mystical glance at these seventh and eighth days than in referring to them as the day and the hour of fulfillment, since it encloses the mysteries and the principles of all things. Absolutely no heavenly or earthly power can know these days before experiencing the passion, only the blessed divinity which created them.[57]

56. The sixth day reveals the principle of being of things, the seventh indicates the manner of the well-being of things, the eighth communicates the ineffable mystery of the eternal well-being of things.[58]

57. Knowing that the sixth day is the symbol of practical activity, let us acquit on this day the whole debt of the works of virtue, so that it can be said of us, "And God saw all that he had done, and behold it was very good."[59]

58. The one who with his body is diligent for his soul in the well-ordered diversity of the virtues fulfills the expectation of the beautiful and praiseworthy work of God.[60]

59. The one who has fulfilled the Preparation of works of justice has arrived at the rest of gnostic contemplation. In it he divinely comprehends the principles of beings and rests from movements of the mind about it.[61]

60. The one who has shared in God's rest on the seventh day for our sake will also share in his activity on the eighth day by our deification, that is, in the mystical resurrection. He also has left behind the linen cloths placed in the tomb and the cloth placed on the head. In contemplating these things, if we are like Peter and John, we believe that the Lord has risen.[62]

61. The Lord's tomb is also to be seen as this world and as the heart

of each believer. The linen cloths are the principles of sensible things along with the modes of virtue. The headcloth is the simple and undiversified knowledge of intelligible things along with the awareness of God one has acquired. Through these things we first know the Word who without them has an understanding which transcends them and is completely inaccessible to us.[63]

62. Those who bury the Lord with honor will also behold him gloriously risen, while to all those who do not he is unseen. For he is no longer caught by those who lay snares, since having no longer the external covering by which he seemed to allow himself to be caught by those who wanted him, and by which he endured the Passion for the salvation of all.[64]

63. The one who honorably buries the Lord will be held in veneration by all the friends of God, for he has kept him as is fitting from public display and from shame in not leaving him as a subject of blasphemy to the unbelievers who nailed him to the wood. Those who posted seals at the tomb and stationed soldiers before it are odious for this deed. They have reproached the risen Word as if he had been stolen, and bought off with money for betrayal the counterfeit disciple who represents the showy manner of virtue, as well as the soldiers for a slander against the risen Savior. The gnostic knows the meaning of these words; he is not unaware of how often the Lord is crucified, is placed in the tomb, and rises again. He treats as dead the passionate thoughts which are posted next to the heart by the demons and which in temptations divide as garments the ways of moral comeliness. He penetrates as seals the images which press in on the soul and predispose it to sin.[65]

64. When any greedy person, in carefully feigning virtue, succeeds in acquiring the object he wants, he renounces the mode by which he was previously thought to be a disciple of the Word.

65. When you see certain arrogant people who cannot bear to have those who are better than themselves praised, and who scheme to suppress the spoken truth by confining it by countless temptations and wicked slanders, it occurs to me that it is by them that the Lord is once again crucified, put into the tomb and guarded by soldiers and seals. Throwing them upside down, the Lord rises up again, all the more conspicuous in being attacked because of the silent serenity he maintained throughout his sufferings. For he is the strongest of all inasmuch as he is and is called the Truth.[66]

66. The mystery of the Incarnation of the Word bears the power of all the hidden meanings and figures of Scripture as well as the knowl-

edge of visible and intelligible creatures. The one who knows the mystery of the cross and the tomb knows the principles of these creatures. And the one who has been initiated into the ineffable power of the Resurrection knows the purpose for which God originally made all things.[67]

67. All visible things need a cross, that is, a capacity which holds back the participation in what is active in them according to sense. All intelligible things need a tomb, that is, the total immobilization of the activities of the mind in them. For when this natural activity and movement with respect to all things is taken away along with their participation, the Word which alone exists by itself as if he had risen from the dead is manifested anew, having in outline all which is from him, though absolutely nothing has any kinship with him in any natural relationship. For it is by grace and not by nature that he is the salvation of those who are saved.[68]

68. Age, time, and place belong in the category of the relative. Without them nothing of what is included in them exists. God is not of the category of the relative because he does not have anything at all included in him. If, then, the inheritance of those who are worthy is God himself, the one who is rendered worthy of this grace will be above age, time, and place. He will have God himself as a place, according to what is written, "Be for me a protecting God, a strong place which saves me."[69]

69. The end has altogether no resemblance to the middle, otherwise it would not be an end. The middle is all that comes after the beginning and before the end. Thus if all ages, times, and places and all that they include are after God who is the beginning without a beginning, and as they are much behind him as infinite end, they do not differ in any way from the middle. Rather, God is the end of those who are saved, and no middle shall be contemplated by those who are saved when the ultimate end is reached.

70. The whole world is limited by its own principles and we attribute place and age to whatever it contains. It has modes of thought naturally inherent in it which can produce a partial understanding of God's wisdom over all things. So long as they serve for understanding, they cannot be anything but middle and thus partial understanding. But when what is partial ceases with the appearance of what is perfect, all mirrors and hidden meanings pass away; once the truth arrives face to face, the one who is saved will be above all worlds, ages, and places in which he was once nurtured as a child, and will reach his end in God.[70]

71. Pilate is the figure of the natural law; the crowd of Jews a figure of the written law. The one who does not surpass by faith the two laws cannot receive the truth which surpasses nature and reason, but really crucifies the Word. As a Jew he regards the Gospel as a scandal, or else as a Greek supposes that it is foolishness.[71]

72. When you see Herod and Pilate forming a friendship with each other to destroy Jesus, then realize that there is the same association between the demon of fornication and that of vainglory which join together to put to death the principle of virtue and knowledge. For the demon of vainglory in feigning spiritual knowledge leads one to the demon of fornication, while that of fornication, taking on an air of purity, leads one back in turn to the demon of vainglory. This is why it is said, "Having clothed him in a bright cloak, Herod sent Jesus back to Pilate."[72]

73. It is good that the mind does not make allowance for the flesh nor devote itself to the passions. "For," it is said, "we do not gather figs from thorns," that is, virtue from the passions, "nor grapes from thistles," that is, joyous knowledge from the flesh.[73]

74. The ascetic who is tested by the patient endurance of temptations, who has purified himself by the training of his body, and who has become perfect by the diligence in sublime contemplations has become worthy of divine consolation. "For the Lord," says Moses, "has come from Sinai (that is, temptations) and has appeared to us from Seir (that is, bodily pains) and has stopped at the mountain of Paran with the multitude of Cadesh (that is, at the mountains of faith with multitudes of holy thoughts)."[74]

75. Herod is intent on the principle of prudence of the flesh; Pilate on the principle of the senses; Caesar on the principle of sensible things; the Jews on the principle of earthly thoughts.[75] When therefore the soul adheres through ignorance to the sensible, it delivers the Word over to the senses for death, proclaiming in its own way by acknowledging the royal character of corruptible things. The Jews say in fact, "We have no other king but Caesar."[76]

76. Herod is intent on the place of activity of the passions; Pilate on the deceptive habit stemming from them; Caesar on the master of the world of darkness; the Jews on the soul. Thus when the soul, in submitting to the passions, hands virtue over into the hands of wicked behavior, it evidently rejects the kingdom of God and seeks after the corrupting tyranny of the devil.

77. The subjection of the passions does not suffice to the soul for spir-

itual joy if it has not acquired the virtues for the fulfilling of the commandments. "Do not rejoice," is it said, "in the fact that the demons are subject to you," that is, the activities of the passions, "but in the fact that your names are written in heaven";[77] that is, they are translated in the place of detachment by the grace of adoption through the virtues.

78. The abundance of virtues through action is absolutely necessary to the gnostic. "For," it is said, "let him who has a purse," that is, spiritual knowledge, "take it, and likewise the bag," that is, the abundance of virtues which lavishly maintains the soul. "The one who has none (clearly the purse and bag, that is, of knowledge and virtue), let him sell his cloak and buy a sword." He should, he says, deliver his flesh with haste to the labors of the virtues and wisely take in hand for God's peace the struggle against the passions and the demons, that is, the behavior which, according to God's word, separates as a sword the better from the worse.[78]

79. In appearing at the age of thirty, the Lord teaches the discerning through this number, as in a hidden way, mysteries which concern him. Indeed, the number thirty considered mystically points to the Lord as Creator and Provider of time, nature, and the intelligibles which are above visible nature. Of time by the number seven, since time is divided into weeks; of nature by the number five, for nature is fivefold and divided into five by the senses; of the intelligibles by the number eight, for the realm of intelligibles is above the period measured by time. He is Provider by the number ten, by the holy decalogue of commandments which introduces men to the good and by the fact that the Lord by this letter mystically introduced his name when he became man. Thus in adding five, seven, eight, and ten we arrive at the number thirty. The one, therefore, who knows how to follow the Lord worthily as a leader will not be unmindful of the reason by which he also will appear as having the age of thirty years, that is, as being able to announce the Gospel of the kingdom. For in an irreproachable way he creates through spiritual exercises the world of virtues as if this were some visible reality, without changing the compass which from this soul follows as some sort of time from contrary things; when by contemplation he gathers without stumbling the knowledge of the intelligibles, and will have been able carefully to place this habit in others also, then will he also be by the Spirit thirty years of age, as if this were his bodily age, manifesting simultaneously with his own benefits the influence which he has on others.[79]

80. The one who has given himself over to the pleasures of the body

is neither active in virtue nor does he properly move toward knowledge. Thereby he does not behave as a man, that is, according to common sense, so that as soon as the water moves he throws himself into the pool, that is, into virtue which receives knowledge and heals every ill on condition that the sick man be not preceded, having delayed by sluggishness, by another who prevents him from reaching healing. This is why for thirty-eight years he is laid up with his sickness. For the one who does not contemplate the visible creation to glorify God nor reverently raise up his thought to intelligible nature remains ill for about the same number of years. In fact, the number thirty taken naturally signifies sensible nature, just as considered practically it signifies practical virtue. The number eight considered naturally denotes the intelligible nature of incorporeal beings, just as contemplated gnostically it means the all-wise theology. The one who does not move by these toward God remains paralyzed until the Word comes to teach him the rapid manner of his cure in saying, "Get up, take up your pallet and walk." He urges him to take away his mind from the love of pleasures which dominate him, to take up his body on the shoulders of the virtues and to return home, to heaven of course. For it is good that what is worse be raised up to the better on the shoulders of the practice of virtue rather than for the better to be carried to the worse through the ease of the love of pleasure.[80]

81. So long as we have not, in our thinking, genuinely transcended the essence which is our own and that of all that is after God, we have not yet acquired an inflexible habit of virtue. But when our dignity will have been restored to us by love we will then know the power of the divine promise. For there, one must believe, are the worthy in an unchangeable repose, there where the mind has anticipated them in rooting its power through love, for the one who does not transcend himself or whatever can be in any way apprehended and who does not settle in a silence beyond all thought is absolutely incapable of being free from mutability.[81]

82. Every thought certainly expresses several or at least a duality of aspects, for it is an intermediary relationship between two extremes which joins together the thinker and the object thought of. Neither of the two can completely retain simplicity. For the thinker is a subject who bears the power of thinking in himself. And what is thought of is a subject as such or dwells in a subject, having inherent in it the capacity of being thought of, or else the essence whose faculty it is which formerly existed. For there is no being at all which is by itself a simple

essence or thought to the extent of also being an undivided monad. As far as God is concerned, if we say that he is an essence, he has not naturally inherent in him the possibility of being thought because he is not composed; if we say that he is thought he has no essence which by nature is capable of being a subject of thought. But God is himself thought by essence, and wholly thought, and solely thought. According to thought he is himself essence, wholly essence, and solely essence. He is entirely above essence and entirely above thought, since he is an invisible monad, simple and without parts. Thus the one who still in some way possesses any thought has not yet left the dyad; but the one who has completely abandoned it has arrived in some fashion into the monad in having supremely relinquished the power of thinking.[82]

83. In the multiple there is diversity, unlikeness, and difference. But in God, who is eminently one and unique, there is only identity, simplicity, and sameness. It is therefore not wise, before leaving the multiple, to apply oneself to contemplations which concern God. This is what Moses shows in pitching the tent of thought outside the camp and then conversing with God.[83] It is precarious to attempt to speak the ineffable in verbal discourse, for this type of language is twofold and manifold. It is safest to contemplate without words and only in the soul the one who is, for he consists in indivisible unity and not in the multiple. For the high priest, who was assigned to enter the Holy of Holies behind the veil only once every year,[84] teaches that only the one who has crossed the court and the holy place and has arrived at the Holy of Holies, that is, who has gone beyond the whole nature of the intelligible and the sensible realities and has purified himself from every particularity stemming from his origin, can encounter God with a soul naked and stripped of representations of him.[85]

84. The great Moses, having pitched his tent outside the camp, that is, having installed his free will and his understanding outside the visible, begins to adore God. Having entered the darkness, the formless and immaterial place of knowledge, he remains there to accomplish the most sacred rites.

85. Darkness is a formless, immaterial, and incorporeal state which bears the exemplary knowledge of beings. The one who enters into this state as another Moses understands things invisible to his mortal nature. Through this state he depicts in himself the beauty of the divine virtues just as a handwriting is a good imitation of the beauty of the archetype; he descends, offering himself to those who want to imitate his

virtue and showing by this the generous and ungrudging grace received in exchange.[86]

86. Those who purely pursue the divine way of life find the greatest benefit in knowledge about it. They no longer change their will along with things, but with a sound firmness undertake readily everything which accords with the principle of virtue.[87]

87. Baptized in Christ by the Spirit, we have received the first incorruptibility of the flesh; we await the final incorruptibility of Christ in the Spirit, that is, in keeping undefiled the first incorruptibility by a free gift of good works and by a voluntary death; according to this final incorruptibility no one who enjoys it will lose the benefits he has acquired.[88]

88. God, who in his mercy for us has desired that the grace of divine virtue be sent down from heaven to those who are on earth, has symbolically built the sacred tent and everything in it as a representation, figure, and imitation of Wisdom.[89]

89. The grace of the New Testament is mysteriously hidden in the letter of the Old. This is why the Apostle says that the Law is spiritual.[90] Thus the Law is rendered old and obsolete by the letter and becomes useless, but it is made young and thoroughly active by the Spirit. For grace is completely free of old age.[91]

90. The Law is the shadow of the Gospel and the Gospel is the image of the good things to come. For the former checks bad activities and the latter provides good actions.

91. We say that the entire Holy Scripture is divided into flesh and spirit, as if it were a spiritual person.[92] For the one who says that the text of Scripture is flesh and that its meaning is spirit or soul does not stray from the truth. The wise man is certainly the one who abandons the corruptible and belongs wholly to the incorruptible.

92. The Law is the flesh of the spiritual man which is Holy Scripture, the Prophets are the senses, and the Gospel is the spiritual soul. Through the flesh of the Law and through the sense of the Prophets the soul is activated and expresses its own power in its activities.[93]

93. The Law is the shadow and the Prophets are the image of the divine and spiritual benefits contained in the Gospel. The Gospel itself has shown us this truth which is present to us through the Scriptures, which hitherto was covered with shadow in the Law and prefigured by the Prophets.

94. The one who fulfills the Law in his way of life and conduct leaves

unaccomplished the performance of evil in sacrificing to God the activity of irrational passions. In this stage he is sufficiently close to salvation through the spiritual infancy he possesses.[94]

95. The one who is instructed by the words of the Prophets rejects the activities of the passions, and puts off as well the submission to those which are encountered in the soul, lest by seeming to abstain from the wickedness of the worse (I mean here the flesh) he unwittingly activates it too much in the better (that is, in the soul).

96. The one who sincerely embraces the evangelical life has cut off from himself the beginning and end of evil, and pursues in word and deed every virtue. He offers a sacrifice of praise and confession in having freed himself from every burden of the activity of the passions and is now free in his mind from the struggle against them. Now he has only an insatiable happiness which nourishes the soul with the hope of the blessings to come.

97. To those who apply themselves with the utmost zeal to the divine Scriptures the Word as Lord appears under two forms: first, a general and public sight not reserved to a small number of which it is said, "We have seen him, he had neither form nor beauty";[95] the second is more hidden and accessible to a small number, to those who have already become as Peter, James, and John, the holy apostles before whom the Lord was transfigured in a glory overpowering the senses, in which "he is beautiful in appearance before the sons of men."[96] Of these two forms, the first is fitting for beginners, the second is proportioned to those who have become perfect in knowledge, insofar as this is attainable. The former is the image of the first coming of the Lord to which the letter of the Gospel refers and which purifies by sufferings those who are in the stage of striving. The latter is a prefiguring of the second and glorious coming in which is understood the Spirit. It transfigures the gnostics by wisdom with a view toward their deification. By this transfiguration of the Word in them, they behold with unveiled faces the Lord's glory.[97]

98. The one who by virtue has unshakably held firm against sufferings bears active in himself the first coming of the Word which purifies him from all blemishes. But the one who by contemplation has transported his mind to the angelic state bears the power of the second coming which renders him free from passion and decay.

99. Sensibility[98] accompanies the man of striving who succeeds in the virtues only with difficulty; insensibility accompanies the gnostic who has withdrawn his mind away from the flesh and the world toward

God. The former, in striving by effort to unbind the soul from the bonds of the natural relation to the flesh, has his free will continually beset with difficulties and gives up. But the latter, who by contemplation has pulled out the nails of this relationship,[99] can be held back by absolutely nothing; he has already purified himself from passion and has become strong against anything attempting to overpower him.

100. The manna given to Israel in the desert is the Word of God, which prepares those who eat it for every spiritual delight and which is transmuted to every taste in accordance with different desires of those who eat it. For it includes all the qualities of spiritual food.[100] That is why for those who are born from above through the Spirit from an incorruptible seed it becomes true spiritual milk.[101] For those who are infirm it is an herb[102] which soothes the passive faculty of the soul; for those who have through habit trained the soul's spiritual sense to discern good and evil, he gives himself as solid nourishment.[103] The Word of God has also other infinite powers which cannot be spoken of here below. The one who has died and who has been judged worthy of being set over many or all things will receive all or some of the Word's powers, because he was faithful in a few things in this life.[104] For the highest of any of the spiritual gifts given by God in this life is a modest and trifling thing in comparision with those to come.

Second Century

1. There is one God because one Godhead, one, without beginning, simple and supersubstantial, without parts and undivided, identically monad and triad; entirely monad and entirely triad; wholly monad as to substance, and wholly triad as to hypostases. For the Father, Son, and Holy Spirit are the Godhead, and the Godhead is in Father and Son and Holy Spirit. The whole is in the whole Father and the whole Father is in the whole of it; the whole is in the Son and the whole Son is in the whole of it. And the whole is in the Holy Spirit and the whole Holy Spirit is in the whole of it. The whole is the Father and in the whole Father; and the whole Father is the whole of it. And the whole is the whole Son and the whole is in the whole Son and the whole Son is the whole of it, and the Son is in the whole of it. And the whole is the Holy Spirit and in the Holy Spirit and the Holy Spirit is the whole of it and the whole Holy Spirit is in the whole of it. For neither is the Godhead partly in the Father nor is the Father partly God; nor is the Godhead partly in the Son nor the Son partly God; nor

is the Godhead partly in the Holy Spirit nor the Holy Spirit partly God. For neither is the Godhead divisible nor are Father, Son, and Holy Spirit imperfectly God. Rather the whole and complete Godhead is entirely in the entire Father and wholly complete it is entirely in the entire Son; and wholly complete it is entirely in the entire Holy Spirit. For the whole Father is entirely in the whole Son and Holy Spirit, and the whole Son is entirely in the whole Father and Holy Spirit; and the whole Holy Spirit is entirely in the whole Father and Son. This is why there is only one God, Father, Son, and Holy Spirit. For there is one and the same essence, power, and act of the Father and Son and Holy Spirit, and no one of them can exist or be conceived without the others.[105]

2. Every concept involves those who think and what is thought, subject and object. But God is neither of those who think nor of what is thought for he is beyond them. Otherwise he would be limited if as a thinker he stood in need of the relationship to what was thought or as an object of thought he would naturally lapse to the level of the subject thinking through a relationship. Thus there remains only the rejoinder that God can neither conceive nor be conceived but is beyond conception and being conceived. To conceive and to be conceived pertain by nature to those things which are secondary to him.[106]

3. Every concept has its motion about substance, as a quality clearly has its place in a substance. For it is not possible that what is completely free and simple and existing by itself could admit something which is not free and simple. But God is altogether simple in both ways and is a substance which is not present in a subject and a conception which has nothing of the subject in him, is not of those things which conceive or are conceived because he is obviously above essence and thought.

4. Just as straight lines which proceed from the center are seen as entirely undivided in that position, so the one who has been made worthy to be in God will recognize in himself with a certain simple and undivided knowledge all the preexisting principles of things.[107]

5. Formed by its objects, the one concept gives rise to many concepts when each of the objects takes formal shape.[108] But when it has gone beyond a multitude of sense experiences and thoughts which have formed it, it becomes completely without form. It is then that the Word which is above thought aptly holds it fast and makes it his own, causing it to cease from those forms produced from thoughts of another

sort; thus the one who experiences this "rests from his works just as God did from his."[109]

6. The one who achieves a perfection attainable to men here below bears as fruit for God love, joy, peace, endurance for the future, incorruption and eternity, and things similar to these. And perhaps the first things belong to the one who is perfect in the active life while the second belong to the one who through genuine knowledge has gone beyond created things.[110]

7. Just as sin is the fruit of disobedience so is virtue the fruit of obedience. And just as a transgression of the commandments is a concomitant of disobedience and a separation[111] from the one who enjoined them, so does the keeping of the commandments and union with the one who gave them follow obedience. Therefore the one who has observed a commandment out of obedience has both fulfilled righteousness and also has preserved unbroken the union of love with the giver of the commandments. But the one who out of disobedience transgresses a commandment has both committed sin and separated himself as well from loving union with the giver of the commandments.

8. The one who rallies from the division caused by disobedience first separates himself from the passions, then from passionate thoughts, then from nature and the things of nature, then from concepts and knowledge derived from them, and finally getting away from the abundant variety of the reasons concerning Providence he reaches in a way which transcends knowledge the very Word of God himself. In him the mind considers its own stability and "rejoices with unutterable joy,"[112] as a peace comes from God which surpasses all understanding[113] and which continually keeps secure the one who is worthy of it.

9. The fear of hell trains beginners to flee from evil, the desire for the reward of good things gives to the advanced the eagerness for the practice of virtues. But the mystery of love removes the mind from all created things, causing it to be blind to all that is less than God. Only those who have become blind to all that is less than God does the Lord instruct by showing them more divine things.[114]

10. The word of God is like a grain of mustard seed; before its cultivation it appears to be very small, but when it has been properly cultivated it shows itself to be so evidently big that the noble reasons of creatures of sense and mind come as birds to rest in it.[115] For the reasons of all things are set in it as finite beings, but it is limited by none of

these beings. Thus the Lord said that the one who has faith as a mustard seed could move a mountain by his word, which means to chase away the might of the devil from us and to change over from his sway.[116]

11. The grain of mustard seed is the Lord, who is sown by faith in the Spirit in the hearts of those who receive him. The one who carefully cultivates it through the virtues moves the mountain of earthly purpose by driving away from himself with authority the tenacious habit of wickedness. Then the reasons and forms of the commandments, which are the divine powers, will come as birds from heaven to rest in him.

12. In building the summit of good things on the Lord as a foundation of faith we must lay down gold, silver, and precious stones, that is, a pure and unalloyed theology, a bright and shining life, and divine notions as pearl-like thoughts; not wood, hay, or straw, that is, idolatry, which is the passionate seeking after things of sense, nor impassioned imaginings, which are as deprived of wise understanding as stalks.[117]

13. The one who seeks after knowledge sets the immovable foundations of the soul firmly on the Lord, as God says to Moses, "You stand with me."[118] Now it should be known that there is a distinction among those who stand before the Lord, if only this Scripture be acknowledged by those eager to learn, "There are some standing here who will not taste death until they see the kingdom of God coming in power."[119] For the Lord does not always appear in glory to those who are standing before him; rather, he comes in the form of a servant[120] to beginners, and to those who are strong enough to follow him in climbing the lofty mountain of his transfiguration before the creation of the world. Thus it is possible for the Lord not to appear in the same form to all those who meet him, but to some in one way and to others in another way, that is, by varying the contemplation according to the measure of faith in each one.[121]

14. When the Word of God becomes bright and shining in us, and his face is dazzling as the sun, then also will his clothes be radiant, that is, the clear and distinct words of the Holy Scripture of the Gospels now no longer veiled. Then Moses and Elijah will stand beside him, that is, the more spiritual meanings of the Law and the Prophets.[122]

15. Just as the Son of Man, as it is written, is coming with his angels in the glory of the Father,[123] so is the Word of God transformed in the worthy with each advance in virtue as he comes with his angels in the glory of the Father. For the more spiritual meanings in the Law and the Prophets, of which Moses and Elijah are the personal figures, appear

with the Lord in his transfiguration and retain a degree of the glory in them and make manifest the power contained in those who are worthy.

16. The one who is instructed for a time about the reason of the monad fully recognizes as well the reasons of Providence and judgment associated with it. Thus he judges it a good thing, as did St.Peter, that three tents be made by him for those who appear, that is, the three ways of salvation: virtue, knowledge, and theology. The first one requires the practice of courage and chastity, of which the blessed Elijah is a figure. The second is the righteousness of natural contemplation which the great Moses showed in his life. The third is the pure perfection of wisdom which the Lord revealed. Tents are spoken of because there are other appointed places better and more distinguished than these which those who are worthy will receive in the future.[124]

17. The active man is said to dwell on the level of flesh as one who through the virtues cuts away the attachment of the soul to the body and drives away from himself the deceitfulness of material things. The man of knowledge is likewise said to dwell in the same flesh as one who still contemplates the truth in mirrors and enigmas. For not yet are the self-existing forms of blessing beheld by him as they are, in a face-to-face enjoyment. For in comparison with the goods which lie in the future, every saint goes around crying, "I am but a wayfarer and a pilgrim before you as were all my fathers."[125]

18. The one who prays ought never to halt his movement of sublime ascent toward God. For just as we should understand the ascents "from strength to strength" as the progress in the practice of the virtues, "from glory to glory"[126] as the advance in the spiritual knowledge of contemplation, and the transfer from the letter of Holy Writ to its spirit, so in the same way the one who is settled in the place of prayer should lift his mind from human matters and the attention of the soul to more divine realities. This will enable him to follow the one who has "passed through the heavens, Jesus the Son of God," who is everywhere and who in his incarnation passes through all things on our account. If we follow him, we also pass through all things with him and come beside him if we know him not in the limited condition of his descent in the incarnation but in the majestic splendor of his natural infinitude.[127]

19. It is always a good thing to devote ourselves to seeking God, as we have been commanded. For although in the present life we are unable to arrive at the limit of God's depth, yet at least by reaching in some small way his depth we would see the holier among holy things and the

more spiritual among spiritual things. This is clearly indicated in the figure of the high priest who from the holy place which is more sacred than the courtyard enters into the Holy of Holies which is more sacred than the holy place.[128]

20. Each word of God is neither multiple nor wordy but rather is one, though made up of different parts of speech, of which each is a part of the meaning. Thus if one is speaking about truth, even if he could speak about it in such a way that nothing is left out he has spoken about the one Word of God.[129]

21. In Christ who is God and the Word of the Father there dwells in bodily form the complete fullness of deity by essence;[130] in us the fullness of deity dwells by grace whenever we have formed in ourselves every virtue and wisdom, lacking in no way which is possible to man in the faithful reproduction of the archetype. For it is not unnatural thereby that the fullness of deity dwell also in us by adoption, expressed in the various spiritual ideas.

22. Just as our human word which proceeds naturally from the mind is messenger of the secret movements of the mind, so does the Word of God, who knows the Father by essence as Word knows the Mind which has begotten it (since no created being can approach the Father without him), reveal the Father whom he knows. As the Word of God by nature he is spoken of as the "messenger of the great counsel."[131]

23. The great plan of God the Father is the secret and unknown mystery of the dispensation which the only-begotten Son revealed by fulfilling in the incarnation, thus becoming a messenger of the great plan of God the eternal Father. The one who knows the meaning of the mystery and who is so incessantly lifted up both in work and in word through all things until he acquires what is sent down to him is likewise a messenger of the great plan of God.[132]

24. If it was for us that the Word of God in his incarnation descended into the lower parts of the earth and ascended above all the heavens;[133] while being himself perfectly unmoved, he underwent in himself through the incarnation as man our future destiny. Let the one who is moved by a love of knowledge mystically rejoice in learning of the great destiny which he has promised to those who love the Lord.

25. If the Word of God and God the Son of the Father became son of man and man himself for this reason, to make men gods and sons of God, then we must believe that we shall be where Christ is now as head of the whole body having become in his human nature a forerunner to

the Father on our behalf.[134] For God will be in the "assembly of the gods,"[135] that is, of those who are saved, standing in their midst and apportioning there the ranks of blessedness without any spatial distance separating him from the elect.

26. The one who is still satisfying the passionate appetites of the flesh dwells as a maker and worshiper of idols in the land of the Chaldeans. But after some reflection on this matter he becomes aware of behavior which is more proper to nature, leaves the land of the Chaldeans, and goes to Haran in Mesopotamia, that is, the frontier state between virtue and vice which is not yet purified of the deception of the senses. This is what the word Haran means. But if one looks even beyond the understanding of the good which is suitable to the senses, he will press on to the good land, that is, to the state which is free from all vice and ignorance which a faithful God points out and professes to give as a reward of virtue to those who love him.[136]

27. If the Word of God was crucified for us out of weakness and was raised up by the power of God,[137] it is evident that he is always doing and suffering this for us in a spiritual way; because he became all things to all men in order to save all. Well, then, did the holy Apostle while among the weak Corinthians determine that he would know nothing except Jesus Christ, and him crucified.[138] But to the Ephesians who were perfect he writes that God "raised us up with Christ Jesus and seated us with him in the heavens."[139] He speaks of the reality of the Word of God in a manner which corresponds to each one's strength. Thus he is crucified for those who are still beginners in the practice of virtue and who crucify their passionate drives with reverential fear. But he rises and ascends into heaven for those who have completely put off the old self which is corrupted through deceitful desires, who have completely put on the new self which is created in God's image through the Spirit,[140] and who have become the Father's by virtue of the grace which is in them: "high above every principality and power, virtue, and domination, and every name that can be given either in this age or in the one to come."[141] For everything which is less than God, things and names and dignities, will be subject to the one who has come to be in God through grace.

28. Just as before his visible and fleshly appearance the Word of God dwelt spiritually with the patriarchs and prophets prefiguring the mysteries of his coming, so after this presence he comes not only to those who are still infants, spiritually supporting them and bringing them to the age of perfection in God, but he comes also to the perfect and in a

hidden way he delineates in advance in them as in a picture the features of his future coming.

29. Just as the understanding of the Law and the Prophets as precursors of the coming of the Word in the flesh instructed souls about Christ, so has this same glorified Word of God incarnate become a precursor of his spiritual coming and he instructs souls by his words about the acceptance of his visible divine coming. This coming he always effects by changing those who are worthy from the flesh to the spirit through the virtues. And he will do this also at the end of time, clearly revealing to all what is still secret.[142]

30. So long as I am imperfect and insubordinate in not obeying God through the keeping of the commandments, and have not reached the interior perfection of knowledge, then Christ also must be considered imperfect and insubordinate as related to me and in me. In this case I diminish him and cut him down and fail to grow up with him spiritually, since we are Christ's body, each one a member of it.[143]

31. "The sun rises and the sun goes down," says Scripture.[144] Thus it is also with the Word who is sometimes regarded as up and sometimes as down obviously depending on the dignity and nature and character of those who practice virtue and who are moved toward divine knowledge. Then blessed is he who like Joshua, the son of Nun, can keep the sun of justice from falling in himself, and the complete duration of whose day in the present life is not limited by the evening of sin and ignorance in order to enable him to rout in a lawful way the wicked spirits who are attacking him.[145]

32. When the Word of God is exalted in us through asceticism and contemplation, he draws everyone to himself,[146] sanctifying our thoughts and ideas about the flesh and the soul and the nature of things, as well as these members and senses of the body by virtue and knowledge, and bringing them under his yoke. Therefore the one who is a witness of divine things should quickly ascend and follow the Word until he arrives at the place where he is. For there he draws him, as Ecclesiastes says, "he draws toward his place"[147] those, that is, who follow him as a great High Priest who leads them into the Holy of Holies where "he entered on our behalf as a forerunner."[148]

33. The one who engages in a pursuit of wisdom out of devotion and stands prepared against invisible forces should pray that both the natural discernment (with its proportionate light) and the illuminating grace of the Spirit remain with him. The former trains the flesh in the acquisition of virtue through asceticism while the latter illuminates the

mind to select the companionship of wisdom before all others, according to the Scripture, "He works the destruction of the strongholds of evil and of every pretension which raises itself up against the knowledge of God."[149] Joshua the son of Nun clearly shows this by asking in prayer, "Stand still, O sun, at Gibeon," that is, that the light of the knowledge of God be kept secure for him in the mountain of spiritual contemplation, "and the moon in the valley," that is, that the natural discernment which lies in the frailty of the flesh remain steadfast through virtue.[150]

34. Gibeon is the higher mind, and the valley is the flesh which is weighed down by death. And the sun is the Word who illuminates the mind and inspires it with the power of contemplative experience and delivers it from every ignorance. The moon is the law of nature which persuades the flesh to subject itself lawfully to the spirit by accepting the yoke of the commandments. The moon is symbolic of nature in that it is changeable; but in the saints it remains unchanging through the unchangeable habit of virtue.[151]

35. It is not necessary that those who seek the Lord seek him outside themselves; rather, those who seek him should seek him in themselves through faith in works: "The word is near you, in your mouth and in your heart, that is, the word of faith."[152] Seeking the word of faith is the same as seeking Christ.

36. In considering the loftiness and divine infinity we should not despair that God's love for man cannot reach all the way to us from the heights. Neither when we ponder the infinite depth of our fall in sin should we disbelieve that a resurrection of dead virtue can take place in us. For God can accomplish both these things: He can come down and illuminate our mind through knowledge, and likewise he can raise up virtue in us once again and exalt us to himself through the works of justification. As Scripture has it, "Do not say in your heart 'who shall go up into heaven?' that is, to bring Christ down, or 'who shall go into the abyss?' that is, to bring Christ up from the dead."[153] It is possible to interpret abyss in another way, as everything which is after God, in which the complete Word of God is present to all of them through Providence in a complete way, as life comes to those who are dead. For all things are dead if they have life only through participation. But heaven is to be understood as God's natural hiddenness which takes him beyond everyone's grasp. It can also be interpreted as the meaning of theology, as the abyss cannot unreasonably be regarded in my interpretation as the mystery of the incarnation. Both of these are hard to

understand and to prove in any definite way. It is better to say that
they are completely inaccessible if they are searched after apart from
faith.

37. In the active person the Word grows fat by the practice of the virtues and becomes flesh. In the contemplative it grows lean by spiritual
understandings and becomes as it was in the beginning, God the
Word.[154]

38. The one who is involved in the moral teaching of the Word
through rather earthly examples and words out of consideration for his
hearers is making the Word flesh. On the other hand, the one who ex-
pounds mystical theology using the sublimest contemplative experiences is making the Word spirit.

39. The one who speaks of God in positive affirmations is making the
Word flesh. Making use only of what can be seen and felt he knows
God as their cause. But the one who speaks of God negatively through
negations is making the Word spirit, as in the beginning he was God
and with God. Using absolutely nothing which can be known he
knows in a better way the utterly Unknowable.[155]

40. The one who through asceticism and contemplation has known
how to dig in himself the wells of virtue and knowledge as did the patriarchs will find Christ within as the spring of life. Wisdom bids us to
drink from it, saying, "Drink waters from your own vessels and from
your own springs."[156] If we do this we shall discover that his treasures
are present within us.

41. Those who live as beasts on the level of sense alone make the
Word flesh in a way dangerous to themselves. They misuse God's creatures for the service of the passions and do not contemplate the reason
of wisdom which is manifest in all things to know and glorify God from
his works, as well as to perceive whence and what and why and where
we are going from the things which are seen. Rather we go groping
through the present life in darkness, feeling with both hands nothing
but ignorance about God.[157]

42. Those who hold fast only to the word of Holy Scripture, and
bind the honor of the soul to the bodily service of the law, culpably
make the Word flesh for themselves. They think that God is well
pleased by sacrifices of brute animals. They take much thought for the
body by exterior cleansings but neglect the beauty of the soul by dis-
figuring it with the stains of the passions. Yet it is because of the soul
that every force of visible things has been produced and every divine
reason and law is enacted.[158]

43. The holy Gospel states that the Lord is "destined to be the downfall and rise of many."[159] Let us observe, then, whether the downfall is of those who see creation only as what is visible to the senses and who are satisfied with the mere letter of Holy Scripture because out of folly they cannot pass over the new spirit of grace. But the rise is for those who spiritually understand the created things and words of God and listen to them, as well as those who take care to cultivate by the appropriate dispositions the divine image in the soul.

44. The scriptural fact of the Lord's being set up as the downfall and rise of many in Israel, if considered only in a praiseworthy way, sees him as the downfall of the passions and evil attitudes in each of the faithful, as well as the rising of the virtues and of a thoroughly upright attitude.

45. The one who thinks of the Lord only as the Creator of what is governed by generation and corruption is, like Mary Magdalene, mistaking him for a gardener. This is why the Lord, for our benefit, shies away from the touch of such a person who has not allowed him to ascend to the Father, when he says, "Do not touch me." For he knows that the one who approaches him with such an inferior preconception will be misled.[160]

46. Those who out of fear of the Jews in Galilee have locked the doors and tarry in the upper room, that is, those who out of fear of evil spirits in the region of revelations have closed the doors of the ordinary course of sense and steadily ascend to the height of divine contemplations, receive in a way which transcends knowledge the Word of God who comes to them and makes himself present without the working of sense. Through his greeting of peace he breathes on them and bestows a tranquillity as well as a sharing in the Holy Spirit. Likewise he offers them the power against evil spirits and opens up the significance of his mysteries.[161]

47. For those who search according to the flesh after the meaning of God, the Lord does not ascend to the Father; but for those who seek him out in a spiritual way through lofty contemplations he does ascend to the Father. Let us, then, not always hold him here below though he came down here out of love to be with us. Rather, let us go up to the Father along with him, leaving behind the earth and what is earthly, so that he will not say to us what he said to the Jews who remained unconverted, "I am going where you cannot come."[162] For without the Word, it is impossible to come to the Father of the Word.

48. The land of the Chaldeans is a life given over to passion, in which

idols of sinners are fashioned and worshiped. Mesopotamia is a condition of wavering between opposites. But the promised land is the state of being filled with every blessing. Thus the one who like the old Israel is careless about his condition is again carried off in slavery to the passions, losing the freedom that he had.

49. It is clear that no one of the saints appears to go down to Babylon of his own will, for it is not right or consistent with rational intelligence for those who love God to prefer worse things to the better. But if some of them are carried off to that place by force along with the people, we can understand through them those who not principally but rather through unfortunate circumstance, on account of the salvation and guidance of those who need them, give up the higher meaning of knowledge and go over to the instruction concerning passions. This is why the great Apostle judged that it was more profitable for him to remain in the flesh, that is, in moral instruction, for the sake of his disciples even though he had a great longing to depart from moral instruction and to be with Christ in supernatural and simple mental contemplation.[163]

50. Just as the blessed David with his lyre relieved Saul from being tormented by the evil spirit, so does every spiritual meaning seasoned by gnostic experiences relieve the frenzied mind and free it from an evil consciousness which torments it.[164]

51. "Ruddy with beauty of eyes"[165] like the great David is the one who in the brightness of his life with God has the reason of knowledge in equal brilliance. In this state, both asceticism and contemplation band together, the former made brilliant in the practice of the virtues, the latter illuminated by divine understandings.

52. The kingdom of Saul is an image of the fleshly observance of the Law which the Lord abolished as not bringing anything to perfection: "For," as Scripture says, "the law brought nothing to perfection."[166] But the kingdom of the great David is a prefiguring of the gospel observance, for it completely embraces all that God wills in his heart.[167]

53. Saul is the law of nature which was allotted by God to hold sway over nature in the beginning. When he transgressed the commandment through disobedience by sparing Agag the king of Amalek, that is, the body, and lapsing into the passions, he was displaced in the kingship to allow David to take charge of Israel, that is, the law of the spirit which begets the peace which splendidly builds for God the temple of contemplation.[168]

54. Samuel is interpreted as "obedience to God."[169] So long, then, as

the Word exercises the priesthood in us by obedience, even though Saul should spare Agag (i.e., earthly intention), the Word as priest is jealous in thus slaying him and smites the mind which is prone to sin by putting it to shame as a companion warrior of divine righteousness.[170]

55. When the mind has become proud after being anointed against the passions by the principle of instruction and ceases its diligent search of what is and what is not to be done, it is completely taken over by the passions out of ignorance. Slowly falling away from God through them it passes by involuntary misfortune to demons who make the belly their God.[171] From there, it desires to find comfort from the things which press on it. Such is Saul who did not take counsel with Samuel in everything, but was necessarily perverted to idolatry and insisted on seeking out the witch as some kind of god.[172]

56. The one who prays to receive his daily bread does not exactly receive it as the bread is in itself but as the one who receives it is capable. For the Bread of Life, because he loves men, gives himself to all who ask but not to all in the same way; rather to those who perform great works of righteousness in a fuller way, to those who do less in a smaller way—to each in accordance with his spiritual capacity.[173]

57. The Lord sometimes is away and sometimes close at hand. He is away insofar as face-to-face vision is concerned, but he is close to us in a vision which is indistinct as in a mirror.[174]

58. To the active person the Lord is present through the virtues, but he is absent to the one who has no understanding of virtue. Likewise, to the contemplative he is present through knowledge of things, but absent to the one who falls away from this in any way.

59. The one who passes from an active to a gnostic condition takes leave of flesh. He is snatched up to the clouds of loftier understandings to the diaphanous air of mystical contemplation where he will ever be able to be with the Lord.[175] But far from the Lord is the one who cannot yet contemplate the understandings as far as they can be contemplated with a pure mind without sense activity, who does not take in the simple and direct meaning of the Lord without images.

60. The Word of God is called flesh not only as having become incarnate but as God the Word understood simply in the beginning with God the Father, who possesses the clear and naked forms of the truth of all things and does not include riddles or enigmas or need allegorical stories. When he is present to men who cannot with their naked mind reach naked spiritual realities, and converses in a way familiar to them in a variety of stories, enigmas, parables, and dark sayings, then he be-

comes flesh. Our mind does not in this first encounter hold converse with the naked Word, but with the Word made flesh, certainly in a variety of languages; though he is the Word by nature he is flesh to the sight, so that many think they see flesh and not the Word even if he is truly the Word. For the understanding of Scripture is not what appears to the many but is otherwise than it appears. For the Word becomes flesh through each recorded word.[176]

61. The beginning of religious discipleship for men is directed at the flesh. For in our first aquaintance with religious devotion we approach it in the letter not the spirit. But gradually going on in the spirit we strip off the grossness of the words to find finer meanings and so arrive purely at the pure Christ, insofar as human beings are able, and can say with the Apostle, "And if we looked on Christ according to the flesh, we no longer look on him in this way."[177] That is to say, by means of the simple encounter with the Word without the veils of the mind covering him, we progress from knowing the Word as flesh to "his glory as the only-begotten of the Father."[178]

62. The one who is living a life in Christ has gone beyond the righteousness of both the Law and of nature, as the divine Apostle has pointed out in these words, "For in Christ there is neither circumcision nor uncircumcision."[179] By circumcision he meant the righteousness of the Law, and by uncircumcision he signified in an obscure way the equality that comes from nature.

63. Some are reborn of water and the Spirit; others receive baptism in the Holy Spirit and in fire. These four: water, Spirit, fire, and the Holy Spirit, I understand as one and the same spirit of God. For some the Holy Spirit is water because he can cleanse the external stains of the body. For others, however, he is Spirit only because he produces the benefits of the virtues. For still others he is fire inasmuch as he purifies the radically interior defilements of the soul. Finally, for others, as the great Daniel tells us, he is Holy Spirit because he bestows wisdom and knowledge. Thus on the basis of the difference of the subject's activity, one and the same Spirit is given different designations.[180]

64. The Law established the Sabbath, "so that," it says, "your ox and your servant can rest."[181] Both of these symbolically mean the body. The body is the beast of burden of the active state, compelled in ascetical practice to bear the necessary onus of virtuous activity. The servant is the contemplative state because it is already possessed of contemplations and carries out the orders of the mind in a spiritual and mystical way. For both of these the Sabbath is the fulfillment of the good ac-

complished both by asceticism and contemplation, a fulfillment which grants a rest suitable to each.

65. The one who accomplishes virtue with conspicuous knowledge keeps his body as a beast of burden and drives it on by reason to perform its duties, and regards the servant as the way of the practice of virtue, that is, the way of life in which virtue comes about, which is purchased with the money of discerning attitudes. The Sabbath is the state of both soul and body, that is, the immutable condition which is tranquil in virtue and peaceful.

66. The Word of God seems to be chaff and hay to those who still devote most of their care to the bodily forms of virtue because it turns the emotional part of their soul to the service of the virtues. But to those who are advanced in the contemplation of the true comprehension of divine things he is bread, which turns the spiritual part of their soul to perfect godlikeness. Thus we find the patriarchs providing along the way both bread for themselves and fodder for their asses.[182] And the Levite in the book of Judges says to the old man who received him as a guest in Gibeah, "We have bread for us and straw for our asses . . . your servants do not lack anything at all."[183]

67. The Word of God is both spoken of and is dew, as well as water and fountain and river, as it is written.[184] That is, according to the underlying force of these terms he both is and becomes these things. For to some he is dew because he can extinguish the fire and energy of the bodily passions which externally lie about them. To those who are internally burning with the poison of wickedness he is water, not only because he is destructive of a hostile force by way of antidote, but also as ready to share life-giving powers for perfect being. Likewise he is a fountain as giving wisdom to those who keep the habit of contemplation ever gushing forth. He is a river for those who pour out like a river the religious and upright and saving teaching as giving abundant drink to men, cattle, beasts, and plants, so that even men might be deified in being raised to the contemplation of what is spoken of, and those who have become brutish by the passions might become human through the exact proof of virtuous behavior and resume their natural rationality.[185] Also that those who have become wild beasts by bad habits and evil actions, having been tamed through a mild and gentle teaching, might return to nature's domesticity. And, finally, that those who like plants have become insensitive to good things might be softened by the depth of the Word's Passover and receive quickening to produce fruit and the strength to sustain themselves, which are the qualities of the Word.

68. The Word of God is a way[186] for those who run well and vigorously the active course of virtue and do not turn aside either to the right out of vainglory or to the left from the inclination of passion, but keep their steps straight on God. Asa the king of Judah did not persevere to the end but we are told that in his old age he became diseased in his feet, as he became feeble in the course of a life lived for God.[187]

69. The Word of God is a door,[188] because he leads on to knowledge those who have rightly accomplished the way of the virtues in a blameless course of asceticism, and shows them, as a light, the brilliant treasures of wisdom. For he is alike way and door and key and kingdom; a way as guide; a key as the one who opens and who is opened for those who are worthy of divine treasures; a door as the one who gives entry; a kingdom as the one who is inherited and who comes to be present in all through participation.

70. The Lord is called light and life and resurrection and truth.[189] He is light as the brightness of souls and as the one who drives away the darkness of ignorance, as the one who enlightens the mind to understand unutterable things, and as the one who reveals mysteries which can be perceived only by the pure. He is life as the one who grants to souls who love the Lord the movement proper for divine things. Again, he is resurrection as the one who raises up the mind from a deathly craving for material things and cleanses it from all kinds of corruption and death. Finally, he is truth as the one who gives to those who are worthy an inflexible disposition toward the good.

71. God the Word of God the Father is mystically present in each of his own commandments. God the Father is by nature completely inseparable in the whole of his Word. Therefore the one who receives the divine commandment and accomplishes it receives in it the Word of God. The one who has received the Word through the commandments has received along with him the Father who is in him by nature, as well as the Spirit who is also in him by nature. For the Scripture says, "Amen I say to you, the one who receives anyone whom I send receives me; and the one who receives me receives the one who sent me."[190] Therefore the one who has accepted a commandment and performed it has received in mystical possession the Holy Trinity.

72. One glorifies God in himself not when he pays him honor with mere words but when he endures for God out of virtue sufferings and trials. In return he is glorified by God with the glory which is in him, recovering the grace of detachment by participation as a reward of virtue. For anyone who glorifies God in himself through the sufferings of

ascetical practice performed for virtue is himself glorified in God through the tranquil illumination of divine gifts in contemplation. For the Lord says when going to his passion, "Now is the Son of Man glorified and God is glorified in him. If God has been glorified in him, God will also glorify him in himself, and will glorify him right away."[191] Thus it seems clear that the divine gifts of grace follow the sufferings endured for virtue.

73. So long as we see the Word of God take flesh in the letter of Holy Writ in a variety of figures we have not yet spiritually seen the incorporeal and simple and singular and only Father as in the incorporeal and simple and singular and only Son. As the Scripture says, "The one who has seen me has seen the Father," and also, "I am in the Father and the Father is in me."[192] It is, therefore, very necessary for a deep knowledge that we first study the veils of the statements regarding the Word and so behold with the naked mind the pure Word as he exists in himself, who clearly shows the Father in himself, as far as it is possible for men to grasp. Thus it is necessary that the one who seeks after God in a religious way never hold fast to the letter lest he mistakenly understand things said about God for God himself. In this case we unwisely are satisfied with the words of Scripture in place of the Word, and the Word slips out of the mind while we thought by holding on to his garments we could possess the incorporeal Word. In a similar way did the Egyptian woman lay hold not of Joseph but of his clothing, and the men of old who remained permanently in the beauty of visible things and mistakenly worshiped the creature instead of the Creator.[193]

74. The meaning of Holy Writ reveals itself gradually to the more discerning mind in loftier senses when it has put off the complex whole of the words formed in it bodily, as in the sound of a gentle breeze. Through a supreme abandonment of natural activities, such a mind has been able to perceive sense only in a simplicity which reveals the Word, the way that the great Elijah was granted the vision in the cave at Horeb. For Horeb means "newness," which is the virtuous condition in the new spirit of grace. The cave is the hiddenness of spiritual wisdom in which one who enters will mystically experience the knowledge which goes beyond the senses and in which God is found. Therefore, anyone who truly seeks God as did the great Elijah will come upon him not only on Horeb, that is, as an ascetic in the practice of the virtues, but also in the cave of Horeb, that is, as a contemplative in the hidden place of wisdom which can exist only in the habit of the virtues.[194]

75. When the mind shakes off the many distractions about things

which are pressing on it, then the clear meaning of truth appears on it and gives it pledges of genuine knowledge after it has driven off the preoccupations bothering it of late as scales on its power of seeing, as with the great and holy apostle Paul.[195] For notions about the mere letter of Scripture and considerations of visible things prejudicial to sense are indeed scales which cling to the clear-sighted part of the soul and hinder the passage to the pure meaning of truth.

76. The divine apostle Paul said he knew in part the knowledge of the Word.[196] But the great evangelist John said that he saw his glory: "We have seen his glory, the glory as the only-begotten of the Father, full of grace and truth."[197] And why did St. Paul say that he knew in part the knowledge of the divine Word? For he is known only to a certain extent through his activities. The knowledge of himself in his essence and personhood remains inaccessible to all angels and men alike and he can in no way be known by anyone. But St. John, initiated as perfectly as humanly possible into the meaning of the Word's incarnation, claims that he has seen the glory of the Word as flesh, that is, he saw the reason or the plan for which God became man, full of grace and truth. For it was not as God by essence, consubstantial to God the Father, that the only-begotten Son gave this grace, but as having in the incarnation become man by nature, and consubstantial to us, that he bestows grace on us who have need of it. This grace we receive from his fullness always in proportion to our progress. Therefore, the one who keeps sacred the whole meaning of the Word of God's becoming incarnate for our sake will acquire the glory full of grace and truth of the one who for our sake glorifies and consecrates himself in us by his coming:[198] "When he appears we shall be like him."[199]

77. So long as the soul makes the passage from strength to strength and "from glory to glory,"[200] progress from virtue to greater virtue, and makes the ascent from knowledge to higher knowledge it does not cease being a sojourner, as it is stated, "My soul has long been a sojourner."[201] For great is the distance and the multitude of steps of knowledge to be passed until it "comes to the place of your wondrous tabernacle, up to the house of God, in a voice of exultation and thanksgiving, and of those keeping festival,"[202] ever adding a voice to voices, a spiritual one to spiritual ones, as it progresses in divine contemplations with rejoicing over the spiritual contemplations, that is, with joy and proper thanksgiving. These festivals are celebrated by all those who have received the Spirit of grace who cry out in their hearts, "Abba, Father."[203]

164

78. The place of the wondrous tabernacle is the virtuous condition which is free of passion and harm in which the Word of God comes and adorns the soul like a tabernacle with various beauties of virtues. The house of God is a knowledge composed of many and varied contemplations, according to which God goes out to the soul and fills it with the chalice of wisdom. The voice of exultation is the joy of the soul over the wealth of virtues. The voice of thanksgiving is gratitude for the glory of the feasting in wisdom. The sound is the continuous mystical doxology which comes about from both exultation and thanksgiving.[204]

79. The one who has genuinely overcome the bodily passions and has done sufficient battle against unclean spirits and has banished their devices from the region of his soul should pray to be given a clean heart and that an upright spirit be renewed deep within him,[205] that is, that he be completely purged of evil imaginings and through grace be filled with divine thoughts. In this way there will come about God's world both great and spiritually luminous brought together by moral, natural, and theological insights.[206]

80. The one who has rendered his heart clean not only understands the meanings of things which are inferior to God but also after passing through all of them can look in some way on God himself, who is the ultimate good. On this heart God comes and deigns to engrave his own words through the Spirit as on the tablets of Moses, to the extent that he has devoted itself through ascetical practice and contemplation according to the mystically given commandment: "Increase."[207]

81. A clean heart might be said to be one which has not at all any natural movement in any way whatever. The Lord comes to it in perfect simplicity and as on a beautifully clean tablet writes his own laws on it.[208]

82. A heart is clean if it presents its memory of God in a condition completely devoid of shape and form and is prepared to be imprinted only by his characters by means of which it becomes visible.

83. The mind of Christ which the saints receive according to the saying, "We have the mind of Christ,"[209] comes along not by any loss of our mental power, nor as a supplementary mind to ours, nor as essentially and personally passing over into our mind, but rather as illuminating the power of our mind with its own quality and bringing the same energy to it. For to have the mind of Christ is, in my opinion, to think in his way and of him in all situations.

84. We are said to be the body of Christ according to the Scripture. "We are the body of Christ, each one a member of it,"[210] not by losing

our own bodies and becoming his, nor because he passes into us in his person or is divided up in our members. Rather it is because the corruption of sin is shaken off in a likeness to the Lord's flesh. For as Christ is by nature sinless in both body and soul by which he is known as man, so can we who believe in him and who are clothed with him in the Spirit be in him without sin by the use of our free will.

85. There are in Scripture both temporal ages and also what comprises the end of other ages according to the Scripture, "But now once and for all at the end of ages, etc."[211] And again there are other ages beyond time after this present temporal age which follow on the end of the ages, according to the Scripture, "That he might show in the ages to come, the overflowing riches, etc."[212] Indeed we find in Scripture a number of ages, past, present, and to come, as well as ages of ages and ages of age, and temporal age and generations joined to age. But to discourse on what Scripture means by temporal ages, or ages of time, or again simply by ages, or ages of ages, or age in the singular, or age of age, would bring us far from the subject. Instead, let us leave these matters for those who are eager to examine them further, and let us return to the original subject matter.[213]

86. We know from Scripture that there is a realm above time which gives evidence of its existence; but to what it is we can give no name; as Scripture says, "The Lord reigns forever and ever and ever."[214] Thus there is something beyond time: the pure reign of God. For it is not correct to say that the reign of God had a beginning or falls under ages and times. Rather we believe that it is the inheritance and the abode and the place of those who are saved as the genuine word of Scripture tells us. It is the fulfillment of those who are moved by a longing for the ultimate object of desire. When they reach it they receive a special kind of repose from all movement, because they will require no further time or period to go through since at the completion of these they arrive at God who is before all ages and whom the very nature of time cannot even approach.[215]

87. So long as one is in the present time of this life even if he be perfect in his earthly state both in action and in contemplation, he still has knowledge, prophecy, and the pledge of the Holy Spirit only in part, but not in their fullness.[216] He has yet to come at the end of the ages to the perfect rest which reveals face to face to those who are worthy the truth as it is in itself. Then one will possess not just a part of the fullness but rather acquire through participation the entire fullness of grace. For the Apostle says, "All of us (i.e., those who are saved) will

be that perfect man in the measure of the age of Christ's fullness";[217] in whom are hidden the treasures of wisdom and knowledge,"[218] "and when he appears what is in part shall pass away."[219]

88. Some seek to know what will be the state of those judged worthy of perfection in the kingdom of God, whether there will be progress and change or a settled state of sameness; and how one should think of bodies and souls. To this one might conjecture an answer by using the example of bodily life where there is a twofold reason for food: for both the growth and sustenance of those who are fed. For until we reach the perfection of bodily stature we are fed for growth; but when the body achieves the measure of its increase it is no longer fed for growth but for sustenance. In the same way there is a twofold reason for food for the soul. For while it is growing it is fed with virtues and contemplations until it no longer passes through all its stages and arrives at the measure of the stature of the fullness of Christ. At this point it leaves off making progress in its increase and growth through various means and is fed directly (in a way which surpasses the mind and thus growth as well) a form of incorruptible food to sustain the Godlike perfection given to it and to manifest the infinite splendors of this food. When it receives through this food eternal blessedness indwelling in it, it becomes God through participation in divine grace by itself ceasing from all activities of mind and sense and with them the natural activities of the body which become Godlike along with it in a participation of deification proper to it. In this state only God shines forth through body and soul when their natural features are transcended in overwhelming glory.[220]

89. Some who are interested in such things seek to know what will be the manner of the difference of the heavenly mansions and promises: whether it is a substantial difference of place or a notional one of spiritual quality and quantity different in each mansion. To some it seems the former, to others the latter. But the one who knows the meaning of "The kingdom of God is within you"[221] and "In my Father's house there are many mansions"[222] will prefer the second opinion.

90. Some seek to know what the difference is between kingdom of God and kingdom of heaven, whether there is a substantial difference between them or a notional difference. To them it should be said that they differ but not in their substance, for both substantially are one, but rather their difference is notional. For the kingdom of heaven is the apprehension of the pure eternal knowledge of beings in their inner meaning of God. On the other hand, the kingdom of God is the imparting through grace of gifts which belong to God by nature. The for-

mer refers to the end of beings, the latter, by a notional change, to what comes after their end.[223]

91. The Scripture "The Kingdom of heaven is at hand"[224] does not, I think refer to temporal nearness for "it does not come with observation nor will they say, 'Behold, it is here.' " Rather it refers to the nearness to it possessed by those who are worthy in a disposition of relationship. As it says, "The kingdom of God is within you."[225]

92. The kingdom of God the Father is in potency in all those who believe, and in act in those who have completely laid aside all life of body and soul in a natural way to gain the mansion of the Spirit, and who can say, "I live now, not I, but Christ lives in me."[226]

93. Some say that the kingdom of heaven is the life which the worthy lead in heaven. Others that it is the state of the saved similar to the angels. Still others claim it is the very form of divine beauty possessed by those who bear the image of the heavenly Being.[227] All three opinions on the subject are in harmony with the truth, it seems to me, for to all there is given a future grace in proportion to their righteousness in quantity and quality.[228]

94. So long as one bravely endures spiritual contests with ascetic discipline, he holds fast to himself the Word who came out from the Father through the commandments to the world. But when he is released from the struggles of the ascetic state against the passions and is pronounced victor over passions and devils, and has passed on through contemplation to the mystical level of knowledge, then he allows the Word mystically to leave the world again and to go to the Father. Thus the Lord says to his disciples, "You have loved me and have believed that I come from the Father. I did come from the Father and have come into the world; again I leave the world and go to the Father."[229] Here he speaks of *world* as the laborious effort required for the practice of the virtues. *Father* refers to the transcendent state of mind and will which is free of material considerations, wherein the Word of God comes to us to give end to the battling against passions and devils.

95. The one who has succeeded through ascetical practice in mortifying the members which are on the earth[230] and through the commandments of the Word has overcome the world of the passions in himself will have no further tribulation since he has already abandoned the world and has begun to dwell in Christ who has overcome the world of the passions and who is the bestower of all peace. For the one who has not put off the attachment to the material world will have trib-

ulation at every turn because he changes his mind along with whatever changes by nature. But the one who has to come to dwell in Christ will not in any way feel material change no matter what it might be. Therefore the Lord says, "These things I have spoken to you so that you might have peace in me. In the world you will have tribulation. But take courage; I have overcome the world."[231] In other words: In me, the Word of virtue, you shall have peace by being delivered from the whirl and confusion of earthly realities and passions, whereas in the world, that is, in the attachment to material things, you shall have tribulation because of their constant change into each other. Thus tribulation comes to both the one who practices virtue in the effort which it involves and also to the lover of the world because of earthly failures. However in the former it is a salutary tribulation while in the latter it is corruptive and pernicious. But the Lord is the comfort of both: for the former, because he puts an end to the struggles connected with the virtues in the detached state of contemplation; for the latter, because through repentance he takes away the firm attachment to corruptible things.[232]

96. The notice on the inscription of the Savior's charge clearly shows us that the one who was crucified is King and Lord of ascetic, natural, and theological ways of wisdom. For we are told that the inscription was written in Latin, Greek, and Hebrew.[233] Now by the Latin inscription I understand the ascetic state, since the empire of the Romans was, according to Daniel,[234] appointed as the mightiest of all earthly empires, and strength is the characteristic of the ascetic state, if anything is. By the Greek inscription I understand natural contemplation because the Greek nation more than anyone else devoted themselves to natural philosophy. And by the Hebrew inscription I understand theological revelation because this nation was manifestly set up from above by God as our ancestors.

97. We are obliged not only to slay the bodily passions but also to do away with lustful imaginings of the soul according to the Scripture, "Early I slew all the sinners of the land that I might destroy out of the city of the Lord all those who work iniquity,"[235] that is, the body's passions and the wanton imaginings of the soul.

98. The one who keeps untarnished the way of virtue with religious and upright knowledge and does not fall away will discover the presence of God in him through detachment. "I will sing and be wise in a blameless path when you come to me."[236] The *psalm* means a virtuous

way of asceticism; *being wise* is the gnostic understanding which comes from virtue whereby one who waits for the Lord in the watchfulness of the virtues experiences the divine presence.

99. It is not necessary that the beginner in devotion be led to the practice of the commandments by goodness alone, but also that he struggle more often in severe trials by keeping in mind the divine judgments. In this way he not only loves by longing for the divine but also resists out of fear of wickedness. "I will sing to you, Lord of mercy and judgment"[237]—so that gladdened by longing he might address God, and being furnished a mouth by fear he might make bold to sing.

100. The one who has joined the body to the soul through virtue and knowledge has become a lyre and a flute and a temple. A lyre, firstly, because he beautifully maintains the harmony of the virtues; next, a flute because through the divine experiences he receives the Spirit's inspiration; finally, a temple because through the purity of his mind he has become the Word's dwelling place.[238]

NOTES

1. The first ten chapters of this initial century serve as a prologue to the entire work. They lay down the theological principles in the light of which all the other chapters are to be read. Sherwood aptly states that they constitute "a forceful summary of the anti-Origenist doctrine of the *Ambigu*" (*ACW* 21, 9). Balthasar has noted the closeness of the vocabulary of this work to that of Gregory of Nyssa: *Die Gnostischen Centurien* in *KL* 600. This work is highly recommended as a scholarly study of Maximus's treatise, and to it these notes are much indebted.

2. An important triad in Maximus that he explains in the following chapter. In the Origenist perspective, beginning and end represent absolute unity; it is movement which is in need of correction. Reacting to this, Maximus in this chapter puts God beyond these and any other category whatsoever.

3. Aristotelian categories are here used to give a metaphysical framework in which Maximus rejects the Origenist understanding of motion. Cf. *Amb.Io.* 2 (1077Cff.).

4. Cf. Dionysius, *Myst. theol.* 5 (1048A).

5. Balthasar explains how Maximus here uses Evagrius, Dionysius, and Gregory of Nyssa in a creative way: KL 601–3. It is manifest that Maximus knew how to derive profit from various streams of Christian tradition.

6. Like the Cappadocians before him, as Balthasar notes, Maximus denies any Neoplatonic hypostasizing of time: KL 603. Cf. *Mystagogy* 5 and n. 43.

7. Cf. Dionysius, *Div.N.* 10 (825BC).

8. Cf. *Amb.Io.* 36 (1312B).

9. Maximus uses the term "believed." God is no object of knowledge as is any other reality. The following chapter explains.

10. Cf. Heb 11:1. In speaking of faith as true knowledge, Maximus is clearly correcting Evagrius, who saw the two as different realities. Cf. Balthasar, KL 606.

11. Rom 11:36. In the Evagrian atmosphere one would have expected the term judgment linked to providence (as in *Chapters on Love* 1:7, etc.) but Maximus, probably under Dionysian influence (KL 607), uses the term goal (*telos*), which does not have the static character of Origenist usage. The theological prologue now completed, Maximus turns to questions of kataphatic concern.

12. After the manner of Gregory of Nyssa, *Hom. op. 2* (PG 44, 132D–133B), 4 (136BC), 16 (184B), *Or.cat.* 30 (45, 77A), and so on. Maximus interprets the biblical "image" as a human reflection of God's infinite freedom. Cf. *Amb.Io.* 37 (1345D).

13. Mal 3:20.

14. Eph 2:22. The double image of wax and mud and the hardening of Pharaoh's heart (Ex 7:13) are taken from Origen (*Princ. 3*, 1, 11) who gets them from Philo (*Quis rer.div.her.* 181:3,41).

15. Cf. *Chapters on Love* 3:25 and note. The image, Maximus notes, pertains to nature, the likeness to deliberate acts. Thus, as we have seen, they are related as logos and tropos. Cf. *Mystagogy* 24, n. 128.

16. Thus does the entire human person come to perfection on all levels of his being. See *Mystagogy*, ch. 2.

17. Cf. *Chapters on Love* 1:3; *Q.Thal.* 54(524B; Laga-Steel 463).

18. Gn 27:20. Balthasar points out graphically the closeness of this chapter (minus the conclusion) with Philo's treatment of the same theme in *Quod deus sit immutabilis* 91–2. "The main idea of the chapter, however, is the typical Alexandrian synergism of man and God." KL 517.

19. This chapter, as well as the foregoing one, bears the influence of Philo, *op. cit.* 93 (Loeb, *Philo* 3, 57). Cf. KL 573.

20. Cf. Nm 14:40; Dt 1:41–44. The example is also used in *Amb.Io.* 40 (1352D).

21. Cf. Ex 12:4ff. The Preparation was the eve of Passover when leavened food was to be eliminated and the paschal lamb prepared. All four evangelists make mention of it in connection with the passion and death of Jesus: Mt 27:62; Mk15:42; Lk 23:54; Jn 19:14, 31, 42.

22. Jos 24:13. The theme of heirs (in Christ: Rom 8:17) is found in Origen and Evagrius. Cf. KG 4:8, 9; 5:36.

23. The first part of this chapter is taken from Philo (*Allegories 2*, 36); the second is influenced by Origen and Diadochus of Photiki. Cf. KL 542–43.

24. Cf. Mt 3:7–8. See *Amb.Io.* 5 (1204B, 1205B), *Q.Thal.* 62 (660B), also further on in 1:76 of the present treatise.

25. Cf. *Q.Thal* 26 (345D–348A; Laga-Steel 181, 153–66). The theme of men being transformed into beasts by the passions is frequent in Gregory of Nyssa: *Beat.* 2 (44, 1216Cf.), 5 (1257D); *Cant.* 8 (44, 944D–945A; Jaeger VI, 250–51.

26. Cf. Mt 7:15.

27. Cf. Gal 2:4

28. Mt 10:8.

29. Cf. Mt 25:24.

30. As did Judas: Mt 27:5.

31. Ex 14:14.

32. Dt 6:4.

33. Ex 14:15. This represents an allegorical interpretation of the crossing of the sea by the Israelites fleeing the Egyptians. The three levels of silence, listening, and crying out are common ones in Origen's tradition and are examined by Balthasar in KL 577–8. The boldness spoken of is the *parresia*, which was met in the *Chapters on Love* and elsewhere.

34. Cf. Jn 6:44, 65. Balthasar says aptly, "For Maximus all gnosis, if it be genuine, is grace." KL 518.

35. Cf. Lk 6:1.

36. Cf. Mt 14:13ff. The language here and in the following chapter is inspired by Origen: KL 546.

37. Cf. Lk 10:19.

38. Cf. Mk 2:27–28. God's resting on the seventh day, and therefore the institution of the Sabbath, was a common theme in Origen and Evagrius: KL 610–12. Maximus here states that the Sabbath repose is not a cessation of human activities but an endless growth in perfection, a reiteration of Gregory of Nyssa's correction of Origenist stasis. Cf. *Perf.* (46, 285BC), Jaeger VII/1, 213–14 *An. et res.* (46, 105BC), and *Cant.* 8 (44, 940D–941C; Jaeger VI, 245—46; 6 (885D–888A; 174); 11 (997D–1000C; 320), and so on.

39. Cf. Ex 31:13. The themes of Sabbath, circumcision, and harvest are here announced for the next eleven chapters. Cf. *Q.Thal.* 65, esp. 756BD and 761A. For references to Philo and Origen see KL 613.

40. Cf. Lv 19:3

41. Lv 23:10.

42. Cf. Dt 34:5.

43. Cf. Jos 5:3

44. Cf. *Q.Thal.* 65 (756C).

45. The notion of loving ecstasy is taken from Dionysius and represents Maximus's correction of the Evagrian scheme.

46. Cf. *Q.Thal.* 65 (756BC); *Abm.Io.* 25 (1273C). Also Evagrius, KG 4:12.

47. There are two harvests, as mentioned in this and the following chapters. The first harvest, as Balthasar explains in *Die Gnostischen Centurien*, is that

of the logoi and tropoi of beings, and is the result of natural contemplation. The second is that of theology, the mystical understanding of God as explained in ch. 43.

48. Lk 10:2

49. Rom 2:29.

50. Gn 2:3. Each of these three images will now be explained.

51. Cf. *Chapters on Love* 2:62. The goal of creaturely existence is the proportionate participation in God's life and activity through deification.

52. Maximus has taken some pains to distinguish between God in himself and God as participated in by creatures. For him this apophatic hermeneutic bears rhythmic repetition.

53. The symbolism of these days which will occupy Maximus for the next several chapters is a very common theme in early Christian writers and even in Philo. We may mention Evagrius, Kg 5:8, 83; 6:7. See Balthasar's discussion in KL 617:19.

54. The exodus and conquest are frequently interpreted in allegory as symbols of the spiritual journey.

55. Eph 2:22.

56. Cf. Jn 14:6. This chapter bears marked Dionysian influence and is an instance of Maximus's correction of Evagrius by the Areopagite.

57. The clue that this chapter is to be interpreted in the light of Johannine theology is given in Maximus's reference to the words spoken by Jesus on the cross, "It is fulfilled " (Jn 19:30). The "experience of the passion" (Riou neglects to translate the latter important term) points to the central role of Christ's suffering in the way to deification. Cf. 1:66. Suffering is the tropos of deification.

58. This triad, which is presented also in the *Chapters on Love*, is also found in *Amb.Io.* 60 (1389Dff.).

59. Gn 1:31.

60. The "well-ordered diversity" of the virtues parallels that of God's creative work in Genesis. Maximus speaks of this cosmos of virtue also in 1:79. The idea is found in Evagrius (*On Prayer* 157), but Maximus's quotation of the Creator in the previous chapter traces ontological diversity to God's will, a subtle denial of the Origenist premise of an original henad and subsequent fall into diversity.

61. Chapters 59 through 67 view Christ's passion and resurrection as symbolic of the spiritual experience. This had already been attempted by Origen in his *Commentary on John* (10, 20) and by Gregory of Nyssa in his *Life of Moses* (2:273–77), and also by Evagrius (KG 1:90, 4:26; 6:40, 42). The Preparation day is that for the feast of Passover, which the evangelists see as leading to the crucifixion and resurrection; cf. Jn 19:14 and above, n. 21. Maximus regards it as the time of "the works of justice." For Gregory of Nyssa it was "the present life during

which we prepare for ourselves the benefits of the life to come" (*V. Moysis* 2:144).

62. Cf. Jn 20:3ff.

63. Cf. also *Q.Thal.* 37 (385BC; Laga-Steel 249) and *Amb.Io.* 49 (1377A).

64. A theme often found in Origen, as Balthasar notes in KL 540.

65. A "richly orchestrated allegory," Balthasar comments, whose themes are found also in the *Ambigua:* 1360AD, 1145AB, 1284C, and so on. KL 627.

66. Cf. Jn 14:6; 3 Esdras (1 Esdras, LXX) 4:35–38. Also Origen, *Commentary on John* 20, 6.

67. Maximus here ties together the mystery of salvations with the mystery of being, economy with theology. Cf. Ep. 25 (613CD). The use of the adverb "originally" is typical of Maximus and is intended to reflect the profound difference between God's creative intention and our destructive sinfulness. The former represents true being, the latter deception. Basing himself on Eph 3:18, Gregory of Nyssa had outlined the cosmic significances of Christ's cross in *Or.cat.* 32 (45,81BC). Compare Pascal: "Jesus Christ est l'objet de tout, et le centre où tout tend. Qui le connaît, connaît la raison de toutes choses." (*Pensée 556*)

68. Any truly apophatic appreciation of God's transcendent being must postulate the reality of grace under the category of relation. Cf. *Chapters on Love.*

69. Ps 71:3.

70. Cf. 1 Cor 13:10–13.

71. Cf. ibid., 1:23.

72. Cf. Lk 23:11–12. Evagrius had linked the two demons in *Praktikos* 13 and 58.

73. Mt 7:16.

74. Dt 33:2.

75. Agreeing in this translation with Ceresa-Gastaldo, *Il Dio-Uomo*, 55.

76. Jn 19:15. For Herod see also *Q.etD.* 16 (90, 800A; Declerck 54).

77. Lk 10:20.

78. Lk 22:36. The spiritual sword is referred to by Evagrius in KG 5:28.

79. On the mystical significance of numbers see Mystagogy 5 and n. 50 (p. 218). These were seen to be signs of deeper, more hidden realities. Cf. KL 641.

80. Cf. Jn 5:2–15. Also *Q. et d.* 64 (837A; Declerck 113).

81. Another instance of Dionysian influence.

82. Cf. Dionysius, *Div.N.* 1, 4; 7, 4.

83. Cf. Ex 33:7.

84. Cf. Ex 30:10; Heb 9:7.

85. This traditional exegesis has its roots in Philo. See *Giants* 52–54.

86. An interesting combination of Evagrian and Dionysian motifs. Cf.

KL 588–9. Maximus's more immediate source, however, may have been Gregory of Nyssa, who interprets Moses' entrance into the darkness as representing (as here) God's transcendent unknowability; cf. *Life of Moses* 1:46, 56, 58, 2:162–65, 169, 315. It is especially in 2:152 and 166 that virtue is linked to knowledge of God.

87. For "will" Maximus uses *gnome*, a term that, as we have already seen, implies insecurity and the possibility of rebelliousness. Balthasar cites an interesting parallel from St. Augustine's *Enarr. in Ps.* 64, 3 (PL 37, 774); KL 636.

88. Cf. *Q.Thal.* 30 (368Dff. Laga-Steel 323). The voluntary character of Christian death leads to resurrection, a reversal of the imposition of death after Adam's sin. This is a common theme in Maximus even before the anti-Monothelite writings. Both Ceresa-Gastaldo (61) and Riou (259) have missed this point; Balthasar's *freiwilliges Sterben* is correct.

89. Balthasar (KL 585) points out the closeness of this to Philo (*Quis rer. div. h.* 112) and to Gregory of Nyssa's *Life of Moses* 2:174 (*SC1³*, 220).

90. Cf. Rom 7:14.

91. Cf. Heb 8:13. Origen had contrasted the carnal understanding of the law with the spiritual and gospel understanding, which remains ever new: *Hom. in Num.* 9, 4; KL 550.

92. This idea is also found in *Mystagogy*, ch. 6.

93. Cf. Origen, *Hom. in Lev.* 6, 2, (SC 286, 272–78).

94. The notion of spiritual infancy is seen in *Mystagogy*, ch. 24, n. 126.

95. Is 53:2.

96. Ps 45:3.

97. Cf. 2 Cor 3:18.

98. I.e., the condition of being subject to feeling.

99. A frequent image in Gregory of Nyssa. Cf. *An. et res.* (46, 97 BC), *Virg.* 5 (348C; Jaeger VIII/1, 277) *Beat.* 8 (44, 1297A).

100. Cf. Ex 16:14ff. Wis 16:20–21. The following Scriptural images were used in the tradition of Philo and Origen. Cf. KL 535–6. Maximus's more direct source, however, may well have been Gregory of Nyssa. Cf. *Life of Moses* 2, 140 (SC 1ter, 192–94; CWS 88) and cant. 9 (44, 960CD; Jaeger VI 270–71).

101. Cf. 1 Pt 2:2; Heb 5:13.

102. Cf. Rom 14:2.

103. Cf. Heb 5:14.

104. Cf. Mt 24:47, 25:21.

105. This trinitarian chapter, the longest of the entire treatise, parallels the theological prologue of the first century (1–10) and like it is meant to serve as theological framework and foundation for the ascetical and mystical chapters to follow. In accordance with contemporary Byzantine standards it is arranged not only in proper theological but also rhetorical structure.

106. Evagrius approaches this subject in KG 4:77 but without the intel-

lectual precision of Maximus, who insists on the unknowableness of God. Cf. Dionysius, *Myst.Theol.* 1, 1 (997AB), (1045D–1048B), and so on.

107. The image of unity at a circle's center, which we have met before, stems from Proclus through Dionysius. Cf. KL 593–94.

108. I.e., one object of thought can be viewed under many aspects and formalities, and thus the thought multiplies.

109. Heb 4:10.

110. Two Pauline lists (cf. Gal 5:22 and Rom 2:7), which Maximus assigns to praxis and gnosis.

111. *Diairesis*. For Maximus this term has the negative connotation of disruption of the harmony of nature brought on by sin. See the Cappadocian references in KL 516.

112. 1 Pt 1:8.

113. Cf. Phil 4:7. Also below, 2:16.

114. This mystical blindness, which Balthasar calls a negative description of love, can be found in Evagrius, *Praktikos* 62. The fear/desire contrast is another instance of Maximus's use of these important categories (*Phobos/Pothos*).

115. Cf. Mt 13:31–32.

116. Cf. Mt 17:20.

117. Cf. 1 Cor 3:12; a theme dear to Origen. See references in KL 549.

118. Ex 34:2.

119. Mk 9:1.

120. Cf. Phil 2:7.

121. A notion already seen in the preceding works, for example, *Mystagogy* 24. Cf Gregory of Nyssa, *Cant.* 3 (44, 828D; Jaeger VI, 96). The Transfiguration theme referred to here and in the next three chapters, very common in patristic spiritual writings, is also seen in 1:97, 98, and 2:28, 74.

122. Mt 17:1–8; Mk 9:2–8; Lk 9:29–36. Cf. *Amb.Io.* 1125D–1128D, 1160CD.

123. Cf. Mt 16:27.

124. For an analysis of the creative use of these Evagrian categories by Maximus, see KL 531–3.

125. Ps 39–13.

126. Cf. 2 Cor 3:18.

127. Cf Heb 4:14. The striking closeness of the latter half of this chapter to Origen's statement in *First Principles* 2, 11, 6 leads Balthasar to believe that in reading Maximus's text we are in effect reading the Greek original of Origen: KL 561.

128. Cf. Ex 26:33; Heb 9:2–3.

129. Cf. Origen, *Comm. on Jn* 5, 5 (SC 120, 380–3). Balthasar considers this to be the central insight of Origen's theology, which approximates even his expression: KL 509–10.

130. Cf. Col 2:9.

131. Is 9:6. This finds a close parallel in Origen, *Comm. on Jn* 1, 38 (SC 120,198).

132. For a discussion of the Isochrist background of this chapter see KL 589–90. This and the following chapters make clear that the Christian's mystical identification with Christ takes place in the order of grace, not of nature.

133. Cf. Eph 4:9–10.

134. Cf. Col 1:18 and Heb 6:20. I do not accept the translations of *kath'emas* offered by Balthasar or Ceresa-Gastaldo.

135. Ps 82:1.

136. This is an allegorization of the migration of Abraham as recounted in Gn 11:31–12:6, although Maximus's etymological explanation is unacceptable. Cf. below, ch. 48.

137. Cf. 2 Cor 13:4.

138. Cf 1 Cor 2:2.

139. Eph 2:6.

140. Cf. Eph 4:22–24.

141. Eph 1:21. Balthasar has pointed out the influence of Origen in these motifs: KL 539.

142. Cf. *Amb.Io.* 16 (1252ff, esp. 1256BC).

143. Cf. 1 Cor 12:27.

144. Eccl 1:5.

145. Cf. Jos 10:12–14. The words I have translated "nature" and "character" are logos and tropos.

146. Cf. Jn 12:32.

147. Eccl 1:5 (LXX).

148. Heb 6:20.

149. Cf. 2 Cor 10:4–5.

150. Jos 10:12.

151. Cf.*Q.et D.* 36 (816AB).

152. Rom 10:8. This quotation had also been used by Origen to draw the same spiritual lesson: *Comm. on Jn.*, Preuschen 4, 47–48.

153. Rom 10:6–7, using Dt 30:12.

154. Cf. Origen, *First Principles*, 1,1, 2, and below, ch. 38–42.

155. Cf. Dionysius, *Div. N.* 5, 10 (PG 3, 825B); *Myst.theol.* 1,1, (998AB), and *Mystagogy*, Introduction, as well as 1:85 together with n. 86 of the present work.

156. Pv 5:15.

157. These themes are found elsewhere in Maximus: *Amb.Io.* 43 (1361B), (1285–1286), 66 (1409), *Q.Thal* 32 (372B; Laga-Steel 325).

158. A chapter under the perceptible influence of Origen.

159. Lk 2:34. Cf. Origen's commentary on this passage: *Hom Lc* 17 (SC 87, 250–56).

160. Cf. Jn 20:15–17. "A little masterpiece of Alexandrian allegory," comments Balthasar, KL 552. Cf. *Amb.Io.* 5 (1132B–D).

161. Cf. Jn 20:19. It is not clear why Maximus refers to Galilee. The disciples were in Jerusalem as were their persecutors.

162. Jn 8:21. See below, ch. 94.

163. Cf. Phil 1:23–24.

164. Cf. 1 Sm 16:23. See *Q.Thal.* 65; (772AB).

165. Ibid., 16:12. Cf. *Q.Thal.* 53 (501C; Laga-Steel 431).

166. Heb 7:19.

167. Cf. 1 Sm 13:14; *Q.Thal.* 65 (769D–773B).

168. Cf. 1 Sm 15:9; *Q.Thal.* 65 (765BC). The law of the spirit begets peace as David begot Solomon, whose name means peace.

169. The etymology is unclear but the term may mean "God's name."

170. Cf. 1 Sm 15:33; *Q.Thal.* 65 (765BC).

171. Cf. Phil 3:19. Saul's anointing is symbolic of the mind's anointing against the passions.

172. Cf. 1 Sm 28:7ff.

173. Cf. Jn 6:35. See *Our Father*. Origen had written the same thing: *Comm. on Jn.* 13, 33; and Gregory of Nyssa: *Cant.* 3 (44, 828D; Jaeger VI, 96).

174. Cf. 1 Cor 13:12.

175. Cf. 1 Thes 4:17.

176. Cf. 2:37; 1:83.

177. 2 Cor 5:16.

178. Cf. Jn 1:14.

179. Gal 5:6; 6:15.

180. For water and fire see Mt 3:11 and Jn 3:5. The reference to Daniel is unclear. This doctrine of designations, says Balthasar, "is the basis of Origen's whole Logology" (KL 547).

181. Ex 23:12. On this theme see Origen, *Comm. on Jn* 13, 33 (SC 222, 144–148).

182. Cf. Gen 24:32.

183. Cf. Jgs 19:19.

184. For these images see Dt 32:2; Sir 15:3, 24:28–29. Cf. Origen, *loc cit.*

185. In accordance with his habitual expression, Maximus states that it is virtue that is natural and rational and vice that goes against both nature and reason.

186. Cf. Jn 14:6.

187. Cf. 1 Kgs 15:23. Also Evagrius, *On Prayer* 120.

188. Cf. Jn 10:9.

189. Cf. Jn 8:12, 11:25, 14:6.

190. Jn 13:20.

191. Jn 13:31. These words are spoken just after Judas has left the table of the Last Supper.

192. Jn 14:9, 10.

193. Cf. Gn 39:12; Rom 1:25. Also *Amb.Th*. prol. (1032–1033).

194. Cf. Kgs 19:12. Elijah renews the primitive purity of God's presence. Again, Maximus is misled on the etymology of the word Horeb, which seems to mean desert or wasteland. Cf. Brown-Driver-Briggs, *Hebrew and English Lexicon of the Old Testament* (Oxford, 1972), s.v. Horeb.

195. Cf. Act. 9:18.

196. Cf. 1 Cor 9:13.

197. Jn 1:14.

198. Cf. Jn 17:10, 19.

199. 1 Jn 3:2.

200. 2 Cor 3:18.

201. Ps 120:5, 6.

202. Ps 42:5.

203. Gal 4:6.

204. As Balthasar notes (KL 562), the style of this chapter has much in common with ch. 24 of *Mystagogy*.

205. Cf. Ps 51:12.

206. Cf. 2:20–21, 78.

207. Gen. 35:11. Cf. Ex 32:16. Also Gregory of Nyssa, *Life of Moses* 2:152 (SC 1 ter, 202).

208. Cf. above, 1:85.

209. 1 Cor 2:16. In line with his Christology, Maximus's theory of deification takes place with no loss of genuinely human activity. The language of "the same energy" would be infelicitous in the wake of the Monenergist movement soon to break, but the content is clear enough in its orthodox dyenergism. Later on, Maximus will establish as a principle that energy or activity is to be referred to nature, not to person: *Pyrrhus* (289ff).

210. 1 Cor 12:27. The centrality of human freedom in Maximus's teaching on deification is here clearly expressed. Interesting to note is the paraphrase of Balthasar, "Was Christus der Natur nach war, können wir durch den Willen werden," KL 541.

211. Heb 9:26.

212. Eph 2:7.

213. These categories were evidently much in discussion in the tradition stemming from Origen; cf. *First Principles* 2, 3, 5. Maximus himself discusses the notion of "age" in *Q.Thal*. 22 (317–22; Laga-Steel 137–43). This allegorical interpretation is unfortunately based on an ignorance of the usage of the superlative in Hebrew.

214. Ex 15:18.

215. This chapter represents a correcting of the Origenist conception of time in the light of Gregory of Nyssa. Cf. *In Ps*. 6 (44, 609BC; Jaeger VI, 188–89); in ps. 6 (44, 609BC Jaeger V, 188–89).

216. Cf. 2 Cor 1:22.

217. Eph 4:13.

218. Col 2:3.

219. 1 Cor 13:10.

220. This is a precious summary of the refutation of the Origenist notion of *stasis*, which Maximus treated at length in the *Ambigua*. For him, the repose of heaven is the untroubled and dynamic enjoyment of God which is the end, that is, fulfillment, of the creature. Cf.*Q.Thal.* 65 (768A). The twofold purpose of eating is found in Origen's *First Pr.* 2, 11, 7.

221. Lk 17:21.

222. Jn 14:2.

223. Evagrius had distinguished and defined each; cf. *Praktikos* 2 and 3.

224. Mt 3:2; Mk 1:15.

225. Lk 17:20–21.

226. Gal 2:20.

227. Cf. 1 Cor 15:49.

228. In the light of the preceding chapters it seems that Maximus is speaking of these three expressions as symbolizing the grades of blessedness in heaven.

229. Jn 16:27–28.

230. Cf. Col 3:5.

231. Jn 16:33.

232. The exegesis of the Lord's words from John brings out a typical position of Maximus on human freedom: it is through the inflexibility of the human will, enabled by grace, in choosing God above anything created that it becomes God's partner in man's deification.

233. Cf. Jn 19:20.

234. Cf. Dn 2:36–45. Traditional interpretation of the fourth kingdom spoken of by Daniel identified it as the Roman empire. This identification is largely abandoned today. See L. Hartman, "Daniel" in JBC 26:16.

235. Ps 101:8.

236. Ps 101:1–2.

237. Ibid., v. 1. Another instance of the happy blending of *Phobos* and *Pothos*, fear and longing (desire). For Maximus, fear is not a mere preparatory stage to love but is itself a component with longing desire of eternal love. Cf. *Chapters on Love* 1:81–82, Balthasar, KL 545.

238. The image of the lyre is also found in *Mystagogy* 5 and *Amb.Io.* Cf. Clement of Alexandria, *Protr.* I, 5 (3–4).

THE CHURCH'S MYSTAGOGY[1]

IN WHICH ARE EXPLAINED THE
SYMBOLISM
OF CERTAIN RITES PERFORMED
IN THE DIVINE SYNAXIS.[2]

INTRODUCTION

How a wise man can become wiser "by taking the opportunity," and how an instructed just man "can receive more instruction," according to the divine Proverb,[3] you have clearly shown by your experience, most venerable of all to me. You have taught me by deed that to which the divine Scripture makes but wise allusion. For you heard me once relate, in a brief and cursory way, the beautiful and mystical reflections of a certain grand old man[4] and truly wise in divine matters, about the holy Church and the holy synaxis performed in it. And as they are especially rich in teaching value you hastened to ask me to make a written account of these things for you, wanting to have my writing as a remedy against forgetfulness and as an aid for the memory, saying that it has time taking its natural toll on it which imperceptibly strips it of all the good things it had stored up, and could even cause the figures and images to disappear. Thus there was great need of a means of refreshing by which the power of the word could be kept always at its peak by keeping memory undisturbed and undiminished. And how to seek a tenacious permanence of what has been heard is wiser than simply to hear it is well known to anyone who gives even a little concern to the nobility of reason and who is not altogether a stranger to its friendship.

To be very frank, I must say that at first I shrank from this proposal of a treatise and tried to beg off. It is not, beloved brothers, that I do not want to give you in every way what you have in mind as far as I am able, but rather because I have not yet been granted a share in the grace which would lead those who are worthy to such a task. Moreover, I do not have experience in the power and practice of discourse, since my education was private, and I have remained quite ignorant of the art of discourse which finds favor in mere eloquence in which many people especially delight while limiting their enjoyment to the hearing, even if it often contains nothing of merit by way of depth. But it is truer and more accurate to say that by the cheapness of our discourse I feared

183

to insult the sublimity and interpretation of that blessed man concerning the divine subject. But finally I yielded to the force of love, which is stronger than everything, and readily accepted the task, preferring by obedience to be ridiculed for presumption and ignorance by those who would complain than to be considered by my delay to be unwilling to share your eagerness for every good thing. And so, I cast my care about speaking upon the Lord,[5] who is the only miracle-worker,[6] the one "who teaches man knowledge,"[7] who clears up the speech of stammerers,[8] who contrives a way for those who are without resources,[9] "who lifts up the poor from the earth and raises the needy from the dunghill."[10] This dunghill is the carnal way of thinking[11] and the foul slime of the passions.[12] The poor man is the one who is poor in spirit or the one who is poor in wickedness and in the habit resulting from it, or else on the other hand, he is still bound to the law of the flesh and the passions who because of this is poor in virtue and knowledge and in need of grace.

But since the symbols of the sacred celebration of the holy synaxis have also been considered by the most holy and truly divine interpreter Dionysius the Areopagite in a manner which is worthy of his great mind in his treatise *Ecclesiastical Hierarchy*,[13] it should be known that the present work will not repeat these same things nor will it proceed in the same manner. It would, in fact, be foolhardy and presumptuous and near madness for those who are not yet able to grasp or understand what he experienced to treat of the same subject, or to bring forward as their own the mysteries that were revealed by the Spirit to him alone. Instead, my subject will be those things which God in his goodness wanted him to leave for others for the interpretation and exercise of the habit of these things in accordance with their desire for divine things. In them the beaming ray of ceremonies, once grasped, becomes understood in proportion to them and draws to itself those who are seized by this desire. And this is so that those who come after him might not remain completely idle during the whole duration of the present life, their reason not being hired[14] to tend this divine vine, that is, for the spiritual tillage of the spiritual vine. It restores to us the spiritual wage of the divine and very royal image which was snatched away from us in the beginning by the evil one through the deception of transgressing the commandment.[15]

But I do not promise to narrate in order everything that the blessed old man mystically contemplated, nor will these words proceed from his contemplation and elaboration of them. For this man, because he was truly wise and a teacher in all learning, had rendered himself free from the bonds of matter and its fantasies by the abundance of virtue and very long and knowing familiarity in divine realities and by his laborious industry, and so really possessed a mind illuminated by divine light and could thus see what others do not see. In addition, he had the gift of words to explain most accurately the object of his contemplations, and like a mirror which is not obscured by any stain of the passions he had the power of both understanding and speaking about things which others could not perceive, so that those who listened to him could be brought to see the whole meaning of his discourse, the whole content of his thoughts clearly perceived in all their meaning and transferred to them through the medium of his words. But such things I remember and can comprehend dimly and speak of even more dimly, but devoutly and with the grace of God who illumines obscure things. For I do not suppose that you who know how to judge rightly should think that I can know and say otherwise than as I can, and as grace from on high endows in accordance with the strength apportioned to me by Providence, even if the giver or rather the teacher is the Most High. Indeed, to expect the same things from those who are not equal either in virtue or in knowledge does not seem to me to be far different from those who try to prove that the moon shines as brightly as the sun or who persist in identifying two things which are not the same, which is impossible.

But let God be the guide of our words and our concepts,[16] the sole intelligence of intelligent beings and intelligible things, the meaning behind those who speak and of what is spoken, the life of those who live and those who receive life, who is and who becomes all for all beings, through whom everything is and becomes but who by himself never is nor becomes in any way anything that ever is or becomes in any manner.[17] In this way he can in no way be associated by nature with any being and thus because of his superbeing is more fittingly referred to as nonbeing. For since it is necessary that we understand correctly the difference between God and creatures, then the affirmation of superbeing must be the negation of beings, and the affirmation of beings must be the negation of superbeing.[18] In fact both names, being and nonbeing, are to be reverently applied to him although not at all properly. In one sense they are both proper to him, one affirming the being of God as cause of beings, the other completely denying in him the being which all beings have, based on his preeminence as cause. On the other hand, neither is proper to him because neither represents in any way an affirmation of the essence of the being under discussion as to its substance or nature. For nothing whatsoever, whether being or nonbeing, is linked to him as a cause, no being or what is called being, no nonbeing, or what is called nonbeing, is properly close[19] to him. He has in fact a simple existence, unknowable and inaccessible to all and altogether beyond understanding which transcends all affirmation and negation.[20] But so much for this; let us come to the subject we propose to treat.

CHAPTER ONE

How and in what manner holy Church is an image and figure of God.

Now that blessed old man used to say that at the first level of contemplation[21] holy Church bears the imprint and image of God since it has the same activity as he does by imitation and in figure. For God who made and brought into existence all things by his infinite power contains, gathers, and limits them and in his Providence binds both intelligible and sensible beings to himself and to one another. Maintaining about himself as cause, beginning, and end[22] all beings which are by nature distant from one another, he makes them converge in each other by the singular force of their relationship to him as origin.[23] Through this force he leads all beings to a common and unconfused identity of movement and existence, no one being originally[24] in revolt against any other or separated from him by a difference of nature or of movement, but all things combine with all others in an unconfused way by the singular indissoluble relation to and protection of the one principle and cause. This reality abolishes and dims all their particular relations considered according to each one's nature, but not by dissolving or destroying them or putting an end to their existence. Rather it does so by transcending them and revealing them, as the whole reveals its parts or as the whole is revealed in its cause by which the same whole and its parts came into being and appearance since they have their whole cause surpassing them in splendor. And just as the sun outshines the stars both in nature and energy so also does it conceal their existence from those who look for their cause. For just as the parts come from the whole, so do effects properly proceed and get known from the cause and hold their particularities still when understood with exclusive reference to the cause and, as was said, according to the singular force of their relationship to it. For being all in all,[25] the God who transcends all in infinite measure will be seen only by those who are pure in understanding when the mind in contemplative recollection of the principles of beings will end up with God as cause, principle, and end of all,[26] the creation and beginning of all things and eternal ground of the circuit of things.

It is in this way that the holy Church of God will be shown to be working for us the same effects as God, in the same way as the image reflects its archetype. For numerous and of almost infinite number are the men, women, and children who are distinct from one another and vastly different by birth and appearance, by nationality and language, by customs and age, by opinions and skills, by manners and habits, by pursuits and studies, and still again by reputation, fortune, characteristics, and connections: All are born into the Church and through it are reborn and recreated in the Spirit. To all in equal measure it gives and bestows one divine form and designation, to be Christ's and to carry his name. In accordance with faith it gives to all a single, simple, whole, and indivisible condition which does not allow us to bring to mind the existence of the myriads of differences among them, even if they do exist, through the universal relationship and union of all things with it. It is through it that absolutely no one at all is in himself separated from the community since everyone converges with all the rest and joins together with them by the one, simple, and indivisible grace and power of faith. "For all," it is said, "had but one heart and one mind."[27] Thus to be and to appear as one body formed of different members is really worthy of Christ himself, our true head, in whom says the divine Apostle, "there is neither male nor female, neither Jew nor Greek, neither circumcision nor uncircumcision, neither foreigner nor Scythian, neither slave nor freeman, but Christ is everything in all of you."[28] It is he who encloses in himself all beings by the unique, simple, and infinitely wise power of his goodness. As the center of straight lines that radiate from him he does not allow by his unique, simple, and single cause and power that the principles of beings become disjoined at the periphery but rather he circumscribes their extension in a circle and brings back to himself the distinctive elements of beings which he himself brought into existence.[29] The purpose of this is so that the creations and products of the one God be in no way strangers and enemies to one another by having no reason or center for which they might show each other any friendly or peaceful sentiment or identity,[30] and not run the risk of having their being separated from God to dissolve into nonbeing.

Thus, as has been said, the holy Church of God is an image of God because it realizes the same union of the faithful with God. As different as they are by language, places, and customs, they are made one by it through faith.[31] God realizes this union among the natures of things without confusing them[32] but in lessening and bringing together their distinction, as was shown, in a relationship and union with himself as cause, principle, and end.

CHAPTER TWO

Why, how, and in what manner the holy Church of God is an image of the world composed of visible and invisible substances.

On a second level of contemplation he used to speak of God's holy Church as a figure and image of the entire world composed of visible and invisible essences because like it, it contains both unity and diversity.

For while it is one house in its construction it admits of a certain diversity in the disposition of its plan by being divided into an area exclusively assigned to priests and ministers, which we call a sanctuary, and one accessible to all the faithful, which we call a nave. Still, it is one in its basic reality without being divided into its parts by reason of the differences between them, but rather by their relationship to the unity it frees these parts from the difference arising from their names. It shows to each other that they are both the same thing, and reveals that one is to the other in turn what each one is for itself. Thus, the nave is the sanctuary in potency by being consecrated by the relationship of the sacrament[33] toward its end, and in turn the sanctuary is the nave in act by possessing the principle of its own sacrament, which remains one and the same in its two parts. In this way the entire world of beings produced by God in creation is divided into a spiritual world filled with intelligible and incorporeal essences and into this sensible and bodily world which is ingeniously woven together of many forms and natures. This is like another sort of Church not of human construction which is wisely revealed in this church which is humanly made, and it has for its sanctuary the higher world assigned to the powers above, and for its nave the lower world which is reserved to those who share the life of sense.

Once again, there is but one world and it is not divided by its parts. On the contrary, it encloses the differences of the parts arising from their natural properties by their relationship to what is one and indivisible in itself. Moreover, it shows that both are the same thing with it and alternately with each other in an unconfused way and that the whole of one enters into the whole of the other, and both fill the same whole as parts fill a unit, and in this way the parts are uniformly and entirely filled as a whole. For the whole spiritual world seems mystically imprinted on the whole sensible world in symbolic forms, for those who are capable of seeing this, and conversely the whole sensible world is spiritually explained in the mind in the principles which it contains. In the spiritual world it is in principles; in the sensible world it is in figures.[34] And their function was like a wheel within a wheel, as says the marvelous seer of extraordinary things, Ezekiel, in speaking, I think, of the two worlds.[35] And again, "The invisible realities from the creation of the world have been perceived and are recognized through the things he has made," says the divine Apostle.[36] And if we perceive what does not appear by means of what does, as the Scripture has it, then much more will visible things be understood by means of invisible by those who advance in spiritual contemplation. Indeed, the symbolic contemplation of intelligible things by means of visible realities is spiritual knowledge and understanding[37] of visible things through the visible. For it is necessary that things which manifest each other bear a mutual reflection in an altogether true and clear manner and keep their relationship intact.

CHAPTER THREE

That the holy Church of God is an image of the sensible world by itself.

Moreover, he used to say that God's holy church in itself is a symbol of the sensible world as such, since it possesses the divine sanctuary as heaven and the beauty of the nave as earth. Likewise the world is a church since it possesses heaven corresponding to a sanctuary, and for a nave it has the adornment[38] of the earth.

CHAPTER FOUR

How and in what manner the holy Church of God symbolically represents man and how it is represented by him as man.

And again from another point of view he used to say that holy Church is like a man because for the soul it has the sanctuary, for mind it has the divine altar, and for body it has the nave.[39] It is thus the image and likeness of man who is created in the image and likeness of God. By means of the nave, representing the body, it proposes moral wisdom, while by means of the sanctuary, representing the soul, it spiritually interprets natural contemplation, and by means of the mind of the divine altar it manifests mystical theology. Conversely, man is a mystical church, because through the nave which is his body he brightens by virtue the ascetic force of the soul by the observance of the commandments in moral wisdom. Through the sanctuary of his soul he conveys to God in natural contemplation through reason the principles of sense purely in spirit cut off from matter. Finally, through the altar of the mind he summons the silence abounding in song in the innermost recesses of the unseen and unknown utterance of divinity by another silence, rich in speech and tone. And as far as man is capable, he dwells familiarly within mystical theology and becomes such as is fitting for one made worthy of his indwelling and he is marked with his dazzling splendor.

Chapter Five

How and in what manner still is the holy Church of God an image and figure of the soul considered by itself.

And he used to teach that it is not only of the whole man, that is, as composed of body and soul joined together, that God's holy Church can be an image but also of the soul considered in itself by reason. For, said he, the soul in general consists of an intellectual and a vital faculty, the former moved freely according to its will, the latter remaining without choice in accordance with nature. And the contemplative power belongs to the intellectual faculty and the active power belongs to the vital faculty. The contemplative power he used to call mind, the active power reason. The mind is the mover of the intellectual faculty whereas the reason provides for the vital faculty. The former, that is, the mind, is and is called wisdom when it directs its proper movements altogether unswervingly toward God. In the same way the reason is and is called prudence when in uniting to the mind the activities of the vital faculty wisely governed by it in sensible direction, it shows that it is not different from it but bears the same divine image by virtue as does the mind. This image, he added, is naturally shared by both mind and reason as the soul was previously proven to consist of mind and reason because it is intellectual and rational and the vital faculty is equally evident in both mind and reason—for it is not licit to think of either as deprived of life—and thus shared by both. By means of it the mind, which is also called wisdom, as we said, increasing in the habit of contemplation in the ineffable silence and knowledge, is led to the truth by enduring and incomprehensible knowledge.[40] For its part, the reason, which we called prudence, ends up at the good by means of faith in the active engagement of its body in virtue. In both these things consists the true science of divine and human matters, the truly secure knowledge and term of all divine wisdom according to Christians.

And to speak more clearly of these things, he used to say that the soul has a contemplative aspect, as has been said, and also an active aspect. The contemplative aspect he called mind and the active he called reason, since these are the primary powers of the soul. Moreover he used to call the mind wisdom and the soul prudence, since these are its primary acts. Going into more detail he used to say that to the soul belong, through its intelligent mind, wisdom, contemplation, knowledge, and enduring knowledge, all directed to truth. Through its rational reason belong reasoning, prudence, action, virtue, and faith, all directed to the good. Truth and goodness, he used to say, reveal God. Truth does this when the divine seems to be revealed in its essence, for truth is something simple, unique, one, identical, indivisible, immutable, impassible, all-seeing, and wholly eternal. Goodness, on the other hand, reveals God when it manifests him in its activities: for the good is beneficent and provident and protective of everything that comes from it. In the opinion of etymologists the word which derives from "to be in abundance," or "to be settled," or "to run" signifies that it is a bestower of being, continuation, and movement to all beings.

Thus these five pairs that we observed in the soul, he spoke of as being understood in the single pair which signifies God. These pairs are the mind and reason, wisdom and prudence, contemplation and action, knowledge and virtue, enduring knowledge and faith. The pair which reveals God is truth and goodness. When the soul is moved by them to make progress it becomes united to the God of all in imitating what is immutable and beneficent in his essence and activity by means of its steadfastness in the good and its unalterable habit of choice. And if I might add a brief but useful consideration, this is perhaps the ten divine strings of the spiritual lyre[41] of the soul which includes the reason resounding in harmony with the spirit through another blessed series of ten, the commandments, which spiritually renders perfect, harmonious, and melodious sounds in praise of God. This is so that I might learn what is the meaning of the ten which sing and the ten which are sung, and how the ten are mystically attuned and united to the other ten—Jesus my God and Savior, who is completed by me who am saved, brings me back to himself who is always filled to overflowing with plenitude and who can never be exhausted. He restores me in a marvelous way to myself, or rather to God from whom I received being and toward whom I am directed, long desirous of attaining happiness. Whoever can understand this by having had the experience of these things will completely come to know in clearly having recognized his own dignity already through experience, how there is rendered to the image what is made to the image, how the archetype is honored, what is the power of the mystery of our salvation, for whom it was that Christ died,[42] and finally how we can remain in him and he in us[43] as he said, and how "the word of the Lord is right and all his works are faithful."[44] But we have sufficiently spoken of these things, so let us return to the train of our discourse.

The mind, he used to say, arrives at contemplation when it is moved by wisdom, by contemplation to knowledge, by knowledge to enduring knowledge, by enduring knowledge to truth. It is here that the mind finds the term of its movement, for in it are included essence, potency, habit, and act. Now he used to say that wisdom is a potency of the mind and that the mind is wisdom in potency, that contemplation is a habit, that knowledge is act, that enduring knowledge (of wisdom, contemplation, and knowledge, i.e., of potency, habit, and act) is the perpetual and unceasing movement toward the knowable which transcends knowledge whose term is truth, the ultimate knowable. And what is admirable is how the enduring reality finds its end once it is included or comes to its term in the truth, that is, in God. For God is the truth toward which the mind moves continuously and enduringly, and it can never cease its movement since it does not find any discontinuity[45] there. For the wonderful grandeur of God's infinity is without quantity or parts, and completely without dimension, and offers no grip to take hold of it and to know what it is in its essence.[46] Now what has no discontinuity or which offers no grip at all is not limited by anything.

As for reason, it is analogously moved by prudence and arrives at action; through action it comes to virtue; through virtue it comes to faith, the genuinely solid and infallible certainty of divine realities. The reason possesses it at first in potency by prudence, and later demonstrates it in act by virtue through its manifestation in works. Indeed, as the Scripture has it, "faith without works is dead."[47] Now no reasonable person would ever presume to say that anything dead or without activity should be counted among the finer things. But when by means of faith it arrives at the good which is its term, the reason ends its proper activities because its potency, habit, and act are now concluded.

He used to say, in fact, that prudence is the potency of reason and that reason is prudence in potency. Also that action is habit, that virtue is act, and that faith is the inward and unchangeable concretization of prudence, action, and virtue (i.e., of potency, habit, and act).[48] Its final term is the good where, ceasing its movement, the reason rests. It is God, precisely, who is the good at which every potency of every reason is meant to end. How and in what way each of these succeeds and is brought to reality, and what is opposed or allied to each of them and in what measure, is not our present purpose to determine or say. Nevertheless, we should know that every soul by the grace of the Holy Spirit and his own work and diligence can unite these things and weave them into each other: reason with mind, prudence with wisdom, action with contemplation, virtue with knowledge, faith with enduring knowledge, without any of these things being inferior or superior to the other in such a way that all excess or defect be eliminated from each of them. To summarize: It means to reduce the ten to one, when it will be united to God who is true, good, one, and unique.[49] It will be beautiful and splendid, having become similar to him as much as it can by the perfecting of the four basic virtues which reveal the divine ten in the soul and include the other blessed ten of the commandments. In fact, the tetrad is the decade in potency, joined together in a progressive series from the one.[50] And moreover it is itself a monad which singly embraces the good as a unity and which by being itself shared without division reflects the simplicity and indivisibility of the divine activity.[51] It is through them that the soul vigorously keeps its own good free from attack and bravely repels what is foreign to it as evil, because it has a rational mind, a prudent wisdom, an active contemplation, a virtuous knowledge, and along with them an enduring knowledge which is both very faithful and unchangeable.[52] And it conveys to God the effects wisely joined to their causes and the acts to their potencies, and in exchange for these it receives a deification which creates simplicity.

For thought is the act and manifestation of the mind related as effect to cause, and prudence is the act and manifestation of wisdom, and action of contemplation, and virtue of knowledge, and faith of enduring knowledge. From these is produced the inward relationship to the truth and the good, that is, to God, which he used to call divine science, secure knowledge, love, and peace in which and by means of which there is deification. This whole reality is science because it is the achievement of all knowledge concerning God and divine realities and virtues which is accessible to men. It is knowledge because it genuinely lays hold of the truth and offers a lasting experience of God. It is love because it shares by its whole disposition in the full happiness of God. Finally it is peace inasmuch as it experiences the same things as God and prepares for this experience those who are judged worthy to come to it. If God is completely without change and has nothing to trouble him (for what can escape his view?), then peace is an unshaken and unmoved solidity and an untroubled happiness. Here the entire soul experiences divine things when it is judged worthy of obtaining divine peace. And this peace makes it pass beyond, if we may speak this way, the limits not only of malice and ignorance, of lying and wickedness and of vices opposed to virtue, knowledge, truth, and goodness which exist alongside the natural movements of the soul,[53] but even the limits of virtue itself, and knowledge, and truth and goodness as we know them.[54] It brings us to rest beyond speech and knowledge in the ultimate truth and goodness of God's embrace in accordance with his unfailing promise, so that there is no longer anything at all which can trouble it or cause it any disturbance in the secret recesses in God. It is in this blessed and most holy embrace that is accomplished this awesome mystery of a union transcending mind and reason by which God becomes one flesh and one spirit with the Church and thus with the soul, and the soul with God. O Christ, how shall I marvel at your goodness? I shall not presume to sing praise[55] because I have not enough strength to marvel in a worthy manner. For, "they shall be two in one flesh," says the divine Apostle; "this is a great mystery, I speak of Christ and the Church."[56] And he adds, "The one who cleaves to the Lord is one spirit."[57]

Thus when the soul has become unified in this way and is centered on itself and on God[58] there is no reason to divide it on purpose into numerous things because its head is crowned by the first and only and unique Word and God. It is in him as the Creator and Maker of beings that all the principles of things both are and subsist as one in an incomprehensible simplicity. Gazing with a simple understanding on him who is not outside it but thoroughly in the whole of reality, it will itself understand the principles of beings and the causes why it was distracted by divisive pursuits before being espoused to the Word of God. It is by them that it is logically brought safe and sound to him who creates and embraces all principles and causes.[59]

Such, then, as we have said are the elements of the soul which spiritually possesses wisdom in potency. From wisdom it is led to contemplation, whence to knowledge. From knowledge it is led to enduring knowledge, whence to truth, which is the term and end of all the blessings of the mind. By reason it possesses prudence; from this it is led to action, from action to virtue, whence to faith whereby it rests in the good which is the blessed term of reasonable activities. Through these the science of divine things is acquired from the unifying encounter of these things with each other. It is to all these things that the holy Church of God clearly adapts itself when likened in contemplation to the soul. By means of the sanctuary it signifies everything that is manifested as existing in the mind and proceeding from it; by means of the nave it indicates what is shown to exist in the reason and projects from the reason. All of these things it gathers together for the mystery accomplished on the divine altar. Whoever has been fortunate enough to have been spiritually and wisely initiated into what is accomplished in church has rendered his soul divine and a veritable church of God. It is perhaps for this reason that the church made by human hands which is its symbolic copy because of the variety of divine things which are in it has been given to us for our guidance toward the highest good.

CHAPTER SIX

How and in what manner holy Scripture is said to be a man.

He used to say further that just as in elevated[60] contemplation the Church is a spiritual man and man is a mystical Church so is the entire holy Scripture taken as a whole a man[61] with the Old Testament as body and the New Testament as spirit and mind.[62] Moreover he said that the historical letter of the entire holy Scripture, Old Testament and New, is a body while the meaning of the letter and the purpose to which it is directed is the soul.[63] And when I heard this I especially admired the exactness of the image and praised as well and as fittingly as I could the one who distributes his graces according to each one's merit. For as man who is ourselves is mortal in what is visible and immortal in the invisible, so also does holy Scripture, which contains a visible letter which is passing and a hidden spirit underneath the letter which never

195

ceases to exist, organize the true meaning of contemplation. And just as that man who is ourselves wastes the flesh in mastering by wisdom the desires and drives of the passions, so does holy Scripture spiritually understood circumcise its own letter. For, says the great Apostle, to the degree that "our exterior man perishes, the interior man is renewed day by day."[64] This can be also thought and said of holy Scripture if we consider it morally[65] as a man. To the extent that its letter withdraws, its spirit is enriched; and to the extent that the shadows of the temporal worship pass, so is there introduced the splendid, brilliant, and shadowless truth of faith. It is in accordance with and by virtue of this truth of faith that it principally is, is written, and is called Scripture, being engraved on the mind through spiritual grace. It is just like the man who is ourselves: He especially is and is called man principally because of his rational and intelligent soul according to and by means of which he is an image and likeness of God his Creator and distinguished in nature from other living things without any appearance of a faculty putting him in relationship with them.[66]

Chapter Seven

How the world is said to be a man, and in what manner man is a world.

And again using a well-known image[67] he submitted that the whole world, made up of visible and invisible things, is man and conversely that man made up of body and soul is a world. He asserted, indeed, that intelligible things display the meaning of the soul as the soul does that of intelligible things, and that sensible things display the place of the body as the body does that of sensible things. And, he continued, intelligible things are the soul of sensible things, and sensible things are the body of intelligible things; that as the soul is in the body so is the intelligible in the world of sense, that the sensible is sustained by the intelligible as the body is sustained by the soul; that both make up one world as body and soul make up one man, neither of these elements joined to the other in unity denies or displaces the other according to the law of the one who has bound them together. In conformity with this law there is engendered the principle[68] of the unifying force which does not permit that the substantial identity uniting these things be ignored because of their difference in nature, nor that their particular characteristics which limit each of these things to itself appear more pronounced because of their separation and division than the kinship in love mystically inspired in them for union.[69] It is by this kinship that the universal and unique mode of the invisible and unknowable presence in all things of the cause which holds all things together by his existence in all things renders them unmixed and undivided in themselves and in relation to each other. And it shows that they exist by the relationship which unites them to each other rather than to themselves, until such time as pleases the one who bound them together to separate them in view of a greater and more mystical arrangement[70] in the time of the expected universal consummation, when the world, as man, will die to its life of appearances and rise again renewed of its oldness in the resurrection expected presently. At this time the man who is ourselves will rise with the world as a part with the whole and the small with the large, having obtained the power of not being subject to further corruption. Then the body will become like the soul and sensible things like intelligible things in dignity and glory, for the unique divine power will manifest itself in all things in a vivid and active presence proportioned to each one, and will by itself preserve unbroken for endless ages the bond of unity.

Thus if any one of these three men—the world, holy Scripture, and the one who is ourselves[71]—wishes to have a life and condition that is pleasing and acceptable to God let him do what is best and noblest of all. And let him as best he can take care of the soul which is immortal, divine, and in process of deification through the virtues, and let him disdain the flesh which is subject to corruption and death and able to soil the soul's dignity by its carelessness. "For," it is said, "the body burdens the soul and its earthen dwelling crushes the thoughtful mind."[72] And again, "The flesh lusts against the spirit and the spirit against the flesh."[73] And again, "He who sows in his flesh will reap corruption from the flesh."[74] And let him be moved to do spiritual battle through knowledge against the incorporeal and intellectual powers and leave aside present and visible things, "for visible things are passing but invisible things are eternal,"[75] and it is in these through the abundant habit of peace that God rests. And let him through an informed study of holy Scripture wisely get past its letter and rise up to the Holy Spirit in whom are found the fullness of all goodness and the treasures of knowledge and the secrets of wisdom.[76] If anyone is shown to be interiorly worthy he will find God himself engraved on the tablets of his heart through the grace of the Spirit and with face unveiled will see as in a mirror the glory of God once he has removed the veil of the letter.[77]

CHAPTER EIGHT

Of what the first entrance of the holy synaxis and the ceremonies which follow it are symbols.

After the concise exposition of the views expressed by the blessed old man concerning holy Church, our discourse can proceed by making an even briefer interpretation, as we can, of the holy synaxis.[78] According to his teaching, then, the first entrance of the bishop into the holy Church for the sacred synaxis is a figure and image of the first appearance in the flesh of Jesus Christ the son of God and our Savior in this world. By it he freed human nature which had been enslaved by corruption, betrayed through its own fault to death because of sin, tyrannically dominated by the devil. He redeemed all its debt as if he were liable even though he was not liable but sinless, and brought us back again to the original grace of his kingdom[79] by giving himself as a ransom for us. And in exchange for our destructive passions he gives us his life-giving Passion as a salutary cure which saves the whole world. After this appearance, his ascension into heaven and return to the heavenly throne are symbolically figured in the bishop's entrance into the sanctuary and ascent to the priestly throne.[80]

CHAPTER NINE

What is the meaning of the entrance of the people into the holy church of God.

The venerable old man used to say that the entrance of the people into the church with the bishop represents the conversion[81] of the unfaithful from faithlessness to faith and from sin and error to the recognition of God as well as the passage of the faithful from vice and ignorance to virtue and knowledge. For entrance into the church signifies not only the conversion of infidels to the true and only God but also the amendment of each one of us who believe but who yet violate the Lord's commandments under the influence of a loose and indecent life. Indeed, when any person is a murderer, or adulterer, robber, haughty, boastful, insolent, ambitious, greedy, slanderous, resentful, inclined to outbursts and anger, a drunkard, and in a word—lest I weary my discourse by enumerating all kinds of vice—when someone is entangled in any kind of vice but should cease voluntarily to be held by its attention and deliberately to act according to it and changes his life for the better by preferring virtue to vice, such a person can be properly and truly considered and spoken of as entering with Christ our God and High Priest into virtue, which is the church understood figuratively.

CHAPTER TEN

What is symbolized by the divine readings.

The master used to say that the divine readings from the sacred books reveal the divine and blessed desires and intentions of God most holy.[82] Through them each one of us receives in proportion to the capacity which is in him the counsels by which he should act, and we learn the laws of the divine and blessed struggles in which by consistent fighting we will be judged worthy of the victorious crowns of Christ's kingdom.[83]

CHAPTER ELEVEN

What the divine chants symbolize.

He used to say that the spiritual enjoyment of the divine hymns signified the vivid delights of the divine blessings by moving souls toward the clear and blessed love of God and by arousing them further to the hatred of sin.

CHAPTER TWELVE

What the salutations of peace signify.

The wise man declared that by the salutations of peace which are issued from within the sanctuary on the signal of the bishop at each reading[84] are indicated the divine favors imparted by the holy angels. By them God determines the combats of those who fight bravely for the truth against opposing forces by breaking off the invisible struggles and by giving peace in the destruction of the body[85] and by giving to the saints the grace of detachment in return for their labors for virtue. And once delivered from this warfare they turn the forces of the soul to spiritual cultivation, that is, to the accomplishment of the virtues.

Through these forces they disperse the armies of evil spirits under the command of God the Word, who scatters the sharp and wily machinations of the devil.

CHAPTER THIRTEEN

Of what specifically are the reading of the holy Gospel and the mysteries that follow it a symbol.

Immediately after these things the sacred order of the holy Church prescribes that there should take place the reading of the divine Gospel which specifically proposes to those who are zealous some suffering on behalf of the Word. Then the word of gnostic contemplation comes to them from heaven as High Priest to constrict their fleshly understanding as a sort of sensible world by restraining the reasoning still inclining to earth, and in driving them away from there it leads them, by the closing of the doors and the entrance into the holy mysteries, to the vision of spiritual principles and realities.[86] And after having shut their senses and having become outside of the flesh and the world, he teaches them unspeakable things as they are reconciled first with each other and with him through the kiss of peace and offer him in return for his numerous benefits toward them the grateful confession for their salvation which is intimated by the creed of faith. Next, having set them in the number of the angels through the Trisagion[87] and having bestowed on them the same understanding of sanctifying theology as theirs, he leads them to God the Father, having become adopted in the Spirit through the prayer whereby they were rendered worthy to call God Father. And again after that, as having through knowledge passed all the principles in beings he leads them beyond knowledge to the unknowable Monad by the hymn "One is Holy," and so forth,[88] now divinized[89] by love and made like him by participation in an indivisible identity to the extent that this is possible.

CHAPTER FOURTEEN

Of what the divine reading of the holy Gospel is a symbol in its general meaning. What is generally intimated about the end of this world.

After the divine reading of the holy Gospel the bishop descends from his throne and there takes place the dismissal and sending away of the catechumens and of others unworthy of the divine vision of the mysteries to be displayed.[90] It signifies and figures by itself the truth, of which it is an image and figure, as if proclaiming thereby that after having preached, as is written, "the Gospel of the kingdom in the whole world as a witness to all the Gentiles,"[91] the end will then appear in the second coming of our great God and Savior Jesus Christ from the heavens in glory.[92] "For the Lord himself . . . will come down from heaven at the archangel's voice and the Lord's trumpet," says the divine Apostle.[93] And he will wreak vengeance on his enemies[94] and through the holy angels will separate the faithful from the unfaithful, the just from the unjust,[95] the saints from the accursed and, in short, those who have walked uprightly in the Spirit of God from those who follow after the flesh;[96] and for infinite and endless ages, as the truth of God's declarations affirms, he will render to each one the just reward of the life he has led.[97]

CHAPTER FIFTEEN

Of what the closing of the doors of the holy church after the reading of the holy Gospel is a symbol.

The closing of the doors which takes place after the sacred reading of the holy Gospel and the dismissal of the catechumens signifies the passing from material things which will come about after that terrible separation and even more terrible judgment and the entrance of those who are worthy into the spiritual world, that is, into the nuptial chamber of Christ, as well as the complete extinction in our senses of deceptive activity.[98]

CHAPTER SIXTEEN

What is signified by the entrance into the holy mysteries.[99]

The entrance into the holy and august mysteries, as that great old man used to say, is the beginning and prelude of the new teaching which will take place in the heavens concerning the plan[100] of God for us and the revelation of the mystery of our salvation which is in the most secret recesses of the divine.[101]

For as the Word of God says to his disciples, "I shall not drink of the fruit of the vine until that day when I drink it anew with you in the kingdom of my Father."[102]

CHAPTER SEVENTEEN

What is symbolized by the divine kiss.[103]

The spiritual kiss which is extended to all prefigures and portrays the concord, unanimity, and identity of views which we shall all have among ourselves in faith and love at the time of the revelation of the ineffable blessings to come. In this situation those who are worthy will receive intimate familiarity with the Word of God. For the mouth is a symbol of the Word, precisely through whom all those who share in reason as reasonable beings are united to the first and unique Word who is the cause of every word and meaning.[104]

CHAPTER EIGHTEEN

What is symbolized by the divine symbol of faith.

The profession by all of the divine symbol of faith signifies the mystical thanksgiving to perdure through all eternity[105] for the marvelous principles and modes[106] by which we were saved by God's all-wise Providence on our behalf. Through it those who are worthy are confirmed as grateful for the divine favors, for otherwise they would have no other way of returning anything at all for the numberless divine blessings toward them.

CHAPTER NINETEEN

What is symbolized by the doxology of the Trisagion.[107]

The triple exclamation of holiness which all the faithful people proclaim in the divine hymn represents the union and the equality of honor to be manifested in the future with the incorporeal and intelligent powers.[108] In this state human nature, in harmony with the powers on high through the identity of an inflexible eternal movement[109] around God, will be taught to sing and to proclaim holy with a triple holiness the single Godhead in three Persons.

CHAPTER TWENTY

Of what the holy prayer "Our Father" is a symbol. [110]

The most holy and venerable invocation of our great and blessed God the Father is a symbol of the personal and real adoption to be bestowed through the gift and grace of the Holy Spirit. In accordance with it, once every human particularity is overcome and disclosed by the coming of grace, all the saints will be and be called sons of God to the extent that from that moment they will have radiantly and gloriously brightened themselves through the virtues with the divine beauty of goodness.

CHAPTER TWENTY-ONE

What is signified by the conclusion of the mystical service [111] *when the hymns are sung, that is, "One is Holy," and so forth.*

The profession "One is Holy"[112] and what follows, which is voiced by all the people at the end of the mystical service, represents the gathering and union beyond reason and understanding which will take place between those who have been mystically and wisely initiated by God and the mysterious oneness of the divine simplicity in the incorruptible age of the spiritual world. There they behold the light of the invisible and ineffable glory and become themselves together with the angels on high open to the blessed purity. After this, as the climax of everything, comes the distribution of the sacrament,[113] which transforms into itself and renders similar to the causal good by grace and participation those who worthily share in it. To them is there lacking nothing of this good that is possible and attainable for men, so that they also can be and be called gods by adoption through grace because all of God entirely fills them and leaves no part of them empty of his presence.

CHAPTER TWENTY-TWO

How and in what manner is there conceived the deifying and perfective state of the soul considered in itself, and in what concerns each properly, after what has just been said.

Now let us consider the same things again with reference to the contemplative [114] soul by going through the same things with order and method. And with God leading us by the hand, as it were, let us not hinder the mind which longs and desires to rise a little in religious understanding insofar as it can to a higher contemplation, and to consider and perceive how the divine precepts of holy Church lead the soul, by a true and active knowledge, to its own perfection. [115]

CHAPTER TWENTY-THREE

That the first entrance of the holy synaxis is a symbol of the virtues of the soul.

So, now, you who have become the genuine lover of Christ's blessed wisdom, consider with the mind's eye the first entrance of the holy synaxis from the outside error and confusion of material things as it is written, "Come here, you women who are coming from a sight," [116] I mean of the wandering of the senses in form and shape on the basis of appearance. For one should not speak of true contemplation what I call the mere surface of sensible things, as did the fools whom the Greeks called wise. Among us they would never have been called wise because they could not or would not recognize God from his works. On the basis of this surface appearance of things there has developed a perpetual war of these things with each other to the mutual destruction of all since everything is destroying each other and being destroyed in each other, and the only result is that they are unstable and perish and are never able to meet each other in a tranquil and secure situation.

And consider how the soul in fleeing them headlong comes as into a church to an inviolable shelter of peace in the natural contemplation [117] in the Spirit, and how free of any fighting or disorder it enters it together with reason [118] and before the Word and our great and true High Priest of God. There it learns, by symbols of the divine readings which take place, the principles of beings and the marvelous and grand mystery of divine Providence revealed in the Law and the Prophets, and it receives in each, by the beautiful instruction divinely given in them through the holy angels who spiritually communicate to it the true understanding, the peaceful meanings with the strengthening and preserving enchantment of the divine and ardent desire for God by means of the spiritual appeal of the divine chants singing in it mystically. And consider again how the soul passes beyond this and concentrates on the one and only summit, the holy Gospel, which collects these principles together into one and in which preexist in one form all the principles both of Providence and of existing things in a single burst of meaning. Following this, it is permitted to those who love God to see by a divine perception with the undaunted eyes of the mind the Word of God come to it from heaven and symbolized by the bishop's descent from his priestly throne. He separates as catechumens the thoughts which are still formed from the senses and divisible because of them from its perfect part. And thence again it leaves the world of sense as suggested by the closing of the doors of God's holy church, and leads it to the understanding of immaterial things signified by the entrance into the unutterable mysteries, and understanding which is immaterial, simple, immutable, divine, free of all form and shape, and by which the soul gathers to itself its proper powers and comes face to face with[119] the Word, having united by a spiritual kiss both the principles and ineffable modes of its own salvation and teaching through the symbol of faith to confess this with thanksgiving.

From this moment on the soul is rendered as far as possible simple and indivisible by its instruction, having encompassed by knowledge the principles of both sensible and intelligible things. The Word then leads it to the knowledge of theology made manifest after its journey through all things, granting it an understanding equal to the angels as far as this is possible for it. He will teach it with such wisdom that it will comprehend the one God, one nature and three Persons, unity of essence in three persons and consubstantial trinity, of persons; trinity in unity and unity in trinity; not one and the other, or one without the other, or one through the other, or one in the other, or one from the other, but the same in itself and by itself and next to itself, the same with itself.[120]

The same unity and trinity has a unity without composition or confusion and a distinction without separation or division. It is unity by reason of essence or of being, but not by any composition or joining together or confusion; it is trinity by reason of its mode of existence and subsistence, but not by any separation or diversity or division. For the unity is not divided into the persons nor does it exist in such a way that it can be considered in an external relationship to them. Nor are the persons put together to form a unity nor do they make it up by contraction[121] but it is by itself the same reality, sometimes to be thought of in one way, sometimes in the other. For the holy trinity of persons is an unconfused unity in essence and in its simple nature; and the holy unity is a trinity of persons and in its mode of existence. We are to think of both of these distinctly, as was said, first one way, then the other: one, single, undivided, unconfused, simple, undiminished, and unchangeable divinity, completely one in essence and completely three in persons,[122] and sole ray shining in the single form of one triple-splendored light. In this light the soul now equal in dignity with the holy angels,[123] having received the luminous principles which are accessible to creation in regard to divinity and having learned to praise in concert with them without keeping silent the one Godhead in a triple cry, is brought to the adoption of similar likeness by grace. By this, in having God through prayer as its mystical and only Father by grace, the soul will center on the oneness of his hidden being by a distraction from all things, and it will experience or rather know divine things all the more as it does not want to be its own nor able to be recognized from or by itself or anyone else's but only all of God's who takes it up becomingly and fittingly as only he can, penetrating it completely without passion and deifying all of it and transforming it unchangeably[124] to himself. Thus, as says the very holy Dionysius the Areopagite, it becomes the image and appearance "of the invisible light, an accurate mirror, very transparent, without flaw, undefiled, unstained, receiving in itself, if we are allowed to say this, the splendor of the divine model and purely illuminating in himself, as far as possible, the goodness of the silence of the inner recesses."[125]

Chapter Twenty-Four[126]

What mysteries the enduring grace of the Holy Spirit effects and brings to completion through the rites accomplished in the holy synaxis in the faithful and those gathered in the church out of faith.

This, indeed, is why the blessed old man believed that every Christian should be exhorted—and he never failed to do this—to frequent God's holy church and never to abandon the holy synaxis accomplished therein because of the holy angels[127] who remain there and who take note each time people enter and present themselves to God, and they make supplications for them; likewise because of the grace of the Holy Spirit which is always invisibly present, but in a special way at the time of the holy synaxis. This grace transforms and changes each person who is found there and in fact remolds him in proportion to what is more divine in him and leads him to what is revealed through the mysteries which are celebrated, even if he does not himself feel this because he is still among those who are children[128] in Christ, unable to see either into the depths of the reality or the grace operating in it, which is revealed through each of the divine symbols of salvation being accomplished, and which proceeds according to the order and progression from preliminaries to the end of everything.

Thus we see effected in the first entrance the rejection of unbelief, the increase of faith, the lessening of vice, the bestowal of virtue, the disappearance of ignorance, and the development of knowledge. By the hearing of the divine words there is effected the firm and unchangeable habits and dispositions of the realities just mentioned, that is, of faith, virtue, and knowledge. Through the divine chants which follow there is effected the deliberate consent of the soul to virtue as well as the spiritual delight and enjoyment that these arouse in it. By the sacred reading of the holy Gospel there is brought about the end of earthly thinking as of the world of sense. Then by the closing of doors which follows there is effected the passage and transfer of the soul in its disposition from this corruptible world to the intelligible world, whereby having closed its senses like doors it renders them cleansed of the idols of sin. By the entrance into the holy mysteries we see the more perfect and mystical and new teaching and knowledge of God's dispensation[129] toward us. By the divine kiss there is seen the identity of concord and oneness and love of all with everyone and of each one with himself first and then with God. By the profession of the symbol of faith there is seen the fitting thanks for the marvelous ways of our salvation. By the Trisagion there comes about the union with the holy angels and elevation to the same honor, as well as the ceaseless and harmonious persistency in the sanctifying glorification of God. By the prayer through which we are made worthy to call God our Father we receive the truest adoption in the grace of the Holy Spirit. By the "One is holy" and what follows, we have the grace and familiarity which unites us to God himself. By holy communion of the spotless and life-giving mysteries we are given fellowship and identity with him by participation in likeness,[130] by which man is deemed worthy from man to become God. For we believe that in this present life we already have a share in these gifts of the Holy Spirit through the love that is in faith, and in the future age after we have kept the commandments to the best of our ability we believe that we shall have a share in them in very truth in their concrete reality according to the steadfast hope of our faith and the solid and unchangeable promise to which God has committed himself. Then we shall pass from the grace which is in faith to the grace of vision, when our God and Savior Jesus Christ will indeed transform us into himself by taking away from us the marks of corruption and will bestow on us the original mysteries which have been represented for us through sensible symbols here below. To make it easier to remember, if you wish, let us recapitulate thus the meaning of what has been said by running over it briefly.[131]

Thus the holy church, as we said, is the figure and image of God inasmuch as through it[132] he effects in his infinite power and wisdom an unconfused unity from the various essences of beings, attaching them to himself as a creator at their highest point, and this operates according to the grace of faith for the faithful, joining them all to each other in one form according to a single grace and calling of faith,[133] the active and virtuous ones in a single identity of will,[134] the contemplative and gnostic ones in an unbroken and undivided concord as well. It is a figure of both the spiritual and sensible world, with the sanctuary as symbol of the intelligible world and the nave as symbol of the world of sense.

It is as well an image of man inasmuch as it represents the soul by the sanctuary and suggests the body by the nave. Also it is a figure and image of the soul considered in itself because by the sanctuary it bears the glory of the contemplative element and by the nave the ornament of the active part. The first entrance of the holy synaxis which is celebrated in the church signifies in general the first appearance of Christ our God, and in particular the conversion of those who are being led by him and with him from unbelief to faith and from vice to virtue and also from ignorance to knowledge. The readings which take place after it signify in general the divine wishes and intentions in accordance with which everyone should conform and conduct himself, and in particular the teaching and progress in the faith of those who are believers, and the firm disposition of virtue of those who are active in accordance with which, by submitting themselves to the divine law of the commandments, they set themselves bravely and unshakenly against the devil's wiles and escape his adversary works; finally it signifies the contemplative habits of those who have knowledge, in accordance with which, by bringing together as much as possible the spiritual principles of sensible realities and of Providence in what concerns them, they are borne without error to the truth.

The divine melodies of the chants indicate the divine delight and enjoyment which comes about in the souls of all. By it they are mystically strengthened in forgetting their past labors for virtue and are renewed in the vigorous desire of the divine and wholesome benefits still to be attained.

The holy Gospel is in general a symbol of the fulfillment of this world; in particular it indicates the complete disappearance of the ancient error in those who have believed; in the active, the mortification and the end of the law and thinking according to the flesh; and in those who have knowledge, the gathering and ascent from the numerous and various principles toward the most comprehensive principle, once the most detailed and varied natural contemplation has been reached and crossed.

The descent of the bishop from the throne and the dismissal of the catechumens signifies in general the second coming from heaven of our great God and Savior Jesus Christ and the separation of sinners from the saints and the just retribution rendered to each. In particular it means the perfect assurance of believers in faith which is produced by the Word of God become invisibly present to them, whereby every thought which still limps in some way regarding faith is dismissed from them as are the catechumens. Thus for the active ones there results perfect detachment by which every passionate and unenlightened thought departs from the soul, and for those with knowledge the comprehensive science of whatever is known by which all images of material things are chased away from the soul.

The closing of the doors and the entrance into the holy mysteries and the divine kiss and the recitation of the symbol of faith mean in general the passing away of sensible things and the appearance of spiritual realities and the new teaching of the divine mystery involving us and the future concord, unanimity, love, and identity of everyone with each other and with God, as well as the thanksgiving for the manner of our salvation. In a particular way it means the progress of the faithful from simple faith to learning in dogmas, initiation, accord, and piety. The closing of the doors indicates the first thing, the entrance into the holy actions the second, the kiss the third, the recitation of the creed the fourth. For those at the active stage it means the transfer from activity to contemplation of those who have closed their senses and who have become outside the flesh and the world by the rejection of activities for their own sake, and the ascent from the mode of the commandments to their principle, and the connatural kinship and union of these commandments in their proper principles with the powers of the soul and the habit which is adapted to theological thanksgiving. For those who have knowledge, it involves the passing of natural contemplation to the simple understanding according to which they no longer pursue the divine and ineffable Word by sensation or anything that appears and the union with the soul of its powers and the simplicity which takes in under one form by the intellect the principle of Providence.

The unceasing and sanctifying doxology by the holy angels in the Trisagion signifies, in general, the equality in the way of life and conduct and the harmony in the divine praising which will take place in the age to come by both heavenly and earthly powers, when the human body now rendered immortal by the resurrection will no longer weigh down the soul by corruption and will not itself be weighed down but will take on, by the change into incorruption, potency and aptitude to receive God's coming. In particular it signifies, for the faithful, the theological rivalry with the angels in faith; for the active ones, it symbolizes the splendor of life equal to the angels, so far as this is possible for men, and the persistence in the theological hymnology; for those who have knowledge, endless thoughts, hymns, and movements concerning the Godhead which are equal to the angels, so far as humanly possible.

The blessed invocation of the great God and Father and the acclamation of the "One is holy" and what follows and the partaking of the holy and life-giving mysteries signify the adoption and union, as well as the familiarity and divine likeness and deification which will come about through the goodness of our God in every way on all the worthy, whereby God himself will be "all in all"[135] alike to those who are saved as a pattern of beauty[136] resplendent as a cause in those who are resplendent along with him in grace by virtue and knowledge.

He used to call faithful, virtuous, and knowing the beginners, the proficient, and the perfect, that is, slaves, mercenaries, and sons, the three classes of the saved.[137] The slaves are the faithful who execute the Lord's commandments out of fear of threats and who willingly work for those who are obeyed. Mercenaries are those who out of a desire for promised benefits bear with patience "the burden and heat of the day,"[138] that is, the affliction innate in and yoked to the present life from the condemnation of our first parents, and the temptations from it on behalf of virtue, and who by free choice of will wisely exchange life for life, the present one for the future. Finally, sons are the ones who out of neither fear of threats nor desire of promised things but rather out of character and habit of the voluntary inclination and disposition[139] of the soul toward the good never become separated from God, as that son to whom it was said, "Son, you are always with me, and everything

I have is yours."[140] They have become as much as possible by deification in grace what God is and is believed by nature and by cause.

Let us, then, not stray from the holy Church of God which comprehends in the sacred order of the divine symbols which are celebrated, such great mysteries of our salvation. Through them, in making each of us who conducts himself worthily as best he can in Christ, it brings to light the grace of adoption which was given through holy baptism in the Holy Spirit and which makes us perfect in Christ. Instead, let us with all our strength and zeal render ourselves worthy of the divine gifts in pleasing God by good works not being occupied as are "the pagans who know not God,"[141] with the passion of concupiscence,"[142] but as the holy Apostle says, "putting to death our members which are rooted in earth: fornication, impurity, passion, evil desire and covetousness which is idolatry, from which comes God's wrath on the sons of disobedience, and all wrath, animosity, foul language, and lying, and to sum up, putting aside the old man which is corrupted by the lusts of illusion with his past deeds and lusts, let us walk in a manner worthy of God who has called us to his kingdom and his glory, having clothed ourselves with heartfelt compassion, with kindness, humility, meekness, and patience, bearing with one another in love and forgiving one another if one has a complaint against the other just as Christ has forgiven us, and over all these let us clothe ourselves with love and peace, the bond of perfection, to which we have been called in one body, in short, the new man who is constantly renewed in full knowledge according to the image of the one who created him."[143] For if we lived in this way we would be able to arrive at the goal of the divine promises with a good hope and to be filled "with the knowledge of his will in all wisdom and spiritual understanding, . . . being fruitful and increasing in the knowledge of the Lord, strengthened with all power according to the might of his glory for edification and long-suffering with joy, giving thanks to the Father for having made us worthy to share the inheritance of the saints in the light."[144]

The clear proof of this grace is the voluntary disposition of good will toward those akin to us whereby the man who needs our help in any way becomes as much as possible our friend as God is and we do not leave him abandoned and forsaken but rather that with fitting zeal we show him in action the disposition which is alive in us with respect to God and our neighbor. For a work is proof of a disposition. Now nothing is either so fitting for justification or so apt for divinization, if I can speak thus, and nearness to God as mercy offered with pleasure

211

and joy from the soul to those who stand in need. For if the Word has shown that the one who is in need of having good done to him is God—for as long, he tells us, as you did it for one of these least ones, you did it for me—[145]on God's very word, then, he will much more show that the one who can do good and who does it is truly God by grace and participation because he has taken on in happy imitation the energy and characteristic of his own doing good.[146] And if the poor man is God, it is because of God's condescension[147] in becoming poor for us and in taking upon himself by his own suffering the sufferings of each one and "until the end of time,"[148] always suffering mystically out of goodness in proportion to each one's suffering. All the more reason, then, will that one be God who by loving men in imitation of God heals by himself in divine fashion the hurts of those who suffer and who shows that he has in his disposition, safeguarding all proportion, the same power of saving Providence that God has.

Who, then, is so slow and lazy with regard to virtue as not to desire divinity when one can acquire it at such small cost and so readily and easily? For a firm and secure protection of these things and an easy way to salvation outside of which none of these benefits will be kept truly without harm by the one who has them is the personal attention to our actions whereby in learning to regard and consider what concerns us alone we free ourselves from the hollow hurt caused by others. For if we learn to see and examine ourselves alone we will never interfere in another's concerns whatever they might be because we acknowledge God as the only wise and just judge who judges wisely and justly all things that exist according to the principle of their being not according to the manner of their appearance.[149] Men might also make a judgment by looking vaguely at appearances but the truth and meaning of existing things are not at all to be found there. God, on the other hand, who looks at the soul's hidden motivation and its unseen desire and the principle of these by which the soul is drawn, and its goal, that is, the foreseen end of every action, judges rightly, as was said, all the actions of men. And if we are zealous in succeeding in this and stay within our limited compass without becoming involved in external things we shall not permit the eye, ear, or tongue either to see, hear, or speak at all, if possible, what is the business of others, or at least in getting involved with compassion rather than with passion, we allow ourselves to see, hear, and speak them for our profit and only insofar as it seems good to the divine Word who controls them. For nothing slips more easily toward sin than these organs when they are not disciplined by reason, and on the other hand nothing is more apt to salvation when it commands, controls, and leads them toward where it ought and chooses to go.

Therefore, let us to the best of our ability not be careless in obeying God who calls us to eternal life and to a blessed end through the observance of his divine and saving commandments "to receive mercy and find grace as an aid in time of need."[150] "For grace," says the divine Apostle, "is with all who love our Lord Jesus Christ in incorruptibility,"[151] that is, those who love our Lord with the incorruptibility of virtue and the pure and sincere dignity of life, or to speak more clearly, those who love the Lord by doing his will and by not transgressing any of his commands.

Conclusion

These things I have explained to the best of my ability as I have been taught, as the reward of obedience, not daring to touch on matters more mystical and sublime. But should any devout person desire to know them let him read what has been divinely worked out by Saint Dionysius the Areopagite and he will find the true revelation of ineffable mysteries granted to the human race through his divine intelligence and tongue "for those who are to inherit salvation."[152] And if these things have not fallen far off from your desire, it is thanks to Christ the giver of good things and to you who insisted that they be said. But if they have fallen far short of your expectations, what shall I do or suffer, I who have not had the strength to say them? For weakness should not be punished but pardoned.[153] You must rather approve and not blame me for having yielded to you and accepted the task, especially you to whom it is enjoined to love for the sake of God. And God is pleased with anything which is genuinely offered from the soul to the best of its ability even if this seems small in comparison with great things. He did not reject the widow who offered her two small coins[154] and whatever the widow and her two coins signified. It could be the soul widowed from wickedness which has forsaken the old law as a husband but is not yet worthy of sublime union with the Word of God, but yet offers as a pledge the coins of reason and conduct in due proportion; or else faith and good conscience, or habit and exercise in good things, or contemplation and activity corresponding to them, or knowledge and virtue in proportion, or means which are slightly higher, I mean those in the natural and the written law. When the soul has attained these it gives them up in surpassing and abandoning them as all it has to live on, wishing only to be united to the Word of God. And it accepts to be widowed of violent modes and usages and customs according to nature and law as one becomes widowed of a spouse. Or the meaning could be hinting by means of the letter in which the story is told at something else which is more spiritual than these, understandable only to those who are pure of mind. For everything which seems great to men in virtue is small when compared to the reason which is initiated in theology. But even though they are small of ordinary material and of little worth they still bear just as much as gold coins, the very precious material that the rich offer, the same royal stamp[155] besides the intention of her who offers it wholeheartedly.

In imitation of this woman I have myself offered to God and to you, Beloved, these thoughts and words that come from an intelligence and tongue poor and of little worth on the subject you asked me about. I offer them to you as small coins, beseeching your venerable and holy soul first not to request any further writing of anything I may have spoken of for two reasons. First, because I have not yet acquired that pure and enduring fear of God[156] nor the firm habit of virtue, nor the steadfast and tranquil settling of true righteousness whose weight in a special way confers authority to the words; and second, because being still tossed about by great waves of passion as by a raging sea,[157] and being still very far from the harbor of divine detachment and having an uncertain end of life,[158] I do not want to have my written words to stand as an accuser in addition to my deeds. But finally, having accepted the gift of my obedience, if you wish, commend me by your prayers to Christ the great and only God and Savior of our souls, to whom be "glory and power"[159] with the Father and the Holy Spirit forever. Amen.

NOTES

1. A mystagogy, generally speaking, is an initiation into a mystery. It can mean the accomplishing of a sacred action, especially the celebration of baptism or the eucharist, or an "oral or written explanation of the mystery hidden in Scripture and celebrated in the liturgy" (R. Bornert, *Les Commentaires byzantins de la divine liturgie du 7e au 15e siècle* [Paris, 1966], p. 29). For Maximus the term mystagogy signifies a liturgical contemplation of the mystery of the Church, i.e., of the new creation in Christ (ibid., p. 90). While it is not meant to be a description of the eucharistic rite and, indeed, gives few rubrical details, it is yet a most important testimony of seventh-century liturgy. Relying

214

for the most part on the present treatise of Maximus, F. Brightman is able to reconstruct a sketch of the contemporary eucharistic liturgy: *Liturgies Eastern and Western* I, appendix P, 534–39.

A translation of the present work by Dom Julian Stead, O.S.B., has recently appeared: *The Church, the Liturgy, and the Soul of Man* (Still River, Mass., 1982).

2. Literally, "assembly," "gathering." In this context it refers to the liturgical service, more properly to the readings, hymns, and prayers, but generally (from the fourth century onward) to the whole rite. Cf. J. Jungmann, *The Mass of the Roman Rite* (New York, 1959), p.131 Also M. Hanssens, *Institutiones liturgicae de ritibus orientalibus*, II (Rome, 1930), pp. 24–34 for patristic uses of the term.

3. Cf. Prv 9:9.

4. What is the identity of this "grand old man" to whom Maximus ascribes the teachings in this treatise? It could perhaps be St. Sophronius, patriarch of Jerusalem, who had been his superior at a monastery in Carthage. On him cf. C. von Schönborn, *Sophrone de Jérusalem* (Paris, 1972). Or he could be an earlier acquaintance of Maximus (cf. T. Nikolaou in OCP 49 [1983], 407–418). He could, however, be a literary fiction to whom Maximus refers, out of modesty, his own ideas. In any case he would be following the example of Ps. Dionysius, who makes constant reference to his master Hierotheos, whose real existence is disputed.

5. Cf. Ps 55:23; 1 Pt 5:7.

6. Cf. Ps 136:4.

7. Ps 94:10.

8. Cf. Is 35:6; Wis 10:21.

9. Cf. Wis 14:2.

10. Ps 113:7 and I Sm 2:8.

11. Cf. Rom 8:7.

12. Considered as a dysfunction of man's natural energy. Maximus had already defined passion as an "irrational movement of the soul," *Chapters on Love* 1:35. For Gregory of Nyssa the divine image in us is hidden under the "vile coverings" of wickedness: beat. 6 (44, 1268B–1272C).

13. A fully annotated English translation of this work by W. Campbell has recently been published (Washington, 1982).

14. Cf. Mt 20:7.

15. On the notion of image in Gregory of Nyssa see R. Leys, *L'image de Dieu chez Saint Grégoire de Nyssa* (Paris-Bruxelles, 1951).

16. A traditional invocation at the outset of such a treatise. Cf. *Cel. Hier.* 2, 5, PG 3:145B; Gregory of Nyssa, *Life of Moses* 1, 3 (SC13, 46).

17. In the use of apophatic language to refer to God Maximus is here indebted to Ps. Dionysius. Cf. *Div. N.* 5, 10 (825B) and 7, 3, (872A).

18. Cf. Ps. Dionysius, *Myst. theol.* 3 (1033C) and 5 (1048B).

19. Cf. *Myst. theol.* 1, 1 (998AB); *Cel. Hier.* 9, 4 (261B). It is essential in

Maximus's mind to posit the limits of theological language before embarking on the series of analogies and symbolic references in the present treatise. In this matter he found helpful the language of the Areopagite. Conceptual orthodoxy is a necessary grounding for mystical authenticity. What Maximus is describing in this work is a genuinely Christian sacramental experience.

20. Dionysius had explained that the universal Cause "transcends all affirmation by being the perfect and single cause of all beings, and transcends all negation by the preeminence of its simple and absolute nature which is free of every limitation and beyond all of them" (*Myst. Theol.* 5 [1048A]; also 3 [1033C]). Cf. P. Sherwood, DS 3, 298. The scholion on the fifth chapter of the *Mystical Theology*, attributed to Maximus, significantly refers to Gregory Nazianzen's statement that neither divinity nor unbegottenness nor fatherhood defines God's essence (*schol myst.* th. 5 [PG 4, 429B]; cf. schol. d. n. [200C]).

21. For Maximus the goal of this mystagogical instruction is to introduce one to the mystical knowledge (gnosis) and appreciation of the liturgy. Like Origen, then, he is concerned for the intelligibility of the mystery, which is a valid object of knowledge because it has principles (logoi) which can be apprehended. Cf Amb. Io. 10 (1120A, 1128A); *Q. Thal.* 59 (608A); Bornert, 90. This is accomplished through contemplation, a word that is found very frequently in Maximus. Indeed, J. Lemaitre, R. Rogues, and M. Viller have counted more than 800 instances of this word in the works of Maximus as compared with 45 in Dionysius: DS 2, 1762.

22. Cause, beginning, and end represent an important triad in Maximus's system.

23. The absolute centrality of God's word is thus posited as the key to the whole of creation. Maximus uses Dionysian language to express this fundamental Christian insight. Cf. *Chapters on Knowledge* 2:4, 32.

24. I.e., in their created identity apart from sin and its effects. The regular use of this word in Maximus reflects his view of nature as essentially untainted by sin. See *Our Father*, n. 85.

25. Cf. 1 Cor 15:28.

26. Again the triad, but in slightly different expression. Cf. Amb. Io. 5 (1188BC), as well as the conclusion of the present chapter. Dionysius had mentioned this triad in relationship to God: *Div. Na.* 4, 4 (PG 3;697C, 700A).

27. Acts 4:32.

28. Gal 3:28; Col 3:11. In this first chapter, especially, does Maximus establish the ecclesial hermeneutic of the contemplations to follow. Cf. Riou, 127: "The Church, which is born of water and blood issuing from the pierced side of Christ, is itself the Mystagogy of the Spirit." Progress in mystical awareness is no discrete enlightenment of the gnostic but rather a full and willing participation in the cosmic redemption mystically wrought in the Church as Body of Christ. Cf. Dalmais, "Théologie et mystère liturgique dans la Mystagogie de S. Maxime le Confesseur," *Studia Patristica* 13 (1975), 145–53.

29. This image, which Maximus uses also in *Chapters on Knowledge* 2:4, is referred to by Dionysius in *Div. N.* 5, 6 (3, 821A). This latter probably got it from Proclus, *De Decem Dubit.* (ed. Cousin), p. 826. In the Enneads (6, 18, 19), Plotinus had spoken of the center as the father of the periphery: cf. Balthasar, KL 593–94.

30. Cf. Amb. Io. 35 (1313B) and *Div. N.* 11, 1 (3, 948D–949B). While using the same image as Dionysius, Maximus makes explicit the reference to Christ (here as Wisdom), which is lacking in the former. Cosmic reconciliation is to be understood only through the cruciform mediation of Christ, "the power of God and the wisdom of God" (1 Cor 1:24). Maximus here uses Neoplatonic language to convey a biblical truth.

31. Maximus will return to this theme and underline the reconciling role of Christ in *Q. Thal.* 53(501AB; Laga-Steel 431) and 48 (433C; Laga-Steel 333).

32. Maximus uses the adverb that Chalcedon had used to describe the union of divine and human natures in Christ. The point is clear: the incarnation of God in Christ is the principle and medium of sacramental incorporation into the Church, his body.

33. I.e., mystagogy, one of the rare times Maximus uses this word. Cf. Bornert, 29–31.

34. *Eccl. H.* 1, 2 (3, 372AB). The world according to Dionysius is arranged in hierarchies, each being an "orderly arrangement [*diakosmesis*] of all sacred realities taken collectively": *Eccl. H.* 1, 3, (373C). On the human level, the ecclesiastical hierarchy "abounds in a great variety of sensible signs from which we are hierarchically led according to our capacity up to the oneness of deification—to God and divine virtue"; 1, 2 (373AB).

35. Cf. Ez 1:15, 22; 10:9–17. Maximus regards this as an apt image to symbolize what Riou calls the "synergistic union . . . by collaborative compenetration," which excludes both emanation and fusion. Cf. p. 62.

36. Rom 1:20.

37. Cf. *Eccl. H.* 4, 5 (480C), where Dionysius attributes this knowledge and understanding to the seraphim.

38. *Diakosmesis*, the ordered harmony spoken of above (see n. 33). Cf. *Cel. Hier.* 2, 1 (137A); *Eccl. H.* 1, 3 (373C); 3, 2 (425C); 3, 3, 15 (445B).

39. Origen had compared the spirit of every good man to an altar "from which arises an incense which is truly and spiritually sweet-smelling, namely the prayers ascending from a pure conscience." *Cels.* 8, 17. Cf. *h. in Lev.* 9, 1 (SC 287, 72–74). The image had already been used by Philo (*Opif.*, 37). In his second oration on Easter, Gregory Nazianzen had urged his flock: "Let us sacrifice ourselves to God; or rather let us go on sacrificing throughout every day and at every moment" (*Or.* 45, 23; PG 36, 656B). Christian writers were evidently aware of the biblical roots of this notion of sacrifice: cf. Rom 12:1; Eph 5:2; Phil 2:17, 4:18; Heb 13:15, 16; 1 Pt 12:5.

40. This is a paradoxical expression to signify that this mystical gnosis is beyond the conceptual realm.

41. Cf. Ps 144:9. Evagrius had identified this lyre as "the active soul which is moved by the commandments of Christ," while the harp is "the pure mind which is moved by divine knowledge" (KG 46, 48 [ed. Guillaumont] PO 28/1). It is characteristic of Maximus to link, as he does here by mentioning the commandments, the active and ascetical with the contemplative and mystical. Cf. also *Chapters on Knowledge* 2:100. On the number ten see below, n. 50.

42. These words are found in an instruction of St. Dorotheus on certain words of Gregory Nazianzen on Easter: PG 88: 1821–1829A.

43. Cf. Jn 15:4.

44. Ps 33:4.

45. *Diastema*. The term was used (along with *diastasis*) by Gregory of Nyssa to characterize created nature as opposed to God. Cf. *hom. op.* 16 (PG 44, 181Bff.), 17 (187Aff), *virg.* 12 (Jaeger 8/1, 302), etc. Cf. R. Leys, *L'Image de Dieu chez Saint Grégoire de Nysse* (Paris-Bruxelles, 1951), p. 85; B. Otis, "Gregory of Nyssa and the Cappadocian Conception of Time," *Studia Patristica* 14, part 3, pp. 327–57. Maximus here follows Gregory in his correction of the Origenist error of satiety in the contemplation of God.

46. Maximus is here close to what Gregory of Nyssa says of perfection: *Life of Moses*, 1, 5 ff. (SC 13, 48 ff).

47. Jas 2:26, 17.

48. Characteristic triads.

49. Cf. *Div. N*, 5, 6 (820D).

50. For Pythagoras and his followers numbers symbolized all reality. The four elements, earth, water, air, and fire, comprised the whole cosmic order, and the sum of numbers one through four equaled ten, a number they regarded as sacred. Philo sees the number four as "involving deep principles both of physics and ethics." Indeed, "10 and 14 are said to be 'all' or 'totality' among numbers; 10 being so in realized actuality, and 4 potentially" (*Noah's Work as a Planter* 29 [Loeb Classical Library, Philo III, 273–77]). Gregory of Nyssa presumes the perfection of the number ten in *Life of Moses*, 1:5 (SC 1 ter, 48).

51. Cf Amb. Io. 31 (1293).

52. Maximus unites the pairs (prudence-wisdom, action-contemplation, etc.) in a dynamic unity.

53. Thus the vices are seen by Maximus to be not natural to man but rather apart from his true nature.

54. Here Maximus views the mystery of our mystical union with God in its true apophatic dimension. He is eager to correct the error of Origenists and others who do not sufficiently appreciate the theological depth of the Christian calling. Cf. Amb. Io. 2 (1069AB) and Riou, 49–50. Christian perfection is to be beyond perfection.

55. Perhaps an allusion to the troparion introduced by the patriarch Sergius in 624 and still sung in the present liturgy of the Byzantine rite (although

not by the Greeks): "Let our mouths be filled with your praise, Lord, so that we may sing your glory, because you have deigned to make us sharers in your holy (divine and lifegiving) mysteries. Keep us in your holiness so that the whole day through we may meditate on your righteousness." Text in Brightman, 342 and 536–37. The words in parentheses were added after the time of Maximus. Cf. Casimir Kucharek. *The Byzantine-Slav Liturgy of St. John Chrysostom* (Allendale, N.J., 1971).

56. Eph 5:32.

57. 1 Cor 6:17.

58. Dionysius speaks of three movements of the soul: a *circular* motion, by which it separates itself from external things and concentrates its spiritual powers; a *spiral* motion, when it advances to God through the use of discursive reasoning; and a *direct* motion, when it moves straight upward to pure and simple contemplations: *d. n.* 4, 9 (705AB); sch. d. n. (PG 4:257CD).

59. The logoi of creatures can be understood only in the Logos in whom they have existence.: Amb. Io. 2, 5, etc. On the logoi see I. Dalmais, "La Théorie des 'Logoi' des Créatures chez s. Maxime le Confesseur," RSPT 36 (1952): 244–49; also, P. Sherwood, *Earlier Ambigua*, 155–80.

60. I.e., anagogic.

61. Cf. *Q. Thal.* 64 (728A).

62. This had become a traditional image since Origen; e.g., *First Princ.* 4, 2, 4.

63. Cf. Origen, *On Leviticus*, 5, 1 (SC 286, 204–06); *Comm. on Mt.* 10, 14 (SC 162, 196–98).

64. 2 Cor 4:16.

65. I.e., tropologically. Thus Maximus sees a threefold initiation into the Christian mystery represented in the liturgical, cosmic, and scriptural mystagogies: Amb. Io. 66 (1409AB), 37 (1320) 27, (1285A), 42 (1360C). Cf. Bornert, 91.

66. As Soteropoulos remarks, Maximus has spoken in this chapter of Scripture as both anagogically and tropologically a man. In the first case the use is proper, in the second it is spiritual and symbolic. *He Mystagogia*, 218 n. 2. Cf. Riou, 156.

67. Cf. Origen, *On Lev.* 5, 2, (SC 286, 212). The notion of man as microcosm or epitome of the world dates back to pre-Socratic days and is a commonplace of Greek philosophy and religion. Cf. R. Allers, "Microcosmus, from Anaximandros to Paracelsus," *Traditio* 2 (1944): 319–407. Gregory of Nyssa criticizes the religious value of the notion in *The Making of Man*, 16, 1 and 2 (44, 180Aff). A helpful discussion is found in Thunberg, *Microcosm and Mediator* (Lund, 1965), pp. 140–52.

68. The *principle* of the unifying force is correlated to the *mode* of invisible and unknowable presence a few lines below. This is an illustration of the

logos-tropos distinction used frequently by Maximus. In an important thesis, Felix Heinzer has analyzed the crucial role of this distinction as well as its Cappadocian background: see *Gottes Sohn als Mensch* (Paradosis 26) (Freiburg, 1980).

69. The natural differences in beings, says Dionysius, are to be ascribed to God, who preserves them in his Providence: *Div. N.* 9, 5 (912D). Maximus here sees this as a corrective to the Evagarian error of a proportioned fall from an original henad. The identity, he affirms, must come not on the level of nature but on the level of love. This refutation of Origenism is basic to the appreciation of Maximus's theological contribution. Cf. Amb. Io. 2 (1069A), 5 (1176BC), 10 (1217A–1221B). Helpful analyses are given in Sherwood, EA, 21–29; Balthasar, KL, 122–131, & Riou 45–54.

70. I.e., economy.

71. This division is taken by Maximus from Origen, e.g., *Commentary on John* 13, 42 (SC 222, 178–184), who speaks of logoi. He uses it also in Amb. Io. 16 (1245AB) and 28 (1285C–1288A).

72. Wis 9:15. The Platonic theme is here reinterpreted in the light of biblical truth. In imitation of the author of the book of Wisdom himself, Maximus appropriates Greek philosophy in the service of Christian teaching. The lesson is bolstered by the Pauline texts that follow.

73. Gal 5:17.

74. Gal 6:8.

75. 2 Cor 4:18.

76. Cf. Col 2:3, where this is spoken of Christ. The theme of going beyond the letter of Scripture to its spirit is typical of Origen's tradition. Cf. Daniélou, *Origène*, book 2.

77. Cf. 2 Cor 3:18, 16.

78. The preceding chapters were concerned with giving an exposition of the symbolic meaning of the church as both a building and a construction of souls. With Chapter 8 we begin the second and longer half of the treatise, where Maximus attempts a spiritual interpretation of the ceremonies of the eucharistic liturgy as they unfold.

79. Bornert sees here a literary dependence on the ancient liturgy of St. John Chrysostom: p. 109.

80. Dionysius had spoken of this theme as symbolized in the prayers following the "Holy, holy, holy": *Eccl. H.* 3, 11 (440C–441c); cf. Bornert, 101. The term, "bishop" in the present translation is a rendering of *archierevs*, high priest.

81. The theme of conversion, or return, is a central one in Neoplatonic philosophy and is often used by Origen and his tradition e.g., *First Pr.* 3, 1, 17; *Cels.* 1, 9; In Jer. 1; 1, 4, 6; 5, 2 (SC 232, 196f, 274p; 280p.), etc. Maximus utilizes it by adapting it for the Christian scheme of redemption. The Christian life is a process that begins with this turning away from vice to the newness of

a virtuous life. But for Maximus, the process itself is worshipful. All creation is involved in a cosmic liturgy. As is clear from the present text, the seventh-century liturgy began with the entrance of both bishop and people into the church. This entrance, now reserved to the clergy, is called the "Little Entrance."

82. Maximus discusses these desires and intentions of God in Amb. Io. 2 (1085AC).

83. As Bornert points out, Maximus refers to the readings of Scripture done in a liturgical setting what Origen teaches of the reading of Scripture in general; cf. Bornert, 102. Both see the readings as enlightening for the moral struggle.

84. This is the only indication we have of a blessing of the assembly by the bishop at this point in the liturgy: Bornert, 106 n. 7. Maximus gives another symbolism to this blessing in *qu. dub.* 68 (PG 90, 841D–844A; Declerck 158), seeing the bishop on the height of his throne as Christ ascended into heaven and sending his peace to men.

85. Cf. Rom 6:6. The Combefis text in Migne adds, "of sin":91, 692A.

86. This is a theme one finds in Origen. Cf. M. Harl, *Origène et la fonction révélatrice du Verbe incarné* (Paris, 1959), p. 342. It is also seen in Evagrius: cf. eighth letter attributed to Basil (PG 32, 257C; Loeb 1, 72).

87. See ch. 19.

88. The hymn sung at communion. See below, ch. 21.

89. The Combefis text reads "unified": 692C.

90. Dionysius sees this as symbolic of separating the perfect from the imperfect: *Eccl. H.* 3, 3, 6 (432C–433B).

91. Mt 24:14.

92. Cf. Ti 2:13; Mr 24:30.

93. 1 Thes 4:16.

94. Cf. Lk 18:8.

95. Cf. Mt 13:49.

96. Cf. 2 Pt 2:10.

97. Cf. Rom 2:6.

98. For the rectification and fulfillment of human activity, see the letter of Maximus to Marinus (PG 91:33A–36A), where he bases himself on Gregory Nazianzen, *Or.* 14 (On Loving the Poor).

99. The great entrance is "the rite of transferring the holy gifts from the table of Prothesis to the altar" (Solovey, 223). From the *Quaestiones et Dubia* of Maximus we learn that the number of loaves and chalices to be brought up was an odd one, to represent the mystery of God's simplicity: *q.d.* 41, 820A (Declerck, 10–11).

100. Or economy; i.e., our deification.

101. Bornert sees in this explanation a direct reference to the oration of

the Proskomide in the liturgy of St. Basil, which is also found in the liturgy of St. James. This would indicate a dependency of Maximus's commentary on the liturgical text itself. Cf. Bornert, 109.

102. Mt 26:29.

103. In the Byzantine rite today the celebrant kisses the holy gifts and the altar, then the other priests, while the deacon exhorts the faithful to love one another. See text in Brightman, I, 382. Based on St. Paul's frequent admonition (Rom 16:16; 2 Cor 13:11–12; 1 Thess 5:26; Phil 4:21; Ti 3:15), the kiss of peace was adopted very early into the liturgy. Justin Martyr in the early second century makes mention of it in his first Apology 1:65. Dionysius refers to it in *Ecc. H.* 3, 2 (425C); 3, 3, 8 (437A).

104. God's Word is the ultimate Logos in whom all the logoi of creation have a share.

105. Like Dionysius, Maximus sees the Christian life as an eternal liturgy of thanksgiving in God's presence. Cf. *Eccl. H.* 3, 3, 7 (436C) and 3, 2 (425C).

106. Logoi-tropoi.

107. "Holy God, Holy Mighty One, Holy Immortal One, have mercy on us." A very ancient hymn (it is mentioned in the acts of the council of Chalcedon), it is still sung today in the Byzantine rite. Cf. Solovey, 183–87. Up until the recent liturgical reforms it was sung (in Greek) in the Roman rite on Good Friday.

108. I.e., the angels. The notion is based on the Gospel saying of Christ, Lk 20–30. Cf. Gregory of Nyssa, *Pss. titt.* 9 (PG 44:484B; Jaeger V, 66); Dionysius, *Div. N.* 1, 4 (592BC. The scholion on this point speaks of the present life of turning away from earthly pleasures as already a reflection of angelic life: schol. div. nom. (4, 197D–200A, 204BC), 4, 2, (241CD). The notion has been encountered several times already in these works.

109. Cf. *Cel. Hier.* 7, 1 (205B), 4 (212A). The angels are deiform, says Dionysius. In a scholion attributed to him, Maximus explains that they are indeed godlike because they are free in the habitual possession of virtue: schol. c. h. (65D). Inflexibility of will is seen as an immunity from sin and therefore as true freedom.

110. In taking up a discussion of the Lord's prayer at this point, Maximus passes over in silence the anaphora, or eucharistic prayer. No satisfactory reason for this has been offered, and the omission is intriguing. Cf. Bornert, 107–8. Perhaps one reason for the omission is that by this time the anaphora was recited silently. Indeed, a century previously the emperor Justinian attempted by legislation to thwart the movement toward a silent anaphora (novel 137; *Corpus Juris Civilis*, Berlin, 1895, 3:699), but unsuccessfully, Cf. P. Trembelas, "L'audition de l'anaphore eucharistique par le peuple," in *L'Eglise et les Eglises*, Mélanges Dom L. Beauduin (Chevetogne, 1955), t. 2, 207–20. To explain Maximus's silence, Riou points to a more intrinsic reason, viz., that the the true anaphora is the configuring anamnesis of Christian martyrdom (p. 165).

111. Or hierurgy, the term meaning liturgy used by Dionysius: *Eccl. H.* 3, 1 (425B).

112. "One is holy, one is Lord, Jesus Christ, to the glory of God the Father." Still sung in the Byzantine liturgy, this hymn is found as early as the middle of the fourth century in Cyril of Jerusalem's *Mystagogical Catecheses* 5, 19 (PG 33, 1124B). The Maurist editor refers to Gregory of Nyssa, *C. Eun.* 2 (PG 45:485). Cf. Also *Constitutiones Apostolorum* (ed. Funk) (Paderborn, 1905), pp. 516–7. The acclamation is also found in Didymus, *De Trinitate* 3:13 (PG 39:861A).

113. Mysterion, i.e., the eucharistic elements. The expression is that of Dionysius, *Eccl. H.* 3, 1 (425A).

114. Literally, gnostic.

115. Maximus proposes to deepen the appreciation of the liturgical mystery in a manner akin to Dionysius, who follows each of his chapters of the *Ecclesiastical Hierarchy* with a "contemplation." Thus Bornert can assert that for Maximus (as for Origen) the liturgical mystagogy is less an initiation into the liturgical mystery than an introduction into the mystery using the liturgy as a starting point (p. 92).

116. Is 27:11. The LXX reading that Maximus follows is very different from the Hebrew text on which most contemporary translations are based.

117. Natural contemplation, which correlates with biblical and spiritual contemplation mentioned just following.

118. Maximus typically uses the same word, logos, to express the three realities mentioned here: reason, the Word, principles. The Word of God, he is saying, is the universal key to understanding, as well as the key to understanding the universe.

119. Reading *Katanta* of Combefis rather than *Kata noun* of Soteropoulos.

120. Even in describing the high point of mystical union, Maximus uses credal language. Clearly for him the theological precision is necessary for the correct intelligibility of the mystical reality.

121. *Synairesis*, the term associated with Sabellius and Marcellus. Cf. Gregory Nazianzen, *Or.* 22, 12 (PG 35:1145A), 43, 30 (36:537A), 42, 16 (476C); Sophronius, *Synodicon* (PG 87:3152D).

122. Maximus is fond of expressing the Catholic teaching on the Trinity in the Cappadocian manner in its full dogmatic force. Cf. *Chapters on Knowledge* 2:1 and *Our Father*; Amb. Io. 62 (1400D–1401A; opusc. 13 (91, 145B–149A).

123. A frequent theme in Maximus, as we have seen. As Maximus explicitly states, the likeness is not on the level of nature but on that of grace. The Logos unites all the elements of creation while retaining the particularity of their natures.

124. A necessary adverb to indicate that however much man is identified with God through grace, he never forfeits his basic human nature.

125. *Div. N* 4, 22 (724B) and *Cel. Hier.* (165A). Dionysius uses this lan-

guage to speak of angels in view of proving that there is no evil in them. In this he is influenced by Proclus. See *de mal. sub.* 212.37, 212.21, 213.15. Maximus again mentions the image of the mirror in Amb. Io. 5 (1137B).

126. Chapter 24 presents a literary problem. It contains two summaries, one of the rites and the other of the mystical and typological interpretation of the church and the liturgy, to which are added certain ascetical and mystical remarks. After considering both intrinsic and extrinsic difficulties, Bornert concludes that the summaries are rather the work of one or several scholiasts while the ascetical and mystical appendices are the work of Maximus himself (87–90). Riou is rather inclined to see the interpolation in the threefold interpretation based on whether one is a simple faithful, active, or contemplative (168, n. 40).

127. Since the earthly liturgy is a sacrament of the heavenly liturgy, the angels are present in mystery. Origen had spoken of them in *h. in Lc* 23, 8 (SC 87, 320–22).

128. The theme of spiritual childhood found in Scripture (e.g., Rom 9:8, Gal 3:26) is referred to by Origen, *Comm. on Mt* 15, 6 (GCS 10, 362–3) and Evagrius, *Gnostikos* 128 (in Bousset, *Apothegmata*, 312) and *Practikos*, prol., and by Dionysius, *Eccl. H.* 5, 2 (501B). Cf. also *Chapters on Knowledge* 1:94.

129. I.e., economy.

130. Cf. *Eccl. Hier.* 3, 3, 12 (44B). Maximus habitually distinguishes between the image and likeness of Gn 1:26, comparing them as the logos of nature and the tropos of virtue. The Christian religious life is a call to add "to the natural beauty of the image the voluntary good of likeness" (*Chapters on Knowledge* 1:13; cf. also 1:11; Amb. Io. 2 (1084A), 5 (1192C–1193C); *Chapters on Love* 3:25).

131. What follows is a recapitulation of liturgical instruction in which different significations are given to each rite depending on whether one is in the simple (faithful), active, or contemplative stage. The latter two terms have been employed to translate practikos and gnostikos (or theoretikos).

132. Using here the textual reading in Migne.

133. The Combefis text in Migne is more compact here, and thus we revert to Soteropoulos.

134. *Gnome.* The imprecise language is an indication that the *Mystagogy* (like the commentary on the Lord's prayer) antedates the Monothelite crisis. Maximus will later retract this ambiguous vocabulary in favor of more precise expressions.

135. Cf. 1 Cor 15:28.

136. This expression is taken from Dionysius, *Eccl. Hier.* 3, 3, 2 (428C).

137. These categories were commonly employed by contemporary spiritual writers.

138. Mt. 20:12.

139. Cf. Maximus, Ep. 2 (90, 401D–404A); *Chapters on Love* 4:32, 36; *Chapters on Knowledge* 1:36.

140. Lk 15:31.

141. 1 Thes. 4:6.

142. Ibid. v. 5.

143. This is a weaving together of various Pauline texts: Col 3:5–6; Eph 5:6; Col 3:8; Eph 4:22; Col 3:9; 1 Thes 2:12; Col 3:12–13 (Maximus adds, "in love"), 12–15, 10. The renewal of the creature in Christ is seen here in its concretely moral implications.

144. Col 1:9–12.

145. Cf. Mt 25:40–41.

146. In accordance with the triad essence-power-act.

147. Cf. 2 Cor 8:9.

148. Cf. Mt 28:20.

149. Once again Maximus utilizes the distinction logos-tropos.

150. Heb 4:16.

151. Eph. 6:24.

152. Heb 1:14.

153. Cf. *Div. N.* 4, 35 (736A), where Dionysius says the same thing. The attribution to God's grace of any benefit to be derived from the treatise is common enough; cf. Gregory of Nyssa, hom. in 1 Cor 15:28 (PG 44:1325).

154. Cf. Mk 12:42–43.

155. A common patristic image.

156. Cf. Ps 18:10.

157. In Origen's tradition the sea represents the dangerous realm of instability: *hom.* 16 in Jer., 1 (SC 238, 132); *Comm. in Mt.* 13,17.

158. Cf. Amb. Io. prol. (1064A).

159. Rv 1:6.

BIBLIOGRAPHY

WORKS OF MAXIMUS

Migne, J. PG 90–91.

Questiones ad Thalassium I (ed. Carl Laga and Carlos Steel). Corpus Christianorum, Series Graeca 7. Louvain, 1980.

Quaestiones et Dubia (ed. J. H. Declerck). Corpus Christianorum, Series Graeca 10. Louvain, 1982.

Capitoli sulla carità. (ed. Aldo Ceresa-Gastaldo). Rome, 1963. Critical text with Italian translation. Other translations: KL 414–481 (H. Urs von Balthasar); SC 9 (J. Pegon); ACW 21 (P. Sherwood); The Philokalia II (G. Palmer, P. Sherrard, K. Ware).

The Ascetic Life: Translations in ACW 21 (P. Sherwood) and P. Deseille, *L'Evangile au Désert* (Paris, 1965), pp. 162–193.

Mystagogy: C. Soteropoulos. He Mystagogia tou Agiou Maximou tou omologetou (Athens, 1978). Critical text. Translations in *Irenikon* 13 (1936): 466–72; 595–97; 717–20; 14 (1937): 66–69; 182–85; 282–84; 444–48; 15 (1938): 71–74; 185f.; 276–78, 390F.; 488–92 (= L'Initiation chrétienne [Paris, 1963], 251–91) (M. Lot-Borodine) R. Cantarella. "S. Massimo Confessore, La Mistagogia" ed. Altri Scritti. Florence, 1931. KL 366–407 (H. Urs von Balthasar). Dom Julian Stead. *St. Maximus the Confessor, the Church, the Liturgy, and the Soul of Man.* (Still River, Mass., 1982).

The Lord's Prayer; A. Riou, *Le Monde et L'Eglise selon Maxime le Confesseur,* pp. 214–39. *The Philokalia* (G. Palmer, P. Sherrard, K. Ware), pp. 285–305.

Chapters on Knowledge; KL 509–643. A. Ceresa-Gastaldo. *Il Dio-Uomo.* Milan, 1980. A. Riou. *Le Monde et L'Eglise selon Maxime le Confesseur,* pp. 240–61 (First Century). *The Philokalia* II, 114–63.

Letter 2; I. H. Dalmais. "St. Maxime le Confesseur, Docteur de la charité," VS (1948), pp. 296–303.

Also E. von Ivanka. *Maximos der Bekenner, All-eins in Christus.* Einsiedeln, 1961. P. B. Hermann. *Weisheit, die betet.* Wurzburg, 1941.

227

BIBLIOGRAPHY

STUDIES

Aubineau, M. "Textes de Marc l'Ermite, Diadoque de Photicé, Jean de Carpathos, et Maxime le Confesseur dans le codex Harleianus 5688." OCP 30 (1964): pp. 256–59.

Balthasar, H. Urs von. *Kosmische Liturgie, Das Weltbild Maximus des Bekenners.* Second ed., Einsiedeln, 1961 (contains several other pertinent works and translations).

———. *Liturgie Cosmique*, Paris, 1947. French translation of first edition of above.

Berthold, G. "Did Maximus the Confessor Know Augustine?" SP XVII (1982): pp. 14–17.

———. "The Cappadocian Roots of Maximus the Confessor." In MC, pp. 51–59.

———. "Maximus the Confessor and the Filioque," SP. In. press.

Bornert, R. *Les Commentaires Byzantins de la divine liturgie du VIIe au XVe siècles.* Paris, 1966.

Brock, S. "An Early Syriac Life of Maximus the Confessor." AB 91 (1973): pp.299–346.

Canart, P. "La Deuxième Lettre à Thomas de saint Maxime le Confesseur." *Byzantion* 34 (1964): pp. 415–45.

Candal, M. "La Gracia increada del Liber Ambiguorum de san Maximo." OCP (1961): 131–49.

Caspar, E. "Die Lateransynode von 649." *Zeitschrift fur Kirchengeschichte* 51 (1932): 75–137.

Ceresa-Gastaldo, A. "Appunti dalla biographia di S. Massimo Confessore." *Scuola Cattolica* 84 (1956): pp.145–51.

Congar, M. J. "La déification dans la tradition spirituelle de l'Orient." In *Chrétiens en Dialogue.* Paris, 1964, pp. 257–72.

Croce, V. *Tradizione e ricerca. Il metodo teologico di san Massimo il Confessore.* Milan, 1974.

Dalmais, I.-H. "S. Maxime le Confesseur, Docteur de la Charité." VS (1948): pp. 194–201.

———. "La théorie des 'Logoi' des creatures chez s. Maxime le Confesseur." RSPT 36 (1952); pp. 244–49.

———. "L'oeuvre spirituelle de s. Maxime le Confesseur." VS Suppl. 21 (1952): pp. 216–26.

———. "La doctrine ascétique de s. Maxime le Confesseur d'après le Liber Asceticus." *Irenikon* 26 (1953); pp. 17–39.

———. "Un traité de théologie contemplative: Le commentaire du Pater Noster de s. Maxime le Confesseur." RAM 29 (1953): pp. 123–59.

———. art. "Divinisation: II. Patristique Grecque." DS 3, pp. 1376–1389 (1957).

———. "L'Anthropologie spirituelle de saint Maxime le Confesseur." *Recherches et Debats* 36 (1961): pp. 202–11.

———. "Saint Maxime le Confesseur et la crise de l'origénisme monastique." In *Theologie de la Vie Monastique.* Paris, 1961, pp. 411–21.

———. *"La fonction unificatrice du Verbe Incarné dans les oeuvres spirituelles de Saint Maxime le Confesseur."* Sciences Ecclésiastiques 14 (1962): pp. 445–59.

———. "Place de la Mystagogie de S. Maxime le Confesseur dans la théologie liturgique byzantine." SP V, pp. 277–283.

———. "L'Héritage évagrien dans la synthèse de s. Maxime le Confesseur." SP VIII (1966): pp. 356–63.

———. "Le vocabulaire des activités intellectuelles, volontaires, et spirituelles dans l'anthropologie de S. Maxime le Confesseur." In *Mélanges Offerts au P. M.-D. Chenu.* Paris, 1967, pp. 189–202.

———. "Mystère liturgique et divinisation dans la Mystagogie de saint Maxime le Confesseur." In *Epektasis, Mélanges patristiques offerts au Card.* J. Danielou. Paris, 1972, pp. 55–62.

———. "Théologie de l'Eglise et mystère liturgique dans la Mystagogie de saint Maxime le Confesseur." SP VIII (1975): pp.145–53.

———. art. "Maxime le Confesseur." DS X, pp. 836–42.

Daniélou, J. *Platonisme et Théologie Mystique. Essai sur la doctrine spirituelle de Gregoire de Nysse.* Paris, 1954.

Devréesse, R. "La Vie de S. Maxime le Confesseur et ses Recensions." AB 46 (1928): pp. 5–49.

———. "Le texte grec de l'Hypomnesticum de Théodore Spoudée." AB 53 (1935): pp.49–80.

———. "La fin inédite d'une lettre de Saint Maxime." *Revue des Sciences Religieuses* 17 (1937): pp. 23–35.

———. "La Lettre d'Anastase l'Apocrisiaire sur la mort de S. Maxime et des ses Compagnons d'exil." AB 73 (1955): pp. 5–16.

Disdier, T. "De vita contemplativa secundum doctrinam s. Maximi Confessoris." Dissert. Pont. Or. Inst. Rome, 1928.

———. "Les fondements dogmatiques de la spiritualité de saint Maxime le Confesseur." EO 29 (1930): pp. 296–313.

———. "Une oeuvre douteuse de saint Maxime le Confesseur." EO 30 (1931): pp. 160–78.

———. "Elie l'Ecdicos et les hetera kephalaia attribués a s. Maxime le Confesseur et a Jean de Carpathos." EO 31 (1932): pp. 17–43.

Diekamp, F. *Die Gotteslehre des heiligen Gregor von Nyssa*. Munster, 1895.

———. *Die origenistischen Streitigkeiten in sechsten Jahrhundert*. Munster, 1899.

Dionysius the Pseudo-Areopagite. *The Divine Names and Mystical Theology*. Tr. James Jones. Milwaukee, 1980.

———. *The Ecclesiastical Hierarchy*. Tr. Thomas L. Campbell. Washington, 1981.

Dölger-Beck."Diskussions-Beitrage zum XI Internationalen Byzantinischen-Kongress." Munich, 1961.

Evagrius Ponticus. *The Prakticos, Chapters on Prayer*. Tr. J. E. Bamberger. Kalamazoo, Mich., 1978.

Garrigues, J.-M. "La Personne composée du Christ d'après Saint Maxime le Confesseur." *Revue Thomiste* 74 (1974); pp. 181–204.

———. "L'enérgie divine et la grâce chez Maxime le Confesseur." *Istina* 19 (1974): pp. 272–96.

———. *Maxime le Confesseur. La Charité, Avenir Divin de l'Homme*. Paris, 1976.

———. "Le sens de la primauté romaine selon Maxime le Confesseur." *Istina* 21 (1976): pp. 6–24.

———. "Le Martyre de Saint Maxime le Confesseur." *Revue Thomiste* 76 (1976): pp. 410–52.

Gauthier, R. A. "S. Maxime le Confesseur et la psychologie de l'acte humain." RTAM 21 (1954): pp. 51–100.

Geanakoplos, D. J. "Some Aspects of the Influence of the Byzantine Maximos the Confessor on the Theology of East and West." *Church History* 38 (1969): pp. 150–63.

Grumel, V. "La comparaison de l'âme et du corps et l'union hypostatique chez Léonce de Byzance et S. Maxime le Confesseur." EO 25 (1926): pp. 393–406.

———. "Notes d'histoire et de chronologie sur la vie de Saint Maxime le Confesseur." EO 26 (1927): pp. 24–32.

———. art. "Maxime le Confesseur." DTC 10, pp. 448–59 (1928).

———. "Recherches sur l'histoire de monothélisme." EO 27 (1928): pp. 6–16, 257–77; 28 (1929): pp. 19–34, 272–82; 29 (1930): pp. 16–28.

Guillaumont, A. Les *"Kephalai Gnostica" d'Evagre le Pontique et l'histoire de l'Origenismechez les Grecs et chez les Syriens*. Paris, 1962.

———. art. "Evagre le Pontique." DS 4, 1731–1744 (1961).

BIBLIOGRAPHY

Hausherr, I. *Philautie. De la tendresse pour soi à la charité, selon Saint Maxime le Confesseur* (OCA 137). Rome 1952.

―――. *Les leçons d'un contemplatif. Le Traité de l'oraison d'Evagre le Pontique.* Paris, 1960.

Heinzer, F. *Gottes Sohn als Mensch. Die Struktur des Menschseins Christi bei Maximus Confessor.* Fribourg, 1980.

―――. (with C. Schönborn, ed.). *Maximus Confessor. Actes du Symposium sur Maxime le Confesseur.* Fribourg, 1982.

Jugie, M. Art. "Monothélisme." DTC 10:2, 2307–2323 (1929).

Lackner, W. "Zu Quelle und Datierung der Maximosvita (BHG³1234)." AB 85 (1967): pp. 285–316.

―――. "Der Amtstitel Maximos des Bekenners." *Jahrbuch der Österreichischen Byzantinistik* 20 (1971); pp. 64–65.

Ladner, G. B. "The Philosophical Anthropology of Saint Gregory of Nyssa." DOP 12 (1958): pp. 58–94.

Lemaître, J.-Roques, R.,-Viller, M. Art. "Contemplation chez les Grecs." 1. Etude de Vocabulaire. DS 2, 1762–1787 (1953).

Lethel, F. M. *Théologie de l'Agonie du Christ.* Paris, 1979.

Loosen, J., *Logos und Pneuma im begnadeten Menschen bei Maximus Confessor.* Münster, 1941.

Lossky, V. "La Théologie négative dans la doctrine de Denys l'Aréopagite." RSPT 28 (1936): pp. 204–21.

―――. *The Mystical Theology of the Eastern Church.* London, 1957.

Lot-Borodine, M. *La Déification de l'Homme selon la doctrine des Pères grecs.* Paris, 1970.

Mahieu, G. "Travaux préparatoires à une édition critique des oeuvres de S. Maxime le Confesseur." Mémoire de licence en Philosophie et Lettres. Louvain, 1957.

Maritch. J. *Celebris Cyrilli Alexandrini formula christologica de una activitate Christi in interpretatione Maximi confessoris et recentiorum theologorum.* Zagreb, 1920.

Michaud. E. "Saint Maxime le Confesseur et l'apocatastase." *Revue Internationale de Théologie* 10 (1902): pp. 257–72.

Miquel, P. "*Peira.* Contribution a l'étude du vocabulaire de l'expérience religieuse dans l'oeuvre de s. Maxime le Confesseur." SP VII (1966): pp. 355–61.

Montmasson, E. "La chronologie de la vie de Saint Maxime le Confesseur." EO 13 (1910): pp. 149–54.

―――. "La doctrine de l'apatheia d'après s. Maxime." EO 14 (1911): pp. 36–41.

Muyldermans, J. *Evagriana*. Paris, 1931.

———. *Evagriana Syriaca*. Louvain, 1952.

Negri, L. "Elementi critologici ed antropologici nel pensiero di S. Massimo il confessore." *La Scuola Cattolica* 101 (1973): pp. 331–61.

Owsepian, G. *Die Entstehungsgeschichte des Monothelismus nach ihren Quellen geprüft und dargestellt*. Leipzig, 1897.

Peitz, M. W. "Martin I. und Maximus Confessor." *Historisches Jahrbuch der Gorresgesellschaft* 38 (1917): pp. 213–36, 429–58.

Pelikan, J. *The Spirit of Eastern Christendom* (vol. 2 of *The Christian Tradition*). Chicago and London, 1974.

———. "Council or Father or Scripture, The Concept of Authority in the Theology of Maximus the Confessor." In D. Neiman and M. Schatkin (ed.), *The Heritage of the Early Church* (OCA 195). Rome, 1973, pp. 277–88.

———. "The Place of Maximus Confessor in the History of Christian Thought." MC 387–402.

Pierres, J. *Sanctus Maximus Confessor: princeps apologetarum Synodi Lateranensis anni 649*. Rome, 1940.

Piret, P. *Le Christ et La Trinité selon Maxime le Confesseur*. Paris, 1983.

Prado, J. J. *Voluntad y Naturaleza. La antropologia filosofica de Maximo el confesor*. Rio Cuarto (Argentina), 1974.

Preuss, K. *Ad Maximi Confessoris de Deo Hominisque deificatione doctrinam adnotationum*. Schneeburg, 1894.

Refoulé, F. "La christologie d'Evagre et l'origénisme." OCP (1961): pp. 221–66.

Riou, A. *Le Monde et l'Eglise selon Maxime le Confesseur*. Paris, 1973.

Roques, R. *L'Univers Dionysien. Structure hierarchique du monde selon le Pseudo-Denys*. Paris, 1954.

Schönborn, C. von. *Sophrone de Jérusalem, Vie Monastique et Confession Dogmatique*. Paris, 1972.

Sherwood, P. *An Annotated Date-List of the Works of Maximus the Confessor*. Rome, 1952.

———. *The Earlier Ambigua of St. Maximus the Confessor and his refutation of Origenism*. Rome, 1955.

———. "Maximus and Origenism." Berichte zum XI Byz. Kongresse, Munich, 1958.

———. "Explanation and Use of Scripture in St. Maximus as manifested in the Quaestiones ad Thalassium." OCP 24 (1958): pp. 202–07.

————. "Survey of Recent Work on Maximus the Confessor." *Traditio* XX (1964): 428, 437.

————. "Notes on Maximus the Confessor." *American Benedictine Review* 1 (1950): pp. 347–56.

————. art. "Saint Maxime et Denys l'Areopagite." DS III, pp. 295–99.

Soppa, W. *Die Diversa Capita unter den schriften des hl. Maximus Confessor in deutschen Bearbeitung und quellenkritischer Beleuchtung.* Dresden, 1922.

Squire, A. K. "The Idea of the soul as virgin and mother in Maximus the Confessor." SP VIII (1966): pp. 456–61.

Starr, J. "St. Maximus and the Forced Baptism at Carthage in 632." *Byz. Neugriechische Jahrbuch 16* (1940): pp.192–96.

Stiglmayer, J. "Der heilige Maximus 'mit seinen beiden Schulern.' " *Der Katholik* 88 (1908): pp. 39–45.

Steitz, C. G. "Die Abendsmalslehre des Maximos Confessor." *Jahrbuch für deutsche Theologie* 11 (1886): pp. 226–38.

Stephanou, E. "La coexistence initiale du corps et de l'âme d'après s. Grégoire de Nysse et s. Maxime l'Homologète." EO 31 (1932): pp.304–15.

Straubinger, H. *Die Christologie des hl. Maximus Konfessor.* Bonn, 1906.

Thunberg, L. *Microcosm and mediator.* Lind, 1965.

Unger, D. J. "Christ Jesus, Center and Final Scope of all Creation according to St. Maximus Confessor." *Franciscan Studies* 9 (1949): pp. 50–62.

Viller, M. "Aux Sources de la Spiritualité de saint Maxime: les Oeuvres d'Evagre le Pontique." RAM (1930): pp. 156–84, 239–68, 331–36.

Volker, W. "Der Einfluss Pseudo-Dionysius Areopagita auf Max. Conf." In A. Stohr, *Universitas* I. Mainz, 1960, pp. 243–54 (= TU 77, Berlin, 1961, pp. 331–50).

————. *Maximus Confessor als Meister des Geistlichen Lebens.* Wiesbaden, 1965.

Weser, H. *S. Maximi Confessoris praecepta de incarnatione Dei et deificatione hominis exponuntur et examinantur.* Berlin, 1869.

Index to Introduction

INDEX

Index to Texts

Aaron, 21
Abandonment, 86
Abraham, 40, 177
Active way, 47, 61
Adam, 104
Adultery, 59
Agag, 158–59
Alms, 38, 43
Ambrose, St., 119n1
Anaphora, the holy, 21
Anastasius, 28n1, 30n25, 31n32
Angels, 64, 66, 74, 79
Anger: and fear, 56; love and, 38, 40–41,
    84; and lust, 107; and pure prayer, 40;
    mentioned, 74, 123n46
Antichrist, 51
Aquinas, St. Thomas, 98n195
Arians, 20
Aristotle, 89n43, 98n195
Asceticism, 154–56, 158, 162, 168–70
Ascetic Life, The, 356
Attachment, 36–37, 59–60, 63, 109, 151,
    169
Augustine, St., 119n1

Balthasar, Hans Urs von, 87–88, 170, 171,
    176, 179
Body: of Christ, 154, 165; the impurity of,
    66; the pleasures of, 142–43; sin and,
    68; and the soul, 36, 57; and virtue,
    161
Bread of Life, 113, 118, 159

Caesar, 141
Cassian, John, 119n1
Catholic Church, 21
Celibacy, 82–83
Christ Jesus: the body of, 154; burying,
    139; the commandments of, 81;

crucified, 139; the friends of, 86; God
and Savior, 192; imitating, 81;
incarnate, 102–03, 169; the
incorruptibility of, 145; the judgment
of, 68; is life, 162; is light, 162; living
in, 160, 168; and love, 39; is mediator,
102, 217n30, 217n39; the mind of, 165;
and nature, 104; the nature of, 23–24,
166; the number of wills of, 23–24,
29n7; the pure, 160; is resurrection,
162; the self-abasement of, 102; is
sinless, 166; is truth, 162; the way of,
78; the Word, 139, 147–70; mentioned,
83, 84, 85, 110, 151, 153
Chrysologus, Peter, 119n1
Church, the Holy: the entrance into, 198–
    99; as the image of God, 186–87, 208;
    as the image of the soul, 190–95; as the
    image of the world, 188–89; represents
    man, 189–90, 195
Church of Constantinople, 25
Circumcision, 135–36
Clement of Alexandria, 94n141, 124n80
Commandments, 46, 80, 81–82, 85
Conscience, examining the, 79
Constans II, 28n4, 30n22
Constantine III, 28n4
Contemplation: asceticism and, 154–56,
    158; demons war against, 60; the habit
    of, 70–71, 82; and knowledge, 132,
    151, 192; love and, 84; the meaning of,
    196; the mind and, 85; mystical, 138;
    natural, 204, 210, 223n117; objects of,
    76; and passions, 146–47; self-mastery
    and, 84; and virginity, 83; the Word
    and, 156; mentioned, 45, 61, 90–
    91n67, 161
Corinthians, 153
Cyprian, 119n1
Cyril of Jerusalem, 119n1

236

INDEX

INDEX

Scriptures, 82, 83, 145–46, 163, 165, 166, 195–97, 221n83
Self-abasement, 102, 120n9
Self-control, 42
Self-love, 47, 55, 62, 69
Self-mastery: the body and, 80; and celibacy, 83; and contemplation, 84; and detachment, 66; and knowledge, 81; love and, 62, 66, 81, 83, 85; over pleasure, 71; purity through, 83; self-love and, 62; mentioned, 73, 77, 89n43
Sergius, 218
Sherwood, Polycarp, 87n2, n4, 89n31
Simplicity, 143–44
Sin: abstaining from, 58; and distress, 43, 53; by habit, 71; humility and, 43; the law of, 117–18; and pleasure, 53; in thought, 57, 58, 68; mentioned, 98n107
Sloth, 42
Socrates, 124n80
Sophronius, St., 215
Soteropoulos, 219n66
Soul: and the body, 36, 37, 65; and God, 206, 212; impurity of, 66; three movements of, 218n58; the perfect, 75; the powers of, 65; purity of, 38, 85; the holy synaxis and, 204–05; and wisdom, 194–95; mentioned, 80, 88n20, 164
Stead, Dom Julian, O.S.B., 215n2
Stephen, St., 39
Susanna, 85
Synaxis, 183, 198, 204–08
Synodicon of Sophronius, 30n23

Temptation, 53, 72, 77, 116–17, 118, 141
Tertullian, 119n1, 122n44
Theocharistos, 19
Theodore, Pope, 18, 27, 29n13
Theodore of Mopsuestia, 119n1

Theology, 155
Theophanes, 30n23
Thought(s), 57–59, 61, 72, 193
Time, 75
Transcendence, divine, 37
Trinity: contemplation of, 80; knowledge of, 45, 61; and the pure mind, 46; the substance of, 76; in Unity, 110–11; mentioned, 49, 84, 106, 162, 223n122
Trisagion, 207, 210
Tritheists, 50
Troilus, 18, 22, 25, 27
Truth, 162, 191
Typos, 20, 22, 24–26, 29n7

Unity, 205, 223n120

Vainglory: disgrace and, 38, 72; and fornication, 174; and greed, 72; and hatred, 62; humility and, 44; and love, 39; a monk's, 73; mentioned, 56, 59, 62, 70
Vanity, 69
Vice, 48–49, 56, 61, 77
Vigils, 39, 49, 57
Virginity, 82–83, 104
Virtue: and the body, 161; the habit of, 143; and humility, 56; and the mind, 55; and obedience, 149; and the passions, 67; mentioned, 61, 146

Will: of God, 112–13, 121n21; the human, 121n30, 125n85; the union of, 121n21, 124n79
Women, 48–49, 59, 63, 80
Word: as Logos, 219n59, 223n118; mentioned, 58, 103, 112, 139, 147–70
World, 54, 86, 188–89, 196–97

240